I0005494

UNDERSTANDING IMPOVERISHMENT

The Consequences of
Development-Induced Displacement

Edited by
Christopher McDowell

Berghahn Books
Providence • Oxford

First published in 1996 by

Berghahn Books

Editorial offices:
165 Taber Avenue, Providence, RI 02906, USA
Bush House, Merewood Avenue, Oxford, OX3 8EF, UK

© 1996 Christopher McDowell

All rights reserved.
No part of this publication may be reproduced in any form or by
any means without the written permission of Berghahn Books.

Library of Congress Cataloging-in-Publication Data

```
Understanding impoverishment : the consequences of development-induced
displacement / edited by Christopher McDowell.
        p.    cm. -- (Refugee and forced migration studies ; v. 2)
    Includes bibliographical references.
    ISBN 1-57181-916-9 (cloth : alk. paper). -- ISBN 1-57181-927-4
(paper : alk. paper)
    1. Forced migration--Developing countries--Congresses.
2. Economic development--Social aspects--Congresses.  3. Poverty-
-Developing countries--Congresses.  4. Refugees--Developing
countries--Congresses.  5. Developing countries--Population-
-Congresses.    I. McDowell, Chris.  II. Series.
HB2160.U53  1996
304.8--dc20                                                  96-42
                                                              CIP
```

British Library Cataloguing in Publication Data

A catalogue record for this book is available from the British Library.

Table of Contents

List of Figures and Maps

Glossary

American Anthropological Association (AAA)
Anti-Slavery International (ASI)
Canadian International Development Agency (CIDA)
Centre for Education, Research and Training (CENDERET, India)
Chittagong Hill Tracts (CHT)
Confederacion Nacional Campesina (CNC, Mexico)
Confederacion Campesina Independient (CCI, Mexico)
Council of the Nahua Peoples from the Alto Balsas (CPNAB)
Deutsche Gesellschaft für Technische Zusammenarbeit (GTZ)
Environmental Impact Assessment (EIA)
Fundação Nacional do Indio (FUNAI, Brazil)
Government of Botswana (GoB)
Government of Orissa (GoO, India)
International Bank for Reconstruction and Development (IBRD)
International Union for the Conservation of Nature and Natural
    Resources (IUCN)
James Bay and Northern Quebec Agreement (JBNQA)
James Bay Development Corporation (JBDC)
Land Acquisition Act (1984) (LLA, India)
National Irrigation Authority (NIA, The Philippines)
Non-Governmental Organisation (NGO)
Norwegian Agency for Development Co-Operation (NORAD)
Ordem de Advogados do Brasil (OAB)
Organisation for the Development of the Senegal River Valley
    (OMVS)

Organisation for Economic Co-Operation and Development (OECD)

Overseas Development Administration (ODA)

Project-Affected Peoples (PAPs)

Refugee Studies Programme (RSP, Oxford)

Regional Commission Against Large Dams (CRAB),

Southern Okavango Integrated Water Development Project (SOIWD, Botswana)

Swedish International Development Authority (SIDA)

Tennessee Valley Authority (TVA)

United Nations (UN)

United Nations High Commission for Refugees (UNHCR)

World Bank (WB)

World Bank Operational Directive (WBOD)

World Bank Operational Manual Statement (WBOMS)

World Bank Review of Projects Involving Involuntary Resettlement 1986-1993 (WBR)

World Food Programme (WFP)

Acknowledgements

I should like to thank Professor Elizabeth Colson who advised in the compilation of this volume and has been involved in the work of the Refugee Studies Programme (RSP) since the early 1980s. Dr Michael Cernea was a driving force behind the First International Conference on Development-Induced Displacement held in January 1995 hosted by the RSP, and he continues to play an important role in the RSP's work on forced displacement and resettlement. It was Dr Barbara Harrell-Bond who realised the importance of understanding the processes behind development-created population displacement and the resettlement of relocated people for the field of refugee studies.

This volume was prepared and published with the financial support of The World Bank and the European Commision. Sarah Rhodes, Monika Porada and Philadelphia Ricketts kindly read the manuscript and assisted in the compilation of the bibliography and figures.

In memory of
Ahmed Abdel-Wadoud Karadawi
(1945-1995)

1

Introduction

Christopher McDowell

A s the dream of any war is to be 'the war to end all wars', devel-opment is predicated on the wish to improve human socio-economic conditions and eradicate scarcity. Born on a par with the hopes and visions of a changed post-Second World War world, the development paradigm, marking a belief in progress and per-fectibility, has dominated social scientific thinking and interna-tional policy on a mass scale. Initiated by the victors, development policies guided and legitimised the re-distribution of power and resources on a global scale. While the Marshall Plan provided one model for re-dressing the costs incurred by those poor countries of the South who sided with the Allied Powers, the Warsaw Pact introduced an alternative model for development and growth; both models contributed to the formation and perpetuation of a 'Third World'.

The last forty years have been called the 'development age'; the end of that era has also been acknowledged as a *fait accompli* (Sachs 1993, Seabrook 1993). Yet although the decision concerning the end of 'development' seems to be unanimous among certain social scientific writings its post-mortem has yet to be written. The aim of this volume is to address some of the more fundamental issues relat-ing to the weaknesses and flaws of the development paradigm as practised both on an international and national level. The subject of this collection is development-induced population displace-ment, the upheaval of communities to make way for large dams, in-dustrial zones, transportation routes, game parks and commercial forestry.[1] It concerns the balance between the benefits of infra-structural development and the costs and pains of being uprooted and consequently resettled, and the risk of impoverishment carried by those forcibly displaced. This volume differs from the blanket critique of development in that while contributors do not shy from exposing the delusion and disappointment of development – the social costs of which are catalogued in detail – the general conclusion of the book is not that development is obsolete. Rather it is argued that the direct and indirect consequences of development – in this case development-induced population displacement – which harm the lives and livelihoods of people in the Developing and Developed World are avoidable, and the harmful effects, which are being more widely recognised and understood, can be mitigated through more enlightened national and international policies.

A number of contributors give priority in their chapters to the World Bank's shocking and conservative estimate that about ten million people annually enter the cycle of forced displacement and relocation in two development 'sectors' alone – namely dam construction and urban/transportation; in the decade covered by the Bank's review of projects involving involuntary resettlement it was estimated that 90-100 million people became development displacees. When compared to the number of current refugees (18-20 million) it can be seen that forced population dislocation resulting from induced development processes is a problem of enormous proportion and significance, though largely a hidden problem.

Involuntary resettlement is not a phenomenon that will disappear in the foreseeable future, as the number of projects that entail the acquisition of land, which is already large, will increase further. Predictions that available finance for infrastructural development is shrinking and will result in a steep decline in dam construction and other 'mega-projects' appears to be misplaced. Neither the World Bank nor, evidence suggests, any of the other international financial institutions, are withdrawing from infrastructural investments in gen-

---

1. The papers in this volume were presented at the first international conference on development-induced displacement organised by the Refugee Studies Programme at the University of Oxford in January 1995. The conference, attended by delegates from twenty-eight countries, included government officials responsible for the design and implementation of policies leading to the removal and resettlement of populations to make way for planned development; academics and consultants who assess the consequences of large dams and other forms of development and their implications for affected people; representatives of funding organisations who provide the capital for infrastructure projects; engineers and managers responsible for overseeing implementation; and NGOs and pressure groups campaigning alongside those forced from their homes.

eral, though there are shifts between sectors. In addition there are considerable private and domestic investment funds for large-scale development. Even with current concerns about the rising costs of construction, opposition on the grounds of environmental and human damage, and poor rates of return on investments (all of which increase risks and diminish profitability), consortia of private institutions are increasingly providing the capital for the building and management of large-scale projects.

Therefore, as the needs grow for the irrigation, electricity and infrastructure necessary to satisfy the demands of growing and increasingly urbanising populations, there remains enormous pressure for infrastructural development. In this book it is argued that whilst it is right to focus attention on the more spectacular, large-scale population-displacing projects one must not lose sight of the thousands of smaller projects which collectively account for even more total displacement. There is an urgent need to direct research towards urban projects which account for more displacement globally than dams. It is often the case that such projects are not guided by national or international policy norms and are not open to professional outside review, but continue to displace and lead to violations of basic human rights. What emerges strongly from this volume is the need for developing countries and financing institutions to respond by abandoning projects that create unnecessary displacement, and where displacement is genuinely unavoidable, to adopt national policies and legal frameworks for resettlement and rehabilitation, and for donor institutions to provide support and incentives for such policies.

The Oxford conference at which these papers were presented was an important step towards uncovering the problem of development-induced displacement and impoverishment, not as an isolated set of processes, but as part of the more general study of displacement, the causes that lead to forced displacement, the consequences in terms of human rights and impoverishment, and the types of assistance provided to uprooted people. This volume represents a commitment to understanding why this problem, which is becoming ever more pressing, is relegated as a peripheral concern; a number of answers are provided.

First, but with some notable exceptions, there has been a lack of official recognition on the part of governments and international agencies that development-induced displacement is a problem at all. Unlike 'traditional' refugees development-affected people have no global agency to protect their interests and provide assistance – certainly the UNHCR is falling ever further behind in its efforts to keep up with the refugee challenge (Myers 1995) – and the task of protecting those who fall victim to development has yet to begin. Without international support governments have failed lamentably to adopt national protective policies and legal frameworks, but have been quick to use the weight of the state to seize lands and enforce what Gautam Appa and Girish Patel (in this volume) term 'unjust and unnecessary displacement' with a denial of, or at best, the offer of insufficient or inappropriate compensation or means for restitution. Large-scale, highly visible infrastructure projects in developing countries assume – often as monuments to powerful interests – a national priority in which a burden of pain is regarded as inevitable and acceptable when weighed against 'national' and what the state defines as 'public' interest in the 'greater good'. As a result, according to Scott, 'investments for engineering, which mark the passage of a political administration, often take priority over the social area where gains are less spectacular and more polemical' (1995:9).

Looking beyond the prevailing development discourse there is a debate about how best the growing food, health, housing and energy needs of developing societies can be met with full regard to people's basic entitlements and the environment. There is an increased awareness of the social, environmental (Goldsmith and Hildyard 1984, see also various publications by the International Rivers Networks), and political (see Scudder in this volume) implications of large dams, raising serious questions about the rationale behind such projects, their adverse impacts and the viability of continued investment in large-scale development that result in involuntary displacement and reap often only short-term and dubious benefits for a few interested parties. The World Bank is the institution at the forefront of evolving policy and operational methods to ensure that potential benefits and negative effects of dams and other development are correctly evaluated (McDowell 1996). The emphasis is on the need for measures to protect uprooted people and to ensure that the social and personal costs borne by those affected are part of a realistic appraisal of the feasibility of development projects funded by the Bank; contributors to this volume have taken up the Bank's challenge.

A second reason for the relative invisibility of development displacees is that the people most vulnerable in the face of powerful state and capital interests are those who occupy the lands (for example, in highland, forest, riverine or other isolated areas) most commonly targeted for development projects. In India it is estimated that forty per cent of the 23 million people displaced by national development are 'tribals' who form only eight per cent of the country's population (Fernandes 1994:32). As Posey describes so clearly in Brazil, it is the Indian population, marginalised by a system that considers them 'relatively incapable' and renders them invisible in decision-taking over resource exploitation on Indian 'protected lands', who are the most vulnerable group in Brazilian society. Indeed, according to Gray, it is indigenous people in general who are particularly affected by the construction of dams 'not only personally, but because of the threats on their lands, lives and cultures'.

Recently, as Oliver-Smith recounts, resistance to development projects requiring the resettlement of marginal populations has attracted far greater attention to the plight of indigenous people and has made them less invisible, though perhaps no less vulnerable. The issue of resistance to development and its implications in terms of social conflict and the planning and execution of resettlement programmes is addressed in this volume by Andrew Gray, Anthony Oliver-Smith, Alicia Barabas and Miguel Bartolomé, and Darrell Posey.

A further explanation for the relative invisibility of development displacees has been the lack of attention on the part of social scientists. It is only in recent years, and to a certain extent only as a result of policies pursued by some development agencies to actively include the social sciences, that anthropologists and sociologists (who comprise eight of the fifteen contributors to this volume) have broken out of the cocoon of their academic disciplines to undertake instead action-oriented applied development work and long term impact evaluations. Increased social science involvement is beginning to combat models centred on economics and technology – which, according to Cernea, have typically overlooked social and cultural variables – by broadly 'putting people first', crafting alternative social arrangements and helping to develop social capital (Cernea 1991c) in a way that is responsive to social and cultural concerns of affected people.

Academics, NGOs and grassroots groups have successfully focused attention on the issue of development-induced displacement as a political issue of significance, but the task remains to convince governments and international agencies of the challenges that lay ahead. Delegates to the Oxford conference contributed to this effort (McDowell 1995; see also Cernea in this volume) by agreeing on a series of recommendations on displacement and resettlement presented at the World Social Summit in Copenhagen in March 1995, and influencing the final Declaration and Programme of Action on poverty eradication. The Summit Declaration gave priority to the need to restore the livelihoods of those displaced by development. Indeed, the element of restitution, of understanding why it is that impoverishment almost inevitably follows displacement, is an important theme throughout this book and one that will be taken up in a follow-on conference in 1996.

There is no denial that involuntary resettlement is hugely disruptive and painful. In the last several decades, studies carried out in many regions of the world have examined how populations are affected when forced from their homes and required to adjust to new physical and social environments, often with diminished capital and other resources. Elizabeth Colson, opening the Oxford conference, said, '... it is not happenstance that some of us have come to speak of "development refugees", for those displaced by development face traumas somewhat similar to those experienced by those uprooted by war or other forms of violence or natural disaster' (opening address, January 1995). As Colson and Scudder's own research in Zambia among the Gwembe Tonga has shown, for people displaced by the Kariba Lake in 1958, there was a rise in mortality rates associated directly with displacement (see Colson 1971). Forced displacement, therefore, whether it is due to development, warfare, political upheaval or natural disaster has physical consequences which have to be better understood before the true costs of displacement and the benefits of development can be known.

A number of papers in this collection address those consequences in terms of the multidimensionality of impoverishment and social disintegration as it affects large numbers of people well beyond those who must undergo relocation (narrowly termed the 'project affected [or impacted] people' [PAPs]). Scudder reminds us that the net of impoverishment is cast wide to include not just those directly affected and their hosts in the place of resettlement, but immigrants into a project area, fisher-folk dependent upon dam reservoirs, and importantly, those residents who are neither relocatees or hosts. It is this last group, often ignored in socio-economic development guidelines, who do not form a part of organised resistance movements and tend to be more vulnerable to manipulation. Appa and Patel, sensitive to the particular problems of those people indirectly affected by involuntary displacement in India, note that it is often the down-stream populations, ignored in project planning and resettlement and rehabilitation schemes, who are likely to lose their jobs, access to resources and become 'environmental refugees' – that is people who can no longer gain a secure livelihood in their traditional homelands because of environmental factors arising out of planned change.

These papers show that the number and range of people affected either directly or indirectly by infrastructural projects that create displacement are large and varied and the resettlement challenge, therefore, is enormous. Cernea, writing from the World Bank, maintains the position that to help those faced with involuntary resettlement the process must be carried out smoothly, efficiently and as fairly as possible. This so-called 'reasonable' and 'ethical' position is described as lying mid-way between those (usually NGOs) who argue that dams should be cancelled if they interfere with the rights of local people and those of borrower governments who consider that the right of 'eminent domain' does not include any responsibilities to those being moved (Gray in this volume). The approach of the World Bank, according to Gray, starts the discussion from the position of mitigating factors, which is fundamentally supportive of the borrowers and does not respect indigenous rights. Groups campaigning on behalf of local people affected by development argue that the World Bank's position is untenable because, as past evidence has shown, what the Bank strives for, i.e., 'socially and economically responsible resettlement that can prevent impoverishment and extend benefits to the regional economy and host population', simply has not occurred, and our present knowledge, based in part on inadequate environment and social impact assessments, is not sufficient to enable this to occur. Not sharing this fatalism, Cernea presents his findings from a long-term examination of empirical evidence provided by social science studies which distinguish the basic processes that occur when people are forcibly displaced. His 'model of the overall impoverishment process' – which aims to provide not only a model of description, but also a model for converting resettlement into a development opportunity – is presented in the opening chapter and applied in the field by Sam Thangaraj whose findings close the volume. The chapters that stand between provide compelling evidence of damaging development and resettlement failure, draw lessons from past mistakes and make recommendations for the future.

Much of the attention on development-induced displacement has been focused on India and Latin America, in large part due to the enormous publicity given to resistance over the Narmada Sardar Sarovar dam and irrigation projects and the harsh lessons learned at Sobradinho (Brazil). This has led people to overlook the fact that displacements by dam projects in Africa (for example the Akosombo in Ghana and the Koussou in Ivory Coast) have affected a much higher proportion of respective countries' populations than the displacements caused by the largest dams in Brazil, China and India in relation to the total populations of those countries (Cernea 1993); and much of this displacement has created considerable human misery.

Véronique Lassailly-Jacob draws on her experience of resettlement schemes in a range of African countries and concludes that much of the impoverishment which follows displacement occurs because resettlement planners work with entrenched ideas dominated by government-desired innovations that ignore local initiatives and fail to enhance local production systems. She describes how mismanaged land acquisition leads relocatees into a dependency on food relief which lasts for several years. She quotes Scudder's findings of Gwembe Tonga resettlement where relocation in the Lusitu area increased population density four-fold resulting, twenty years later, in desertification which turned the area into a dust bowl. In his chapter, Scudder describes some of the adverse impacts of river-basin development projects in Africa and finds that, 'Dam construction is apt to impoverish downstream riverine communities in two ways. One is through the alteration of the annual regime of dammed rivers. The other is due to attempts by immigrants to displace households and communities from their land' (see also Tamondong-Helin in this volume).

Alicia Barabas and Miguel Bartolomé provide further compelling evidence of the ways in which dam construction contributes directly to the disintegration of affected communities and leads to what they earlier termed 'ethnocide' (Bartolomé and Barabas 1992). They describe the vulnerability of local populations to 'outside' manipulative politics which create new leadership systems that obstruct collective organisation, incite intrafamilial and intergenerational conflict over, for example, the possession of resettlement lands, and 'force young people of both sexes to migrate from their familial and communal spheres, bringing about their uprooting and the loss of cultural and ethnic ties'. Theodore Downing, drawing on a 'prolusion of a theory of social geometry' tackles this phenomenon of social disarticulation – what he describes as the 'unravelling of the underlying social fabric' – arising out of involuntary displacement. He expresses unease with the conventional wisdom which prescribes economic actions to mitigate social impoverishment, arguing instead that we should, in a more culturally sophisticated manner, focus on the 'subtle, important social dimensions of such events that might prove crucial to mitigating social impoverishment and perhaps facilitate political and economic restoration'.

In her evaluation of the resettlement of communities displaced to make way for the Pantabangan Dam in Central Luzon, the Philippines, Sue Tamondong-Helin is able to identify the social and cultural impoverishment of relocatees arising out of what Downing calls the 'disruption of order'. In this resettlement attempt no thought was given to the social geometry of the displaced, rather there was a clear lack of political will on the part of the state to resettle the people properly. The consequences were sadly familiar: designated farm lots were insufficient in size and number and sited on unsuitable land which quickly eroded. Formerly farmers, those relocated were unable to pursue their traditional modes of livelihood, and the wage economy of the new town site became heavily dependent on temporary employment with the National Irrigation Authority, the main implementing agency for the dam, and the limited skills training offered were of little practical use. Today, some twenty years after the first relocations, Tamondong-Helin describes a depressed town populated mainly by the elderly, with few employment opportunities, a sporadic water supply and limited public infrastructure.

Tamondong-Helin describes political interference and incompetence embedded in the institutional processes of relocation and displacement in the Philippines. Alan Rew pursues this theme with an analysis of the organisation of resettlement and the reasons for governmental lack of commitment to resettlement operations. An argument is developed to contribute to the solution of practical operational problems and to policy. Thangaraj, in the final chapter, is also concerned with practical issues and describes his attempt to use an existing model for understanding the impoverishment process, to achieve a better outcome for those displaced by consciously counteracting the anticipated and predictable risks of resettlement.

This volume contains a clear call to widen and deepen our understanding of the whole problem of the development process, population displacement and the displacement-resettlement continuum. Although awareness of the harmful impacts of involuntary resettlement is growing, the pace of the awareness needs to be increased, because the rate of planned development activity continues to be high, and safeguards against human rights abuses barely provide minimum protection. Emerging from these contributions is a package of preventive measures, challenging new initiatives, and recommendations for positive action to improve development practice and reduce impoverishment.

PART ONE

THE SCALE OF THE PROBLEM

2

Understanding and Preventing Impoverishment from Displacement

REFLECTIONS ON THE STATE OF KNOWLEDGE

Michael M. Cernea

Introduction

The remarkable progress in social science research on resettlement during the last decade will be defined in this chapter in terms of (a) knowledge acquisition – the addition of considerable in-depth and 'extensive' new knowledge; (b) significant shifts in research trends – from academic inquiry to operational research, from description to prescription, from writing ethnographies of past cases to crafting forward-looking policy frameworks; and (c) development and diversification of research models – particularly an evolution from the stress-centred model to the 'impoverishment/ restoration' model in analysing resettlement.

The impoverishment risks/restoration model consists of eight recurrent and interlinked processes. It reveals how multifaceted impoverishment caused by displacement occurs via induced landlessness, joblessness, homelessness, marginalisation, increased morbidity, food insecurity, loss of access to common property and social disarticulation. The conceptual model of impoverishment through displacement also suggests, *in nuce*, the model for the positive re-establishment of those displaced, which requires turning the impoverishment model on its head. I will analyse in detail the sudden drop and the reversal in the income curve of resettlers during displacement and relocation and point out the financial premise for income recovery.

Two key priorities for future research on resettlement will be identified and recommended: (a) research on the experiences of reconstructing livelihoods, and (b) research on the economics of displacement and recovery.

In my keynote address to the first international conference on the controversial topic of development-induced displacement held in Oxford in January 1995, I stressed that development-caused displacement is a matter of international concern, rather than only of local or national relevance; and that public awareness – explicitly, political and ethical awareness – of the seriousness and complexity of this issue has crossed a threshold. The inclusion in the World Social Summit's Programme of Action (March 1995) of the well-conceived findings and recommendations for policy and actual practice that emerged from the Oxford conference was real evidence of the wider recognition of the seriousness of the problem.[1]

True enough, forced resettlement is an age-old issue: relocation has accompanied human history from its outset. We know that even the

---

1. The World Summit on Social Development: the proposal made in this Keynote Address – to summarise and send the Conference's policy recommendations to the U.N. Secretariat preparing the Summit's Programme of Action – was accepted by the Conference, which created a working group, chaired by Professor Theodore Downing, charged to synthesise the Conference's policy-relevant conclusions. Then, Oxford's Refugee Studies Programme formally submitted the recommendations of the Conference to the January 1995 session of the UN Preparatory Committee of the Summit (held in New York), where they were discussed and supported by several governments and by several national and international NGOs. Among the latter, OXFAM played a leading role. From developing countries, some local NGOs sent their message on resettlement to the Summit and documented it with empirical research data (see, for instance, the article and statement by Balaji Pandey 1995, on the consequences of population displacement in Orissa, India).

As a result (and despite the advanced stage of the Summit's preparation), a statement on development-related displacement was introduced in the Chapter II of the Summit's draft Programme of Action. It urged governments to avoid or minimise displacements whenever possible. Most importantly, it asked governments to adopt 'policy and legal frameworks' for re-establishing those displaced. That statement was subsequently adopted by the Copenhagen Summit on 12 March 1995 as part of its formal final documents, in the Section II devoted to the 'eradication of poverty' and the 'formulation of integrated action strategies' to that end. It says:

> Governments are urged to integrate goals and targets for combating poverty into overall economic and social policies and planning at the local, national and, where appropriate, regional levels by: … (d) Selecting, wherever possible, development schemes that do not displace local populations, and designing an appropriate policy and legal framework to compensate the displaced for their losses, to help them to re-establish their livelihoods and to promote their recovery from social and cultural disruption (Copenhagen Programme of Action adopted by the World Summit for Social Development, Copenhagen, 6-12 March, 1995).

very first human couple was subject to involuntary relocation. Apparently, this happened by divine decision. The first family was relocated out of a wonderful garden, without any consultation or 'participation' in the decision-making process. Certainly, this was a primitive solution to relocation. However, even now, in the twentieth century, we have not escaped much worse, more painful solutions, to which imposed on a mass scale turn into social nightmares. I am convinced, however, that this age-old problem can be better resolved.

Four paramount questions structure my discussion:

Firstly: What is the state of the art in social science research on involuntary resettlement?

Secondly: What is the essence of the displacement/resettlement set of issues?

Thirdly: How do people respond to displacement situations? How are social scientists addressing people's resistance to, or their participation in, resettlement?

And last, but equally important: What are the current priorities, both in research and at the operational level, for improving resettlement?

Knowledge About Resettlement: The State of the Art

Anthropologists and sociologists initiated research on forced population displacements before other disciplines and before such processes became a subject of public policy. Researchers such as David Butcher and other British scholars including Brokensha (Brokensha and Scudder 1968) and Chambers (1970), as well as Roy-Burman (1961) in India and, especially, Gans (1968), Scudder (1973) and Colson (1971) in the United States, have created an initial and rich 'bank of knowledge' about resettlement, to use Elizabeth Colson's phrase. Unfortunately, it is also true that policy makers have not exactly crowded as customers to this golden knowledge bank.

An important change, vastly consequential in the long run, happened in 1980, when the World Bank became the first development agency to adopt an explicit policy concerning involuntary resettlement, a policy formulated by social scientists and grounded in social research (World Bank 1980; see for details Cernea 1988a and b, 1993b). As senior Bank management increasingly regarded resettlement as a 'topic which touches upon the central aspects of the Bank's work' (Qureshi 1989) and upon the Bank's legal obligations (Shihata 1991a and b, 1993), Bank social scientists expanded their resettlement work and, more importantly, the attention of many governments of developing countries was increasingly and forcefully drawn to resettlement issues. Among the 'cognitive results' of this process is a real 'explosion' of social science research on involuntary resettlement, especially during the last ten years, which practically carved out a topical subfield in social science. Books and dissertations, studies and symposia, evaluation reports and policy documents, university syllabi, training courses, and briefs for parliamentary hearings or courts of law have widened the intellectual endeavours focused on resettlement issues, as documented recently by Guggenheim's impressive bibliography (1994).

This surge in research and publications has been largely responsible for the intellectual construction of development-induced displacement as a social problem of worldwide dimensions. However, more than the academic research, it was the growing movement of resistance to displacement at the grassroots, supported by many NGOs, that has powerfully re-cast displacement as a political issue.

How can we summarise the major advances during the last ten years in the social science research on resettlement? The following main characteristics of this progress, in my view, stand out:

First, we have a more intensive knowledge about resettlement today than ever before; we can name it 'thick' knowledge, to paraphrase a widespread term in anthropology. We have made enormous cognitive gains in terms of depth, refinement and detailed understanding of how displacement actually occurs, gains that have exponentially enriched the body of our knowledge on the subject. (We cannot yet say the same, however, about our knowledge of the re-establishment process that follows displacement.)

The main factor that accounts for this *intensive* knowledge is the unprecedented 'hands on' involvement during this decade of scores of social scientists in development programmes that involve displacement. Many development anthropologists have moved from the traditional role of participant *observers* in the process to become participant *actors*, actors who use their expertise to find ways of avoiding or minimising displacement. They also help on the ground to mitigate its adverse consequences by improving the planning, monitoring, supervision, analysis and evaluation of displacement and resettlement operations. This type of operational and action research is still an unheralded contribution. Little is known about it by the social science community at large. But from my vantage point, privileged to read hundreds of field reports, I stand witness to the good analytical quality, intricately detailed field assessments and sharpened practical expertise reached by scores of resettlement social scientists. They make a tangible contribution to protecting the welfare of people caught in forced displacement processes.

Second, our knowledge on resettlement has developed extensively. Traditionally, the building blocks of knowledge in our area were extracted from research on dam displacements (mainly by anthropologists in developing countries) and urban displacements (mainly by sociologists in industrialised countries). What is relatively new during the last decade is the expansion of knowledge about displacements caused in *other sectors* and affecting additional population groups, as well as of forced relocations unrelated to development projects. Such new sectors, involving new issues and a variety of types of resettlement, are: forestry (Turnbull 1987; Fernandes, Das and Rao 1989); mining, especially open-pit mining and the construction of thermal energy plants (the literature on Singrauli is one example); the establishment of biosphere reserves and parks (Brandon and Wells 1992; West and Brechin 1991); the conversions in land use (Lane and Jules 1990); transportation corridors; urban growth and environmental infrastructure in developing countries (Cernea 1989; Jellinek 1991; Davidson et al. 1993); politically mandated mass relocation (Clay 1988; Pankhurst 1992; Diece and Viezolli 1992; de Wet 1993); and resettlement caused by structural adjustment reforms. Attention to the increased diversity of sectoral circumstances and the variety of previously unstudied types of displacements have broadened our empirical basis and the scope of our concepts and reasoning.

Before moving to the third characteristic, I would like to emphasise that in both aspects discussed above a remarkable trend is the growth of resettlement research in developing countries, particularly in India, Brazil, China, Mexico and Argentina (e.g., Fernandes and Ganguly-Thukral 1989; Baboo 1992; Mathur 1994; Bartolomé and Barabas 1990; Joshi 1991; Odidi Okidi 1992; Ribeiro 1994; Scott 1992b; Huang 1984; Wangxiang 1993; for a detailed bibliography see Guggenheim 1994).

Third, resettlement research has advanced from descriptions to prescriptions, and from academic analysis to operational research. Early resettlement writings ventured less into the territory of recommendations, despite their excellence in analysis. The more prescriptive posture of recent work (Bartolome, Cernea, Cook, Fernandes, Guggenheim, Partridge, Scudder, and many others) reflects the growing maturity of this domain, the increased self-confidence of its research-informed practitioners, and the relevance of this type of social knowledge to development's dilemmas. Development/applied anthropology and sociology are making some of their finest contributions ever in this area.

Fourth, resettlement research has crossed the threshold from producing piecemeal ethnographies to crafting policy frameworks.

Ethnographies deal with consummated cases; policies guide future processes. Case studies should remain a staple in our research menu, but there is great gain embodied in the ability to articulate credible policy proposals. Social science concepts and the involvement of professional social scientists have been decisive, not only in the formulation of the World Bank's resettlement policy, but also of the policy of all twenty-four OECD countries' donor agencies, and of sectoral policies in Brazil, Colombia and other countries. This is also true for the growing debate currently going on in India about the adoption of resettlement policies.

We should not overstate the situation, however, the fact that social science can help formulate resettlement policies and has done so in a few places does not mean that this currently happens routinely. Structural and political obstacles continue to impede the incorporation of social science research into policy and law. In scores of developing countries the problem of policy adoption is far from being resolved, or even being approached (Cernea 1995a).

Fifth, resettlement research has succeeded in generating quantified estimates at the global level of magnitudes in development-induced displacements. The most significant estimate, arrived at by our group at the World Bank, has emerged from collecting, verifying and combining a vast body of data. The estimate is still conservative, yet nothing less than stunning: we found that about *ten million people annually* enter the cycle of forced displacement and relocation in two 'sectors' alone – namely, dam construction, and urban/transportation. That means that about 90-100 million people have been displaced during the decade 1986-1993. Compare this with the numbers of refugees, long recognised as a major contemporary problem. Development-caused displacements, that seemed to be piecemeal occurrences and were estimated as totalling far less than the number of refugees worldwide (assessed by UNHCR at 15-20 million), have turned out to be a much larger process than all the world's annual new refugee flows. Refugees and development-displacees, of course, are not 'numbers' that compete with each other, but are global parallel dramas, sometimes intertwined. However, the shock value of numbers and quantifications in our era of sound bites is part of the social construction of involuntary resettlement as a problem and increases public receptivity to the messages of resettlement research.

Note, also, that the ten million figure annually, or 100 million people for the decade, are still *partial* figures: they do *not* include the populations displaced within what I called earlier the 'new sectors': displacements from forests and reserve parks; mining and thermal power plant displacements; and other similar situations. We simply have not yet generated reliable aggregate data for all sectors worldwide. One can only imagine the additional millions that should be counted each year, in order to capture the full magnitude of the problem.

Sixth, research on displacement has shifted its key emphasis from being stress-centred (the Scudder-Colson temporal 'model' of resettlement phases, 1982) to being impoverishment-centred (the Cernea 'model', 1988a and b, 1990a). Through this shift, research conceptualises and theorises better the essence of displacement. The behaviour of displaced and resettled populations can be understood and explained more fully as a response to economic, cultural and social impoverishment than to 'stress'. By incorporating the shock/stress dimension into a comprehensive socio-economic impoverishment model social science research can shift effectively from mainly reporting displacement traumas to predicting trends and prescribing actual remedies. It zeroes in on what must be the practical heart of the matter in resettlement: preventing impoverishment and reconstructing livelihoods.

I believe that these six characteristics capture the essential lines of progress in the state of our art. We can be collectively proud that we have achieved intensive and extensive knowledge expansion; that we have shifted from academic analysis to operational research, and from description to prediction and prescription; that we are moving up from case ethnographies to policy formulation; from investigating discrete cases to quantified assessments of worldwide trends; and that we have changed the focus from stress-centred to poverty-centred theory and operational analysis. However, research about some other important issues remains unacceptably weak. On these we can and must do better. Some of these lines of enquiry will be examined later.

Let me turn now to the second of my four questions: what is the crux of the displacement/resettlement process?

Preventing Impoverishment: Eight Main Risks

The essence of the displacement/resettlement nexus is the development-induced impoverishment of some population segments and the efforts to prevent and overcome it. Progress in knowledge notwithstanding, thorny problems and disastrous effects continue to plague displacement operations in many countries. One major result is impoverishment; another is increased resistance and political tension surrounding involuntary resettlement.

During 1993-94, I had the responsibility of leading a task force mandated to review all 1986-93 World Bank-financed projects involving involuntary population displacement. For comparative purposes, this review also covered many projects not assisted by the Bank. In 1994 more than 120 researchers and NGO representatives engaged in a consultation about the mid-term findings of this review. The study is now completed and published (World Bank 1994a), and I will discuss some of its final findings, pertinent to preventing impoverishment caused by displacements.

An important part of our study focused on how impoverishment happens. In poorly handled displacements, severe impoverishment and social disintegration affect large numbers of people, and heavy costs extend well beyond the immediately affected populations; conversely, socially and economically responsible resettlement can prevent impoverishment and can extend benefits to the regional economy and host populations. Ensuring that involuntary resettlement is avoided or minimised – and when unavoidable, is carried out without impoverishing the people displaced – is necessary on both economic and ethical grounds.

Our study focused on Bank-assisted projects, rather than on the more numerous displacements occurring in the countless projects supported by domestic resources alone. However, since the present chapter addresses resettlement issues as a worldwide problem and is not a World Bank report, let me state bluntly that the worst consequences of forced displacement occur in domestic projects that are not guided by national or international *policy* norms. Our study found that impoverishment and brutal violations of basic human rights happen most frequently in programmes that are not subject to agreements on policy guidelines and to professional outside review, supervision and evaluation. Such domestic projects account for the overwhelming majority – at least 95 per cent! – of the millions and millions of people forcibly displaced worldwide. This fact is the irrefutable argument for the adoption of national policies and legal frameworks for resettlement in all developing countries.

How does impoverishment through displacement occur and how can it be prevented?

I have examined abundant empirical evidence and compared the findings of numerous anthropological, sociological and geographical studies, in order to distinguish the basic processes that occur when people are forcibly displaced. What these comparisons have revealed, beyond the enormous diversity of individual situations, are *patterns* of recurrent characteristics. Initially I defined seven characteristics or sub-processes (Cernea 1990a), and subsequently identified one more, outlining a pattern of eight typical interconnected trends (Cernea 1993b). Together, they constitute the model of the overall *impoverishment process*. This model captures not only the economic, but also the social and cultural impoverishment, reflecting the fact that displaced people lose natural capital, man-made capital, human capital and social capital.

The eight sub-processes that converge in impoverishment are not the only, but rather the most important, ones. In different locations, they occur with variable intensities. Very concisely, these are:

1. *Landlessness.* Expropriation of land removes the main foundation upon which people's productive systems, commercial activities and livelihoods are constructed. This is the principal form of de-capitalisation and pauperisation of displaced people, through loss of both physical and man-made capital.

2. *Joblessness.* Loss of employment particularly affects urban people, but also occurs regularly in rural areas, displacing landless labourers and service workers, artisans and small businessmen. Creating new jobs is as difficult as finding empty lands, and resulting unemployment or underemployment lingers long after physical relocation.

3. *Homelessness.* Loss of housing and shelter is temporary for most displacees, but for some it remains a chronic condition. In a broader cultural sense, homelessness is also *placelessness*, loss of a group's cultural space and identity, or cultural impoverishment, as argued by Downing (1994, 1995) and by students of 'place attachment' (Low and Altman 1992).

4. *Marginalisation.* Marginalisation occurs when families lose economic power and slide downwards: middle-income farm households do not become landless, but become small landholders; small shopkeepers and craftsmen are downsized and slip below poverty thresholds. Relative marginalisation often begins long before the actual displacement; for instance, when lands are condemned for future flooding and are implicitly devalued, new public and private infrastructural investments are prohibited, and the expansion of social services is undercut.

5. *Increased Morbidity.* Serious decreases in health levels result from the outbreak of relocation-related parasitic and vector-born diseases (malaria, schistosomiasis) and from increased stress and psychological traumas. Vulnerability to illness is increased, and unsafe water supply and waste systems tend to proliferate infectious diseases, diarrhoea, dysentery, etc.

6. *Food Insecurity.* Forced uprooting increases the risk that people will fall into chronic food insecurity, defined as calorie-protein intake levels below the minimum necessary for normal growth and work. Sudden drops in food crops availability and/or

incomes are certain during physical relocation, and hunger or undernourishment tend to be lingering long-term effects.

7. *Loss of Access to Common Property.* For poor people, particularly for the landless and otherwise assetless, loss of access to non-individual, common property assets belonging to communities that are relocated (forested lands, water bodies, grazing lands, etc.) represents a cause of income and livelihood deterioration that is systematically overlooked and typically uncompensated in government schemes (with few exceptions, particularly China).

8. *Social Disarticulation.* The dismantling of communities' social organisation structures, the dispersal of informal and formal networks, associations, local societies, etc., is an expensive yet unquantified loss of social capital. Such 'elusive' disintegration processes undermine livelihoods in ways uncounted and unrecognised by planners and are among the most pervasive causes of enduring impoverishment and disempowerment.

This conceptual construct of the impoverishment process has not only *cognitive value*, but *operational* usefulness as well. First, it provides a *risk model* for planning, by synthesising the lessons of many complex past processes and predicting almost certain outcomes if this warning model is ignored. These eight processes must be seen as a set of potential risks – high-probability risks – that will undoubtedly become real if unheeded, or can be avoided if anticipated and purposively counteracted. Knowledge about these risks can influence reality: as with every risk forecast derived from past experience, this conceptual-predictive model can act as a 'self-destroying prophecy' (see Merton 1957). Risk recognition and analysis are crucial for the argument that impoverishment through displacement can be avoided.

Second, and most important, this conceptual construct of impoverishment through displacement contains *in nuce* the model for the positive re-establishment of those displaced. Indeed, if we turn this model on its head, it suggests precisely what needs to be done to restore, and whenever possible improve, the livelihoods and incomes of those displaced. Turned on its head, the model offers the matrix for the subsequent process – the rehabilitation that must follow displacement. In other words, landlessness risks should be met through land-based planned re-establishment; homelessness through sound shelter programmes; joblessness through employment creation; inevitable disarticulation through purposive community reconstruction and host-resettler integrative strategies, while deliberately enabling inasmuch as is feasible those displaced to share in the specific benefits generated by the programme for which they had to relocate.[2]

The basic policy message embodied in the impoverishment/reconstruction model is that the intrinsic socio-economic risks must be brought under control through an *encompassing strategy* and cannot be tamed through *piecemeal* random measures based solely on financial compensation for condemned assets. Such strategies, however, are seldom developed and even more seldom carried out. We must therefore ask: which factors transform these potential risks into sad reality?

Despite variations between countries, I see several similar common causes of failure:

1. *Policy*: the vast majority of development-caused displacements worldwide are carried out through approaches centred on expropriation and not on income re-establishment. Expropriation laws provide for compensation for condemned assets, but they do not aim at, nor do they promise, re-establishment of prior levels (Shihata 1991a and b, 1993; Paul 1988). Even worse, many decision makers and planners do not recognise that approaches essentially limited to compensation are structurally insufficient and prone to failure. In practice, property acquisition procedures do not provide enough resources to enable displacees to purchase replacement lands and other assets and frequently exclude or underpay significant numbers of affected people. Most governments use the might of the law and their institutional instruments to forcibly displace people, but do not sufficiently use their institutional instruments to facilitate 'land for land' alternatives.

2. *Finances*: the financial resources allocated for displaced people usually fall short, often by large amounts. Limited or absent political commitment, budget constraints and inflexible allocation procedures shrink resources further.

3. *Methodology*: the current methodology for the economic and financial analyses of displacement/relocation costs tends to externalise these costs, rather than to internalise them within project budgets. This is not a minor issue. Some tend to dismissively belittle it, but it is one of the well-kept 'secrets' of resettlement misplanning and failure. When resettlement costs are underassessed (whether deliberately or by error), displacees

2. For instance, enabling reservoir resettlers to relocate on the newly irrigated lands rather than around the reservoir, or providing electricity to relocated villages, or earmarking a share of the revenues resulting from selling energy, or providing access to affordable housing in newly constructed urban areas (see also Cernea 1988a, 1991a and b).

and hosts are forced to bear an undue share of the burden, which reduces their living standards.

4. *Weak Institutions:* the institutions in charge typically lack a policy mandate, commensurate organisational capacity and professional social engineering skills.

5. *Authoritarianism:* both the displaced and the host populations are not empowered to participate adequately in the planning and execution of the relocation, especially in negotiating viable solutions. Effective legal mechanisms for negotiating and resolving grievances are often absent or subverted.

The Resettlers' Income Curve

To take this discussion a step further, let us examine and deconstruct the *income curve of resettlers*. This analysis will demonstrate why compensation for lost assets is alone incapable of restoring prior income levels, and why distinct resources should be invested for resettlers' 'take-off'. In this argument, I am drawing upon the Scudder-Colson (1982) analysis of the phases of resettlement and upon an environmental economics analysis by Pearce (1993).

The resettlers' income curve during the displacement-relocation process consists essentially of four segments:

1. a slow-growing or flat segment preceding displacement
2. a sudden downward segment at dislocation
3. a more-or-less flat segment during the adjustment/transition period at the new site
4. an upward segment once income restoration begins (see Figure 2.1).

The horizontal axis of Figure 2.1 indicates time, and the vertical axis indicates income. Without the project, the income development curve of the area population is estimated conservatively at, say, one per cent per year or less. The curve NR (for 'No Resettlement') illustrates the potential path of income and asset accumulation without the project.

When a project displaces people, this income curve – assumed to be rising only slowly – is suddenly interrupted by displacement, at point D. For the affected people this means an immediate decline in income and assets, represented by the downward segment $D\text{-}D_1$, followed by a transition and adjustment phase, represented by the flat segment $D_1\text{-}A$ (for 'Adjustment'), during which the income remains low, as economic activity is just being resumed at the new

Figure 2.1 Resettlers' Income Curve During Displacement and
Relocation

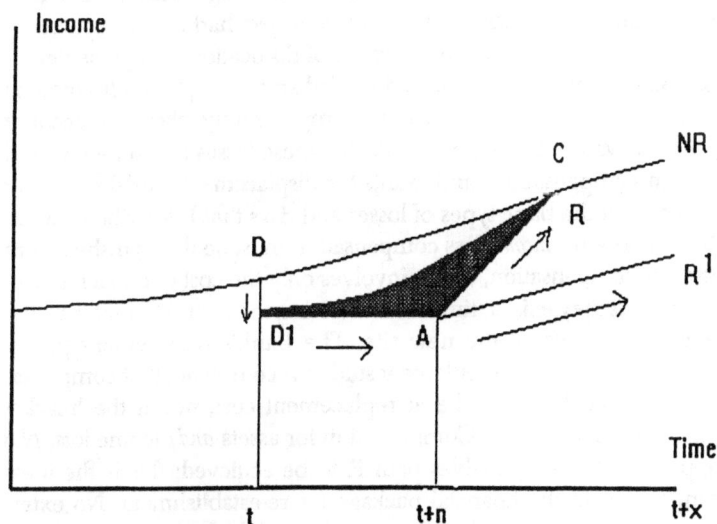

Source: Michael M. Cernea

site during transition. If the resettlement package provided by the
project works, a new development path is established from point A
upwards, represented as path R (for 'Rehabilitation').

To achieve recovery at the same income level as without the project, development path R has to rise faster for a certain period to
catch up to the point at which those displaced would have arrived
spontaneously at time t+x. Path R must therefore be necessarily
steeper than the NR 'normal' curve. Replacement of productive assets
lost alone may, at best, create the material basis for starting on path
R^1, but *additional* investment resources for re-establishment and
restoration are necessary for path R to be steeper than path NR and
catch up with it.

Essentially, this indicates that if the pre-displacement community
was experiencing even slowly rising living standards because of asset
accumulation, the replacement of existing assets is not enough: the
catching up process involves some additional investment and asset
creation. If path R continues to be steeper than NR after t+x, continuing the A-C line beyond the C (catching-up) point would mean
that the resettlers improve over their pre-displacement income.

Figure 2.1 also suggests what would happen if there was only asset
replacement. After the adjustment/transition period between D_1-A

(t to t+n on the time axis), development would recommence along path R^1, but the resettled community would be worse off than it would have been without the project, even though it has resumed its development at the same rate as if the project had never occurred.

The income foregone, lost because of dislocation, is represented in a simplified way by the white and shaded areas (DD_1AC). This income loss is one of the hidden costs of the project, rarely taken into account in the analysis of project costs. Ideally, these losses are to be covered through compensations and grants for displacement hardship, taking into account the basic types of losses and risks that I described earlier. Most important, *income* loss compensation must be distinguished from *asset* loss compensation, which involves only the cost of replacing capital assets as they exist at time t and restoring them, or different income-generating assets, at the new site. The Bank's resettlement policy requires, and various resettlement studies recommend, that compensation for assets lost must be at replacement cost, not at the 'market worth' of the lost assets. Compensation for assets *and* income lost, *plus* support for take-off, enables path R to be achieved; this is the ideal composition of the financial package for re-establishment. No externalisation of any part of these losses to the people displaced must occur.

This analysis also shows that the length of the adjustment transition period is a critical variable, on which the amount of income foregone (lost) by those resettled, and thus the real cost of the project as well, clearly depend. The shorter the transition, the fewer additional costs are caused by the project at large, and the sooner the relocated community gets back on its own feet. When the project is able to deliver a good resettlement package *promptly* to the affected people at dislocation time, the loss tends to be reduced (the white area DD_1c) and project costs are lower. Conversely, if land compensation is underestimated, delivered slowly, and court grievances entail delays in payment, the transition is harder, more painful and additional costs (the full area of DD_1AC) are incurred.

An even better option is to prepare resettlement lands and 'packages' well in advance of dislocation: for instance, China's Shuikou Hydropower project, which I visited in 1994 for the fourth time, shows that establishment of orange orchards by the project is feasible several years beforehand, so they can be at, or close to, first harvest when handed over to resettlers. In this way, transitions can be shortened and income restored faster, with gains to resettlers and savings to the project.

In a sociological perspective, the anatomy of re-establishment costs also highlights the importance of using other levers and resources, of a *non*-financial nature, to reduce costs and accelerate up re-establishment. The process of income restoration is far from being just a cost-compensation transaction: it is a social readjustment process of considerable complexity that also depends upon non-economic factors such as people's forms of social organisation, mobilisation of their energy and innovativeness, participation and motivation, as well as upon the project's institutional efficiency.

In summary, the above analysis leads to important conclusions. The economics of resettlement involve distinct cost categories critical for achieving project results without leaving people worse off; these expenses must be internalised in the overall project budget and financing. Yet current worldwide practice, with limited exceptions, does not use this kind of analysis, externalises significant costs and applies flawed methods in the economic and financial analysis for assessing risks and needed resources. Conversely, when the real costs are fully recognised, important options open up that can help reduce them. The sociological design of resettlement plans should therefore go hand-in-hand with a sound economic and financial analysis of recovery costs and mechanisms for income restoration.

Preventing impoverishment and restoring incomes and livelihoods are not intractable tasks; they are feasible, but very difficult, and require adequate resources, strong political and financial commitment from governments and development sponsors (including the private sector) and intense, strong participation by the populations affected and their organisations.

People's Response: Resistance and Participation

The final question to be considered concerns the currently heightened international interest in resettlement which derives in part from the increasingly organised and publicised resistance to forced displacement in many developing countries. Even if carried out adequately, involuntary resettlement causes social disarticulation. When executed with disregard to people's basic entitlements, it leads to additional social pathologies: avoidable hardship and pain, more losses, social protest, delays of project benefits, sharp political tensions. A Bank field mission reported, for instance, that in the Singrauli Thermal Project in India people opposed the bulldozers which were sent to force them out of their houses and successfully blocked construction of a project building. Another field mission to the Subernarekha Irrigation Project reported strong local protests which have contributed to delaying the impoundment of the Chandil reservoir for two years. In Mexico, protests over the proposed San Juan Tetelcingo project (for which the Bank had previously declined financing) included highway blockades and a large demonstration in Mexico City. In Brazil, community activists formed the Regional Commission Against Large Dams (CRAB), which has since evolved into a national federation of people affected by displacement. In Indonesia, the resistance of many families from the Kendung Ombo reservoir has evolved from refusal to move to court actions all the way to the country's Supreme Court. The anthropological literature, mostly silent about resistance until a few years ago, has started to analyse the growth, structure, patterns and outcomes of expanding social movements opposing displacement (Oliver-Smith 1991a; Good 1992; West 1991 and others).

There are deep causes at the roots of these social conflicts. While surely there are projects where involuntary resettlement can and should be avoided entirely, equally surely, there are many cases where infrastructural projects are indispensable and where developing societies must balance benefits such as safe water supplies, irrigation, efficient transportation systems or urban growth with the costs and pains of resettlement. Many development programmes intrinsically embody or entail this kind of political and economic trade-offs and conflict. These conflicts occur because long-term national or regional interests served by these programmes often cut across the interests of smaller groups, local communities or some individuals. National interests and needs usually prevail. Conflicts emerge because the gains expected from these projects in the long term impose hard-to-bear losses in the short term. As one resettler in India summarised it, 'For their tomorrow, we are giving our today.' Development can never be completely free of conflicts. However, it is unacceptable to unnecessarily exacerbate, instead of reconcile, such conflicts by absence of protective social policies.

The recovery of resettlers' livelihoods is a matter of right and resources. Resource allocation is, in the last instance, a political matter, and not just an economic or financial one. As governmental agencies are using the weight of the state and the force of the law to impose expropriation and displacement, it is incumbent upon governments to also enable those displaced to get back on their feet and share in the benefits for which they are displaced.

Opposition to displacement is not cost-free and painless to those who resist. Government officials or agencies who belittle opposition as the product of a handful of agitators or 'trouble-making NGOs' are deceiving themselves, deceiving the public and distorting the facts. As responsible social research has found, when large numbers of people engage in active resistance to resettlement, they do so because they have no other effective avenues to defend, bargain for and promote their interests. Resettlers' struggles have extracted big improvements in the 'packages' given to resettlers. The story of the Itaparica resettlement in Brazil is a case in point.

The flames of resistance are often ignited not by the hardship of displacement per se, but because the policy and legal vacuums leave few alternatives to political struggle. In a vacuum, abuses and violations go unchecked and unpunished. In a vacuum, one can not breathe. Grievances have little standing in courts. National policy standards are needed in every country to institute norms of fairness, compelling to implementing agencies. Yet the enactment of protective policies is resisted by powerful vested interests. We can often contemplate a socially schizophrenic situation: in the same country people displaced by the same government under two different projects are granted more entitlements and protection under a project co-financed by the World Bank and subject to the Bank's resettlement policy, than their neighbours in the next district displaced by a fully domestic project, to whom the same government denies identical compensation norms. Extending the application of the Bank's policy beyond Bank-assisted projects would be a major step forward.

Recently, market-inspired advocacies increasingly plead the substitution of government agencies with the private (for profit) sector in financing energy investments that entail displacement. Such a trend is in many cases financially sound, but will not diminish the need for protective policies and legal frameworks; if anything, it would reinforce that need. Even more than public sector projects, market economies depend on clear operating rules that apply to all players.

Another factor that exacerbates opposition is the fact that many government agencies decide in secrecy on displacement needs, amounts, procedures, terms and deadlines, without the consultation and participation of those who have their most vital interests at stake. This often forces people to exercise participation by opposition and demonstrative resistance, rather than by bargaining and cooperation in finding the best possible solutions. Not providing information to affected people allows for abuse of entitlements and ends up engendering hostility *vis-à-vis* project authorities.

Is it paradoxical to advocate the 'participation' of people who are displaced in the projects that seek to involuntarily displace them?

Strange as it may appear to some, encouraging and securing the active participation of people in solving the difficult problems of resettlement is essential, in fact even more important than participation in many other types of projects. In substance, there is no paradox: there is acute necessity and mutual interest. Securing genuine participation is indispensable, because without the initiative and mobilisation of the affected people's creativity and energies resettlement cannot succeed. Effective participation is apt to improve the recognition of people's needs, project design and implementation, and particularly the finding of better suited, acceptable solutions.

Participation has prerequisites and takes several forms. The first precondition is to inform the affected populations in time about the need to resettle, about their entitlements, eligibility, options, due process and grievance mechanisms. Next, people and their organisations should be consulted and involved in finding or pondering alternative options and solutions to avoid or minimise displacement, or to identify suitable relocation sites. Further, many NGOs have proven themselves very effective in designing resettlement plans and realistic options, acceptable not only to the people but also to the government, and in mobilising the energies of the resettlers for better implementation, self-help, self-organisation and monitoring of the planned relocation. Starting from 1994, a novel approach is mandated in this respect in World Bank-assisted projects: to improve participation in resettlement, the Bank requires its borrowers to make the resettlement plans available in draft to the public in the project area for review and comment *before* the Bank approves the funding for the new project.

Recent trends in resistance movements are to go beyond project-focused claims and to bring up fundamental issues of resettlement macro-policy. An example comes from India, where a draft national resettlement policy was recently prepared by government agencies for formal adoption. What I find extraordinarily significant is that one Indian NGO has duplicated and sent this draft out to hundreds of various NGOs in all Indian states, to trigger a truly broad national discussion of policy principles for development-necessitated resettlement. One does not need to be a social scientist to predict the heightened awareness such a broad discussion will cultivate, the influence it may have over resettlement operations in many ongoing domestic and internationally assisted projects, and the expanded opportunities for converting good practices and legitimate claims into firm national policy norms.

Current Priorities in Resettlement Research

Despite major progress in social science research on resettlement, which I discussed at the beginning of this chapter, important variables of the resettlement process continue to be understudied and insufficiently known. Let me make a few personal suggestions about overarching priorities on our research front.

The first is to study in more depth the re-establishment segment of the displacement-resettlement continuum. Understandably, the dramas of sudden displacement have attracted more observers than the long, slow, arduous, unspectacular travails of rebuilding livelihoods. However, if social research is to illuminate people's ways out of the displacement dramas, studying the successful adaptive strategies, the rebuilding of production systems and the creation of new social organisation patterns will eventually reduce the hardship and quicken the recovery of future resettlers. Longitudinal studies, comparative studies and short-term impact research stand to discover important responses to many unanswered questions about 'what works' and what does not when dismantled societies, kinship systems and local cultures tend to reassemble, change and function within new encapsulating environments.[3]

An important priority, in my view, stands beyond the confines of sociology or anthropology: it is in the court of our colleagues, the economists. Official misunderstanding or sheer ignorance about the complex economics of displacement and recovery are simply appalling in many agencies and countries. Many pitfalls in current practice can be traced to the sorry state of the economic research on resettlement and to the flawed prescriptions for economic and financial analysis, and for planning, in this domain, as I emphasised earlier. Perhaps anthropologists and sociologists have too-exclusively colonised resettlement ... We must become more inviting of complementary perspectives.

Further, important cognitive gains can be harvested from interdisciplinary and comparative analysis in resettlement. Empirical research in the last decade has advanced mainly in a two-pronged manner: as ethnographic-academic research and as operational action-oriented research. Based on both, more concept-building and new theoretical syntheses are now possible and needed. Unjustified insularity and clogged communication channels between neighbouring research fields, like the deep dichotomy between research on refugees and research on development-displaced people to which I refer elsewhere (Cernea 1996), as well as the yet-unbridged divide between disaster research and displacement research, hamper both knowledge and practice. Here lie other challenges to us for comparative, overarching syntheses.

Evaluation and operational research on resettlement outcomes must be expanded, and not only as an initiative of individual researchers but as a responsibility of governments and institutions. My colleagues and

3. In response to these suggestions the University of Oxford and the Refugee Studies Programme organised a second international conference on resettlement focusing on researching how best to 'reconstruct the livelihoods' of development-displaced peoples and of refugees. The Conference marked a shift from the analysis of impoverishment mechanisms to primarily researching and synthesising the practical experiences of resettlers' coping and adaptation strategies, and the various forms of financial and institutional support that governments can give. Proceedings from that meeting will be published in 1997.

I were gratified to see that our comprehensive evaluation study on policy and performance in the World Bank's resettlement portfolio (World Bank 1994a) has been an instant best-seller and has become influential in both practice and research. To broaden the exchange of policy experiences, a similar multicountry review could be carried out, for instance, around OECD's resettlement guidelines, adopted in 1991. In fact, many bilateral donor agencies, such as GTZ, NORAD, ODA, CIDA, Caisse Centrale, OECF, etc., have long years of experience (that precede the adoption of the OECD guidelines) with projects that entail involuntary resettlement. I am convinced that very useful lessons could be learned and exchanged through such comprehensive agency studies, lessons that are still insufficiently distilled and disseminated. It may well be in the spirit of the World Summit on Social Development to propose that national governmental reviews on population displacement and resettlement become part of the post-Summit work on improving social policies, side-by-side with poverty and other critical issues.

The sober analysis of global development trends tells us that involuntary resettlement will not disappear. It is in fact likely to increase due to urban growth, demographic trends, infrastructural investments, the need to expand irrigation and food production, and also because of policy-induced (as opposed to project-induced) population displacements. Recognising that a certain degree of displacement cannot be avoided does not mean, however, that it should be accepted as a god-ordained tragedy, with little more than a compassionate shrug of the shoulders. If resettlement must happen, then the issue is to change the national and international norms guiding it.

Let me sum up. For this to become a reality, the basic steps are: *first,* the enactment of firm policies and legal frameworks; *second,* the allocation of commensurate resources that will allow internalisation of costs; *third,* the empowerment of resettlers, enabling them to have voice and participation in the decisions and procedures regarding their relocation; and *fourth,* continuation of innovative social research. The urgency and goals of such research are: *to prevent impoverishment and enable those displaced to share in the gains and not just in the pains of development.*

Acknowledgment

Grateful thanks are expressed to Dr.Ruth Cernea for her helpful comments in the preparation of this paper, and to Scott Guggenheim for signals from far away. Gracie Ochieng processed it meticulously, beyond the call of duty.

The views, findings and interpretations contained in this study are those of the author and should not necessarily be attributed to the institutions with which he is associated.

3

Mitigating Social Impoverishment when People are Involuntarily Displaced

Theodore E. Downing

In the previous chapter, Cernea has argued that forced population displacement may lead to eight forms of impoverishment: unemployment, homelessness, landlessness, marginalisation, food insecurity, loss of access to common property, erosion of health status, and social disarticulation (see also Cernea 1990a). Reconfirmed by a wider World Bank review, (World Bank 1994a), each merits preventative measures. This chapter deals with the most conceptually intractable of these problems – that of social impoverishment.[1]

Involuntary population displacement may lead to irreversible social and cultural impoverishment. Resettlement rips routine relations of social time and social space, laying bare critical, but often ignored, dimensions of culture. What is less clear is 'why'? Shamelessly drawing upon my colleagues' work and my experience with resettlement, I offer a prolusion of a theory of social geometry. I argue that involuntary displacement forces people to re-examine primary cultural questions which, under routine circumstances, need not be considered. Key among these is 'where are we'? The social geometry of a people consists of infinite intersections of socially constructed spaces, socially constructed times, and socially constructed person-

1. My appreciation to Thomas Weaver, Edward Hall, Michael Cernea, Scott Guggenheim, Inga-Lill Arronson, Anthony Oliver-Smith, Rohn Eloul and Gilbert Kushner for comments on an earlier version.

ages. And, for many cultures, the geometry also defines 'who are we?' Mitigating social impoverishment begins by reconstructing, in a culturally appropriate manner, the social geometry of the displaced.

Social Impoverishment

Why does involuntary displacement increase the risk of social disorder? When people are refugees from war, famine or natural disasters, social chaos seems macabrely expectable. However, when people are displaced by development projects, social impoverishment seems incongruous, if not grotesque. Provided that relocated persons are granted adequate compensation for lost goods, health care, housing and humanitarian assistance, involuntary resettlement should be little more than a temporary inconvenience. Relatives, friends and neighbours are still alive. Families are not permanently fragmented. New economic opportunities may be provided. Community infrastructure may be upgraded. Movable property may be relocated to the new environs, and exposure to natural hazards reduced. In some cases, some people may be wealthier than they were before.

To their disappointment, politicians, engineers and resettlement specialists have discovered that involuntary resettlement sometimes unravels the underlying social fabric. In resettlement after resettlement, similar patterns reappear (World Bank 1994a, Cernea 1993b). Vital social networks and life-support mechanisms for families are weakened or dismantled. Authority systems are debilitated or collapse. Groups lose their capacity to self-manage. The society suffers a demonstrable reduction in its capacity to cope with uncertainty. It becomes qualitatively less than its previous self. The people may physically persist but the community that was is no more. Social scientists have not reached agreement on what to call this social phenomenon which haunts involuntary resettlement, but I prefer to use Cernea's terminology – social disarticulation (Cernea 1994a).

Discomfort

Despite universal acceptance by resettlement theorists and policy makers that there are social impacts to resettlement and that the negative ones should be avoided, I am uncomfortable with the theoretical underpinnings of resettlement policy, and by extension refugee studies. So-called 'social costs' and 'social impacts' are mentioned again and again without clearly explaining what is meant by 'social'. I am equally uncomfortable with the ease with which only economic actions are prescribed to mitigate social impoverishment. Conventional wisdom is synthesised into prescriptive economic action – holding that social impoverishment, like other forms of impoverishment, can be mitigated by re-establishing disrupted productive activities. Granted that re-establishment of the economy is indispensable to successful economic recovery and poverty abatement, I am still not convinced that destruction of a local economic order is the primary reason for social disarticulations.

Careful examination of the temporal sequencing of resettlement reveals something is amiss. Signs of social disorder appear quite early in the resettlement, often *before* the loss of productive activities, when relocatees are reaping benefits of the temporary employment boom and indemnifications associated with public works. Conversely, communities which are not being resettled undergo transformations of productive activities all the time without the radical social disorder associated with resettlement. Apart from the very serious socio-political consequences associated with the coerciveness of the decision, the fact that people move from one place to another should not lead to the radical social changes which have been witnessed. Nor should we anticipate social changes greater than those normally observed with voluntary migration, trips to the market or visits to a relative. Unlike plants, people move about all the time.

My discomfort increased as I struggled with unanswered, apparently unrelated questions which keep reappearing in resettlement after resettlement, and not coincidentally, in studies of recovery from natural disaster (Oliver-Smith 1986). Why do children seem to recover more quickly than adults? Why do some resettled people return again and again to the shores of a lake covering their inundated home and experience a sense of relief from their visits? And why do disaster victims sometimes refuse to move into shelters, preferring to camp at the location of their former homes? Why do resettlers not occupy houses that architects have carefully modeled after their original houses? And why do resettlers and disaster victims often describe their experience 'like a dream'? I wondered if a focus upon the political and economic dimensions of involuntary resettlement had led us to ignore subtle, important social dimensions of such events – hidden dimensions that might prove crucial to mitigating social impoverishment and, perhaps, facilitate political and economic restoration.

My discomfort could have been easily assuaged if resettlement policy and practice were based on a firm theory of spatial and temporal dislocation which explained why and how social disarticulation occurred. It is not. Fortunately, the building blocks for construction of a powerful theory of social dislocation are scattered about in the form of bits and pieces of observations, concepts and insights from every conceivable discipline and in all the cracks in between. Outside of the arena of displacement, almost every social scientists worthy of note has probably, at some point, struggled with social definitions of time and space although only a handful have worked on the dysfunctional situation where this order is disrupted.

Social Geometry

For most, culture answers what I prefer to call 'primary questions'. Primary questions are: Who are we? Where are we? Why do people live and die? What are our responsibilities to others and ourselves? In everyday life, the answers are routinely provided, leaving it up to the individual to focus upon tactical problems. How might I move to a more desirable location, how might I make minor adjustments within my own backyard? Life focuses upon repairing broken doors, collecting firewood, getting from one well-known place to another, gaining access to restricted places/situations by performing routine events such as going to school, paying for admissions or working for income to facilitate tactical adjustments to life. The routine culture is what social scientists normally describe. In routine culture, people navigate within a space-time continuum in which they chart their positions within socially constructed time, socially constructed space, and among socially constructed personages.[2]

Victims of involuntary resettlement and natural disasters and refugees experience an unexpected destabilisation of routines. In rural cultures whose group and self-definitions are inexorably inter-locked with their knowledge of their local environment, resettlement can devalue their shared survival skills and lead to what Bartolomé and Barabas(1992) have called 'ethnocide'. From the perspective I am proposing, relocatees are forced to re-examine their primary cultural questions – 'where are we?' And, for most, this means, also re-examining 'who are we?'

Properties of Spatial-Temporal Order

The disruption occurs along multiple dimensions of a culturally arbitrary, but nonetheless meaningful spatial-temporal order. I wish to identify ten salient properties of the social space-time continuum, demonstrate how they appear in displacement situations, and then turn to ways in which this knowledge might be used to mitigate social impoverishment. Although my anthropological training tempts me

---

2. Social geometry requires the social scientists to remove their disciplinary blinders which needlessly limit their field of view to social organisation.

to draw on exotic spatial-temporal orders (see Fabian 1992), I will try to draw my examples from an English-speaking culture.

Multi-dimensionality. Most cultures command a vast repertoire of concepts and coordinates of time and space which overshadow the mechanistic, equal interval measures (Bock 1968; Sutro and Downing 1988; Hall 1959; Low 1992; Turner 1990). Within the narrow temporal confines of measuring the time of day, Frake (1993) observes great variation in how societies slice time. Culturally specific interval time systems include variations in the numbers of minutes in an hour, Canonical hours, Jewish hours, astrological signs, Saint's Day cycles and Greek hours. The evolution of Western technology is tightly linked with a struggle to create mechanical analogues of socially meaningful time.

Recent first-hand, cross-cultural evidence has revealed rich variations in constructions of time, especially among indigenous people (Layton 1994). These constructions need not depend upon a written tradition. To highlight only the most obvious constructions, consider festival calendars, planting and harvesting calendars, weekly marketing calendars and so on. In many societies, the organisation of time has become a major political resource and its control varies with competing elements of a society (de Pina-Cabral 1994; Males 1994; Elazar 1994; Rutz 1992).

Space and time are socially defined and ordered in many ways. Time may be linear (1993, 1994, 1995) containing within it sets of repetitive, cyclical orders (Monday, Tuesday, Wednesday ... night/day, lunar cycles and so on). Temporal-spatial orders may be shared with larger groups (a national festive calendar, Mexico City as the capital), or may be regional (market days and regional fairs), local (patron saint's days, unique historical events, harvest calendars) or even familial (wedding anniversaries). Social geometry shows properties of inclusion both temporally (e.g., second, minute, hour, day, year) and spatially (e.g., yard, neighbourhood, barrio, town, county, state, nation, continent). Orders may also be temporally sequential (baby, child, teenager, adult, old) and spatially sequential (gate, courtyard, entrance, house). Complex orderings may involve a sequential intersection of time, space and personages (baptism, confirmation, first communion, marriage). In brief, it follows that societies have many social geometries – alternative logic constructs of order. A social spatial-temporal continuum may be simultaneously 'occupied'. For example, a person might be in Mexico City, at the doorway to the Virgin of Guadelupe and having a birthday.

Intangibility. Cultural spaces and times are often intangible, but real. They need not occupy the physical universe familiar to an engineer. Imagined spatial orders have more meaning, power and importance in the role of human experience than concretely experienced social orders (Riley 1994). We do not need anthropological fieldwork in the Developing World in order to understand this. Millions of Christians share familiarity with places to which they have never been and may never reach – Calvary and Heaven. Social groups can be expected to hold special rights to times and places – an ownership as socially recognised, and often more respected, than a legal title.

Behavioural ordering. Patterns of social behaviour are associated with culturally recognised spaces and times – be they tangible or not. The particular configurations of the geometry create order in the form of finite expectations for social actors and action. They provide human beings with productive rules for acting appropriately in different situations (Hall 1959; Bock 1968). Catholics, for example, expect a Mass at the hinge of a socially constructed time (Sunday, weddings, funerals, political transitions), place (altar in the Church), and personage (Priest). Remove any of the three elements and something is amiss. Economists quickly learn this when they try to provide rural resettlers with a subsidy for crop losses as a protection against social disorder. Harvest is not simply an output of a commodity. It is the association of familiar people at a particular place in a biotemporal cycle.

Prioritisation. Social geometries are also prioritised. Profound differences have been detected between ordinary and extraordinary spatial and temporal orders (Low and Altman 1992). Times and places, just like people, are frequently ranked with some being more valued than others (weekends > workdays, and Sunday > Monday in Christian societies). Prioritised orders often validate fundamental social values and beliefs. For example, the highest valence possible in the Catholic spatial-temporal order occurs when a high valence time in their religious calendar – Easter, intersects a high valence place in their spatial order – the Vatican, and a high valence personage in the social organisation – the Pope. The high valence geometry – Easter/Vatican/Pope – is linked to the expectation of a message for Peace and Hope directed to the World and a High Mass. Barring the Apocalypse, a thousand Easters from now, the intersection of three dimensions should recreate the same sense of awe among the faithful and tangibly demonstrate the eternalness of the Church.

As groups are threatened with forced relocation, they experience unparalleled disruptions of routine behaviours. Their spatial-temporal geometry fails to answer primary cultural questions. Undoubtedly, there are many possible social responses to this unstable situation. One that I have identified is what I might call the 'high-frequency accentuation' hypothesis. In response to the threat, the group increases the frequency of heretofore occasional, high-priority events – attempting to bind the community together. In June of 1994, I had the opportunity to observe support for my hypothesis in a community being relocated by the Zimapan hydroelectric project. Before relocation, people from the small Catholic community of La Vega moved their village patron saint each year from one private household to another and celebrated a special Mass. Immediately following resettlement, the saint began weekly rather than annual visits, moving from one relocated household to the next as the community struggled to reaffirm and re-establish its identity. Whether or not high-frequency accentuation actually mitigates social impoverishment needs further testing.

Moral ordering. Social status and moral correctness is usually associated with access to or exclusion of certain kinds of people from certain places at certain times. Highly structured inclusion (and exclusion) of categories of people to particular places at particular times is the essence of sacredness. In the south-western United States, Brazil, and among the aborigines of Western Australia, anthropologists have found that indigenous people use spatially anchored narratives for moral teachings (Low 1992; Fabian 1992; Basso 1984). In these cases, spatial attachment need not necessarily require or even be related to legal ownership of place.

Gender, age and rank specificity. Perhaps the most obvious finding of social geometry is that specific behaviours and expectations are associated with people of different age, sex and rank being and *not being* in particular places at particular times. Gender differences change over a lifespan (that is, with time). In U.S. culture, Marcus found that men are 'more likely to replay childhood patterns in terms of layout and form of the house, while women are more likely to do this in relation to furniture or movable objects ' (Marcus 1994). A key element of enculturation, the process of learning a culture, involves distinguishing the spatial-temporal appropriate behaviours of sex, age and rank (Pellow 1994; Douglas 1973). Pellow (1994), following Giddens (1984), has shown how the urban courtyards in Accra, Ghana, provide a place for multiple settings in which social conduct is chronically reproduced and where newcomers, particularly women, may learn urban forms of interaction and gain new identities.

Imbeddeness. Forming the basis of routine interaction, social geometries are often as conservative as they are arbitrary. The seven-day week is the most obvious example of an artificial, mathematical rhythm disassociate with nature that sets the cadence for most of the world's cultural activities. Three of the great religions may differ on what day of the week the cycle peaks, but they share conservative agreement as to the number of days in a week. In both the French and Russian Revolutions, unsuccessful and, for some, fatal attempts were made to change the number of days in a week (Zerubavel 1985).

Imbeddedness is also evident within the lifespan of individual members of the culture. Research on environmental memories has discovered the near universality of fondly remembered childhood places, representing the intersection of culturally constructed time and place (Marcus 1994). In more mobile societies, continuity of environmental memories is more rooted in things – movable, storable, shippable – rather than in attachment to a concrete physical space. This finding is particularly important for those working on urban resettlement. Attachment to objects filled with memories substantially increases with age (Marcus 1994; Csikszentimihalyi and Rochberg-Halton 1981). Resettlement practice, but not theory, has long recognised the need for special consideration of more elderly in a society, who seem more likely to show higher mortality and anomie (Ault 1994).

Dissatisfaction with existing orders. Resettlement practitioners are learning that one-for-one restoration of existing spatial arrangements may not necessarily mitigate social impoverishment. Existing spatial and temporal arrangements are not always optimal. Witness how some people periodically rearrange their personal space. At the resettlement which recently took place at the Aguamilpa hydroelectric dam in western Mexico, architects and anthropologists worked side-by-side to design four different house types which followed traditional, indigenous, Huichol design principles (Guggenheim 1993:221). Guggenheim reports, 'the families hated the new houses.' The designers assumed that the Huichol wanted traditional thatched roofs. In response, a Huichol noted that ' thatch may look very refreshing and folkloric for you who come from far away, but you don't have to live with scorpions falling into your soup every time you sit down to dinner.' Thatch was the best material that they could afford. At the Zimapan hydroelectric dam, I discovered that, at the last minute, several male heads of households hastily rearranged meticulously planned, spatial layouts of houselots in a new community to decrease contact with their mother-in-laws! Nor can one expect intrasociety uniformity of satisfaction. Environmental memory research has found that some people choose to reproduce the essence of their childhood spatial arrangements in adulthood, while others choose to create a contrasting environment.

Attachment to space and time. Attachment to space and time can be a powerful binding force for displaced social groups. Oliver-Smith's (1986) work on the cultural responses in the aftermath of a 1970 Peruvian earthquake is an exemplar of the widely reported bereavement and symbolic importance of attachment to place and its role in reconstruction of community identity. Similarly, Setha Low (1992) notes that

> the longing of exiled people and refugees to return to their homeland, and the importance of the symbolic existence of that homeland (as in the case of Israel), suggests that loss or destruction of place is as powerful an attachment as its presence.

In a comparable manner, attachment to time, a particular constructed history, may be an equally powerful force for binding people to one another. Evidence of this is emerging in exciting new research on the values indigenous peoples attached to cultural constructs of 'their past' (Layton 1994). Temporal-spatial identification systems may be quite extensive and subtle, extending far beyond small primary groups and settlements. Recent work in southern Mexico shows that culturally constructed time may be encoded into the landscape and take on concrete architectural form. Archaeologists working at the famous ancient city of Monte-Alban found that the length of adjacent ball-courts and the distances between ceremonial sites were proportionate to the ratio of the number of days in the Zapotec astronomical and ceremonial calendars (Peeler and Winter 1993). In a display of genius foreshadowing modern relativity, the Zapotecs have architecturally united their organisation of space and time.

Control, manipulation and recreation. Landscape architect studies have shown that control over meaningful space: manipulation of that space by means of construction, subtle changes, decoration, modification and the recreation of previous settings in the future, help people to define who they are. In urban areas, for example, the ability of the resettled people to recreate the interior of their home in a new apartment, and to find a parallel in the layout of rooms, increased their chances of positively adjusting to a move (Marcus 1994).

Observational Support

If socio-temporal order gives a society predictability and sets priorities and meaning, its destruction may render social life chaotic, unpredictable and meaninglessness. Involuntary relocation overloads a society with uncertainties and disorder. In large-scale infrastructure projects, such as hydroelectric dams, spatial-temporal dislocation can begin months before the physical relocation – construction work begins, the routine order of daily life and the landscape is fractured by unscheduled high explosives – creating a demonstrable uneasiness among the population (Inga-Lill Arronson, personal communication 1993). From the perspective of social geometry, social dislocations accompanying involuntary resettlement may change some of the spatial-temporal dimensions which define a people's identity, threaten intangible spaces and moral order, modify behavioural orders, set new priorities and have a differential impact on people depending on their age, sex and rank. Hopefully, resettlement may offer some or all of those being resettled an opportunity to correct dissatisfactions with the previous order. I will now examine six discernible patterns.

Relocated and disaster-struck communities show what some might consider an irrational attachment to inexact, prioritised spatial-temporal orders. In central Mexico, three adjacent riverine *mestizo* peasant communities near the Zimapan Dam were relocated to a nearby arid, riverless plateau. Potable water was piped in from twenty-three kilometres away and no water was available for irrigation. Early in the project, resettlers were permitted to rename the principal street in their new town. To the surprise of outside observers, they named their principal street River Boulevard. The local resettlement team reported serious conflicts between rival community claims over who had the right to live on the right bank of 'River Street,' in a position identical to their previous location. A few months later, they selected the new name for their arid, hilltop community: Bella Vista del Rio (Beautiful View of the River). But the river is nowhere to be seen.

Cernea offers another example of ingenuous solutions to spatial-temporal distortion. In Fugian Province, China, involuntary resettlement gave Chinese peasant families a rare opportunity. Young people from large, extended families could obtain new houseplots, but the issue became 'where'? In the local social geometry, house sites adjacent to the main road were more valuable. Only a few could have choice locations and the potential for internal conflict was evident. The dissatisfaction was rectified by the peasants, who revamped their lottery system to permit the drawing of a cluster of 2-3 housesites (Cernea, personal communication November 1994). The element of chance, which plays a powerful role in social geometry, was reintroduced into an over-structured planning exercise.

The power of the continuum – the attachment to prior conceptions of socio-cultural space – has been witnessed again and again in disasters. Following the devastation of Hurricane Andrew in 1990, families in Homestead, Florida, preferred to camp among the ruins of their homes rather than accept government shelter – often maintaining precisely the same spatial arrangements in the streets that were present in their now obliterated apartments. A comparable attachment was witnessed following the 1978 Mexico City earthquake, when families camped in front of the rubble of their fallen apartment houses – in some cases maintaining the same spatial referents which they had to their neighbours. Something is occurring which goes beyond a rudimentary defence of what might remain of one's property.

It follows that re-establishment of spatial-temporal prioritisation and order is an important part of the recovery process. An American television network's videotape crew followed one of the 200,000 families left homeless by this hurricane – the Lucketts (ABC News 1992). The Lucketts are an extended, sixty-five person matriarchal clan who, before the disaster, occupied sixteen homes in Homestead, Florida. Homeless, without belongings, they were temporarily relocated in a high school auditorium. The Luckett clan's women concentrated on re-establishing the routine organisation of the family, focusing on the children. The women stressed that it was important that the children have 'three meals a day, bath, and get to bed on time.' At the shelter, each part of the family organised a small, personal space. The children's behaviour in their socially defined space was of considerable concern as the mothers struggled to establish where they perceived the children should and should not go within the school auditorium and yard. They made and believed in an unstated contract with the relief officials. The matriarch told the interviewer, 'if the children don't get out of line ... don't go where they're not supposed to ... then we won't get kicked out into the streets.' Re-establishment of temporal priorities was evident when the entire gymnasium of relocatees joined in celebrating what might normally be an insignificant familial ritual – a birthday party, as a human-scale temporal regularity returned to an incomprehensible large disaster.

Social geometry provides insights into another problem. Following Hurricane Andrew, the Luckett matriarch stumbled through the ruins of what, a week before, had been her home. She described her post-relocation situation 'like a dream in which you wake up'. In June 1994 in central Mexico, I listened to a distraught young wife describing her loss following our visit to a mountain top where we watched a new reservoir slowly flood what had been, for many generations, her family's home. Using almost identical words, she described her feelings 'like a dream. Someday I will wake up'. In both cases, the women's expressions are more than metaphors. In human experience, dreams are thoughts disoriented in time and space (Friedlander 1940). They represent another geometry which is divorced from the elaborate, ordered conscious geometries which characterise waking life. From the perspective of social geometry, both women's descriptions were correct.

The spatial-temporal order influences which segments of a population will be affected by social dislocation. This sometimes yields unexpected results. Investigations following the devastating 1976 Guatemala earthquake uncovered an unusual age-specific mortality pattern. Eighty per cent of casualties were the penultimate child (Kates 1973). Rural, indigenous Guatemalans suffered heavy casualties. In this culture, it is common for the youngest child to sleep next to the mother, and the penultimate child sleeps with the elder brothers and sisters. The quake struck at 3:05 am on 4 February. The youngest were protected by the parents when the quake hit, but the weakest child, the penultimate child, was the most exposed to danger. Consequently, the socio-spatial and socio-temporal sleeping patterns exposed a particular segment of the population to higher mortality.

For some time, I was puzzled by the apparent resiliency of children to involuntary resettlement and natural disasters. Within days of the disaster, the children of the Luckett clan gleefully played basketball in the relocation camp. Within two weeks of what, to the adults, was a traumatic relocation in Zimapan, Mexico – adults locked themselves in their new suburban-style houses, complete with satellite dishes – children played tag in the new town's streets. I was mistaken. I was not witnessing resiliency, but support for the theory of social geometries. Children have rudimentary spatial-temporal orders (times: play, eat, and rest; space: home, neighbours, street) unaffected by the more complex orders that they will ultimately learn to respect and value. It is a quality which Hotchkiss (1967) identified as the non-person status of a child which permits them almost unrestricted freedom of egress and ingress and, he argues, makes them ideal spies. It is the same quality which makes them more resilient to relocation, since they are less tied to the complex of learned social geometries of adults.

Policy And Other Implications

For over fifteen years, development anthropologists and sociologists – led by their colleagues in the World Bank – have painstakingly crafted a policy framework to mitigate the harmful economic and social impacts of involuntary resettlement (Cernea 1993b; Kardam 1993).[3] An architect of the policy and Senior Advisor on Social Policy at the World Bank notes that resettlement policy has been enhanced by the feedback between theoretical assumptions about change and lessons gleaned from development projects (Cernea 1993b). As feedback and theory have changed, the policy frameworks have been updated and refined (World Bank 1994a). Identification of the eight forms of impoverishment, mentioned at the outset, is a relatively recent example of this knowledge-based policy.

At this point, the theory of social impoverishment seems to be edging ahead of policy development. Presently, resettlement policies pay minimal attention to mitigating spatial dislocation and almost no attention to relieving temporal dislocation. World Bank policy (OD 4.30 para. 7) and OECD guidelines propose identical language – 'reducing dispersion, sustaining existing patterns of group organisation, and retaining access to cultural property (temples, pilgrimage centers, etc.), if necessary through the relocation of that property (OECD 1991).'[4] In the realm of want-to-be policies, the American Anthropological Association White Paper on Involuntary Resettlement goes further, introducing an element of temporality – reducing social costs by making the move as quickly as possible and avoiding temporary holding facilities (American Anthropological Association 1991). In light of the preceding discussion, it is apparent that the policies are culturally unsophisticated. Practice supports this judgement. A simple decision to displace a population to a location proximate to that of origin does not necessarily reduce human and social costs (Lightfoot 1979).

On a positive note, resettlement practitioners who are directly responsible for resettlement operations, as well as many of those who are displaced, are well aware of the dislocation problems that I have identified in this discussion. Some have, with minimal theoretical or policy guidance, forged solutions of their own. In western Mexico, for example, Huichol resettlers worked with anthropologists to record not just sites being inundated, but to create a symbolic reference map for the new sites (Guggenheim 1993:224). In Zimapan, Mexico, the centrality of the bandstand *(kiosk)* to community life was

---

3. By 1995, the policy framework had been extended to only a few other international donors (BID and OECD) and countries.
4. It remains an untested proposition that the sacredness of a site is linked to its geographic coordinates. Certainly major conflicts in Jeruselum could be resolved if it were possible to move or relocate temples and pilgrimage centres (the physical structures) without regard to their physical location.

recognised, and each of the three communities was provided with a spatial area for performing recurring temporal events. Government engineers wisely postponed a scheduled relocation until after the annual village festival and organised a new festival to celebrate the founding of the new town. The relocation was stressful, but peaceful. Comparable sensitivity is reported on the successful resettlement at the Costa Rican Arenal Hydroelectric project (Partridge 1993).

Drawing policy lessons from these isolated cases is risky. The sensitivity of people to social and temporal displacement varies markedly between, as well as within, groups. Some show minimal disorientation. Others become almost culturally dysfunctional. This variation forces policies to identify groups at high risk. It appears that people with long-standing relationships to their environment, especially indigenous populations, will be more likely to need special attention.

The combination of theoretical findings and development experience strongly suggests that social impoverishment of displaced people can be mitigated by intentionally repairing fractured social geometries. The solution requires that resettlement policy step outside the narrow arena of economic rehabilitation and technological fixes. It requires solid, innovative ethnographic work to complement aerial photography, conventional mapping, demographic surveys and socio-economic censuses. In addition, it requires close scientific collaboration between the displaced and the cultural analyst which can never be accomplished in a windshield visit to a relocation area.

Positive actions to reduce social impoverishment include:

Field Reviews. Policy development will emerge from the interchange of the rich, on-going research into spatial-temporal organisation and the growing practical experiences of resettlement projects. Cases of development-induced displacement should be reviewed to uncover serendipitous or intentional actions which helped people re-establish their social geometry. How did they find (new?) answers to primary cultural questions, especially 'where are we?' and 'who are we?' The results of this rich experience should be codified into systematic social knowledge.

Social geometric analysis. A cross-culturally applicable, rapid-assessment methodology must be developed to discover the social geometries of people to become a part of project planning and execution. Minimally, the method would a) identify and prioritise the times and places which people regard as critical to their society, b) identify intra-group differences which are likely to be effected by social dislocation (e.g., religious, gender or class differences), and c) find areas of dissatisfaction which might provide a potential ray of hope for planning a future following displacement. The methodology might adapt techniques used to study 'attachment to space' to the analysis to understand the social geometric matrix of time/space/person. Likely remodelling candidates for creative adaptation are spatial memory studies, environmental autobiographies, role playing, behavioural mapping and favourite-place analysis, as well as more formal ethnographic methods.

Theory building. Much work remains to refine the theory of social geometries, starting with a synthesis of more than a century of insightful intellectual efforts to understand spatial-temporal organisation which is dispersed throughout many disciplines.

Open dialogues. Awareness of the social impoverishment problem may increase by encouraging in-house discussions and workshops within development agencies and non-governmental organisations. Those to be displaced must also be provided with an opportunity to examine and search for ways to protect what might be heretofore hidden dimensions of their culture.

Refinement of operational indicators for project performance. Social impoverishment indicators of spatial-temporal disruptions should provide 'early warnings' of more serious social and economic dysfunction in a displaced population. Development and monitoring of social-geometric indicators may be injected into project cycles. This would include explicit recognition of the threat of social impoverishment and planning for its mitigation. At minimum, operations would include pre-resettlement social geometry surveys and plans to mitigate social impoverishment in culturally acceptable ways, with full participation of members of the affected population in both the initial study and the reconstruction.

Determination of rates of return. It is highly probable that minimising social impoverishment and economic impoverishment are mutually reinforcing actions. A review might be undertaken to determine if the rates of return of projects which resolved socio-temporal disruptions were higher than the rates of return of those that did not, in a fashion comparable to the classic World Bank study by Kottak (1991).

Conclusion

Each year, another ten million people become involuntarily displaced and risk social impoverishment (World Bank 1994a). Social impoverishment occurs when the displaced are unable to answer the primary cultural question – 'where are we'? For many, the answer to this question also defines 'who are we?' Reconstruction of the lives of the displaced demands carefully, coordinated economic *and* social action. It requires a theory capable of explaining how displacement leads to social impoverishment. I advocated a theory of social geometry, finding that the answers to primary questions are encoded in the linkage of socially constructed places, socially constructed time and socially constructed personages. This linkage provides a framework for routine and ritual activities. Weaken the framework, and social impoverishment becomes likely. Reconstruct it, and increase the likelihood of meaningful reconstruction of the lives of the displaced.

4

Development-Induced Impoverishment, Resistance and River-Basin Development

Thayer Scudder

Introduction

Past research on the impacts of river-basin development on local populations has concentrated on those undergoing relocation. Where used, the term 'hosts' refers to those who host the relocatees rather than to those who 'host' the project. Similarly the phrase 'project-impacted people' or 'project-affected people' (PAPs), which is prominent in the literature on India, refers primarily to those who must undergo resettlement. This narrow vision has tended to obscure the fact that often those undergoing removal and their hosts are a minority of those who subsequently may be impoverished by a particular development intervention. Yet even where they constitute a majority, project-impacted people who are not relocatees, hosts or immigrants have been largely ignored by academics, planners, donors and non-governmental agencies alike.

In this chapter, I will use the term project-impacted people to include four major categories. These are a) those whose relocation is required (called relocatees for short); b) those among whom they are resettled (hereafter referred to as hosts); c) all other river-basin residents who are neither hosts nor relocatees (PAPs in this paper); and d) immigrants. Immigrants will not be dealt with in any detail since they, of the four categories, are most apt to be project beneficiaries.

Immigrant examples include those responsible for planning, designing and implementing a project as well as those who come at a later date to exploit project-related opportunities.

Immigrants responsible for the different stages of the project cycle include not just planners and those responsible for project operation and maintenance, but also the construction labour force. Though numbering in the thousands for larger projects, it is the case that with such projects, which are often advertised as a project to benefit local people, few local people have the skills to compete even for jobs as labourers. Construction of China's Three Gorges Project, for example, will probably draw mainly on some 40,000 workers who were involved in the completion of the Gezouba Dam immediately downstream and who, in the late 1980s, were standing by. To take another multi-billion dollar example, local Cree employed during the construction of the La Grande phase of Quebec's James Bay Project comprised less than 3 per cent of the labour force. A far larger number were available but had neither the language (French) nor technical skills.

One of the few major benefits of dam construction for low-income people pertains to fishing the reservoir. Even here, however, fisherfolk tend to be immigrants from other more established fisheries. Such has been the case with most of the larger artificial reservoirs in Africa including those backed up behind the Kariba, Volta, Manantali and Aswan High dams. At Kariba, for example, approximately 50 per cent of those involved in the current artisanal fishery are immigrants, while the owners of all but five of the capital-intensive rigs used for the lucrative open-water sardine fishery (with landings of over 20,000 tons per annum) are also immigrants. On the Volta, Manantali and Aswan High Dam reservoirs, the large majority of fishers are immigrants.

Least analysed by either academics or those responsible for feasibility studies, or more specifically for environmental impact assessments, are river-basin residents who are neither relocatees or hosts. Such project-affected people also tend to be left out of the type of environmental and socioeconomic development guidelines first pioneered by the World Bank. While Bank documents (1980 and 1994a) emphasise the need to deal equitably with relocatees and hosts, they largely ignore other project-impacted people. Yet in situation after situation they constitute the majority of those whose living standards are adversely affected by river-basin development activities. Though there are a few exceptions, such people also tend to be more vulnerable to manipulation and less apt to mount effective, or indeed any, resistance movements. I suspect the absence of resistance movements is due primarily to two factors. One is that those involved tend to be spread out over a much wider area, making alliance forming and political action more difficult. The other is that, with few exceptions, they have yet to receive assistance from national and international conservation, human-rights, and other non-governmental organisations. Where impacted upon by river-basin development, such project-affected people tend to reside in two very different locales. One is within the immediate vicinity of a specific project as in the basin of a large artificial reservoir, adjacent to a large canal, or sandwiched in between a number of projects as in the James Bay case. The other locale is downstream from a particular dam, the impacts of which are apt to extend to the river's delta. That may be over a thousand kilometres of riverine habitat, as in the case of the Kainji and Jebba Dams on the Niger River or Kariba and Cahora Bassa on the Zambezi. Or it may be less than a hundred kilometres, as in the case of Ghana's Volta Dam. Regardless, very serious impoverishment is apt to follow due to habitat change in particular but also to increased competition for land and other resources and for jobs from immigrants.

Impoverishment caused by river-basin development projects is a worldwide phenomenon, the magnitude of which researchers, planners, government officials and donor agencies have been slow to grasp. A major reason for this situation has been the failure of researchers and donors to complete careful evaluations of the impacts of river-basin development projects ten to twenty years after their completion. Granted the fact that such projects are apt to be the largest single expenditure in a nation's development plan, I have always found this fact difficult to understand. Especially puzzling is the failure of the World Bank's Office of Operations Evaluation to carry out such studies.

While relocatees are major victims, at least there is an increasing awareness of their plight as potential 'development refugees'. Over the longer term, however, adverse impacts may be just as serious for other project-impacted people. Long considered a major success story, replicas of the Tennessee Valley Authority (TVA) have been a major U.S. export to Africa, Asia and Latin America. Yet, in a 1984 publication, Chandler persuasively argues that TVA has also impoverished many rural people for the questionable benefit of an urban-industrial elite.

Project-Vicinity Affected People

Introduction

Two cases follow. In the first, project conceptualistion ignored the local population. In the second, the local people were supposed to be the main beneficiaries. Though the first case is more complicated, nonetheless in both cases a strong argument can be made that implementation would have further impoverished an already impoverished population. In both cases the large majority of those involved are neither relocatees nor hosts but rather other project-impacted people living in the project's vicinity.

Hydro-Quebec, James Bay and the Cree

The James Bay Project and the Cree

The James Bay Project provides an excellent case history in that it illustrates the strength of the type of coalition advocating large-scale river-basin development projects, their impoverishing impact on an entire culture area (as opposed to just relocatees and hosts), and the difficulties that local people must face in trying to modify, let alone cancel, projects. Just as TVA was a vision of Roosevelt, the Aswan High Dam and the Volta Dam of Nasser and Nkrumah respectively, and China's Three Gorges Dam to Mao, Chou Enlai and Deng, so was the James Bay complex the vision of Prime Minister Bourassa of Quebec (1985). A provincial parastatal organisation, Hydro-Quebec, was responsible for project planning and design. As Hydro-Quebec's name suggests, the James Bay Project was seen primarily as a single purpose one for the generation of hydro-electric power. A separate parastatal organisation, the James Bay Development Corporation, was subsequently established to 'develop' the area that would be 'opened up' by the project.

As planned, Hydro-Quebec's James Bay Project is one of the five largest contemporary river-basin development projects in the world. If completed, the total generating capacity of more than twelve dams would be about 25,000 megawatts, of which the generating facilities for 10,000 megawatts have either already been completed or are under construction. Between 1971 and 1991 Can.$11 billion have been invested, with the remainder of the complex estimated to cost at least another Can.$40 billion.

Hydro-power is seen as Quebec's major resource for both provincial consumption and for export, with 95 per cent of the province's present installed capacity coming from hydro-power (Hydro-Quebec 1993). Costs to consumers have intentionally been kept low, with the result that Quebec has successfully induced large aluminum and manganese processing industries to set up installations along the Gulf of Saint Lawrence.

Map 4.1 James Bay Power Project as Conceived in the Early 1900s

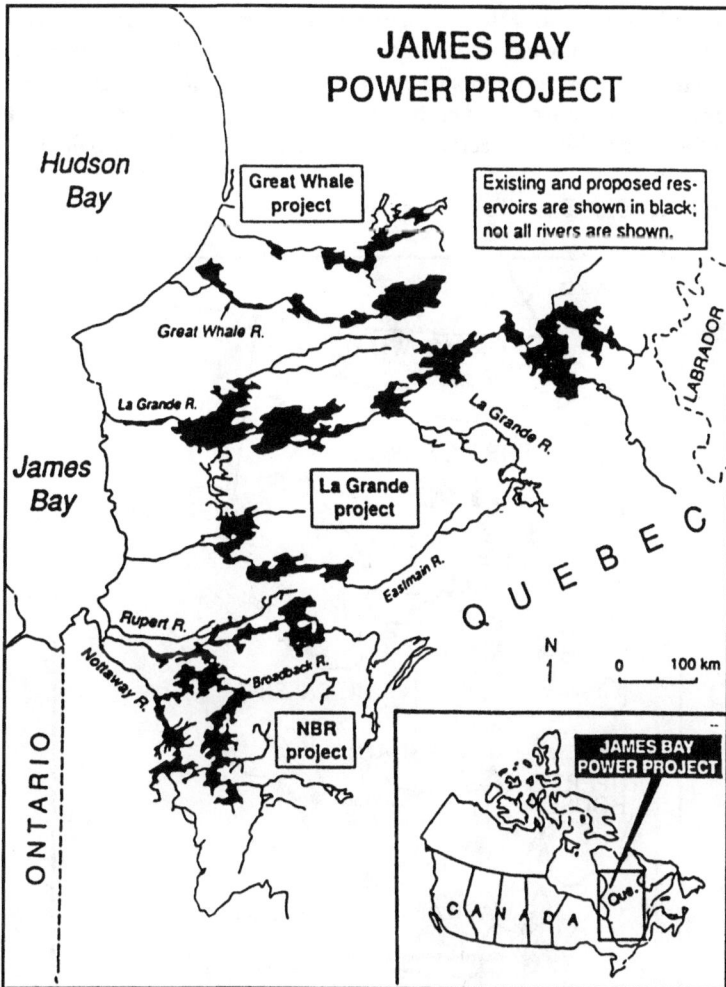

JAMES BAY POWER PROJECT

Hudson Bay

Great Whale project

Existing and proposed reservoirs are shown in black; not all rivers are shown.

LABRADOR

Great Whale R.

La Grande R.

La Grande R.

James Bay

La Grande project

Eastmain R.

Q U E B E C

Rupert R.

Nottaway R.

Broadback R.

N

0   100 km

NBR project

JAMES BAY POWER PROJECT

C A N A D A   Que.

ONTARIO

Source: Probe International

Though subsequent feasibility studies have changed the design of the Grande-Baliene component of the complex, Map 4.1 illustrates the Project as conceived in the early 1990s. The complex can be broken down into roughly three components, of which the La Grande in the middle of the complex area is nearing completion. Feasibility studies for the northern-most component, Grande-Baleine, were completed in 1993 and were in 1995 being reviewed at federal, provincial and local levels. As for the BNR (abbreviated from the three southern rivers) component, Hydro-Quebec's intention has been to bring that on-line by the year 2010. In all, five major river systems are involved with the project, which also incorporates a number of interbasin transfers to augment reservoir storage capacity. The major design change, for example, between the early 1990s and 1994 was to divert the Petit Baliene into a major reservoir to be formed on the Grande Baleine.

Map 4.2 Cree Band Territories, 1971

Source: Salisbury, 1986

Map 4.2 shows the homeland of the James Bay Cree, considered to be one of the most viable indigenous populations in North America. One-third of approximately 11,000 Cree, for example, still support themselves primarily as trappers, hunters and fishers, so that practically the entire homeland is divided into trap lines. It does not require superimposing Map 4.2 upon Map 4.1 to see that, coincidentally, the James Bay hydro-power complex nearly coincides with the boundaries of the Cree homeland.

Advocates of the project point out that virtually no compulsory relocation is required, the engineering works and reservoirs requiring the movement of not a single Cree village. Rather the only relocation, and numbers of people are probably less than a few hundred, pertains to a relatively small number of trap-line camps. Most of those, if not all, can be resited within each family's trapping territory, so that the number of hosts is even smaller. In other words, well over 90 per cent of project-impacted people are neither relocatees nor hosts.

Costing over Can.$250 million, the environmental impact assessment (EIA) for the Grande-Baleine component was completed in 1993. Though a broad review process was established, in June 1994 the President of Hydro-Quebec decided to appoint a six-member international review panel that would present an independent assessment, subsequently made public, to Hydro-Quebec. I was a member of that panel which found that the EIA was inadequate for making decisions as to whether or not to proceed with construction in large part because it had seriously underestimated cumulative impacts of the James Bay complex, as opposed to the Grande-Baleine Project alone, on the totality of the Cree population and the culture of that population.

Sandwiched in-between the French and English-speaking people of southern Quebec and the Inuit to the north, the homeland of the James Bay Cree began to be opened up with the establishment of various Hudson Bay Company trading posts in the latter part of the seventeeth century, with the fur trade having a significant impact on the Cree lifestyle (Feit 1982). Further contact with the outside world came in the mid-1940s with the initiation of family allowances and other federal government benefits, including the first schools. Construction and occupation of U.S. Mid-Canada Line military bases between 1955 and 1964 brought further contact. Throughout this period, however, isolation continued to characterise the Cree homeland. This changed rapidly once the decision was made in 1971 to proceed with the James Bay Project. The major influences were impacts arising from the 1975 James Bay and Northern Quebec Agreement (JBNQA) and road construction.

The 1975 James Bay and Northern Quebec Agreement (JBNQA)

At the time that Quebec's Premier announced the James Bay Project in April 1971, there had been no Cree involvement in project planning or design, nor had any form of social-impact analysis been carried out. With construction already under way by the mid-1970s, the emerging Cree leadership believed, probably correctly, that they had little hope of stopping the first phase of the Project. By agreeing to its implementation and becoming signatories of the JBNQA, at least they received in return a promise of a degree of self government (in particular relation to running their own education and health system and establishing their own police) and an innovative programme for maintaining trapping, hunting and fishing activities.

Such benefits led anthropologist Richard Salisbury and other friends of the Cree to see the JBNQA in a positive light. Certainly it had an impact-mitigating influence. More importantly it led to the formation of the Grand Council of the Cree and the Cree Regional Authority, which provided the Cree with a degree of political self-determination and an institutional structure for facilitating economic development. On the other hand, the land settlement provisions of the JBNQA split the Cree homeland into three categories of land. Category One, aside from sub-surface (mineral) rights, fell under exclusive Cree control. Situated around the village centres of the eight recognised Cree bands (a ninth band was subsequently recognised), these Category One lands included only 2,158 square km, or less than 5 per cent of the former Cree homeland. Category Two lands of 25,130 square km set aside for exclusive Cree hunting, fishing and gathering, covered approximately 15 per cent. Although given preferential access to certain mammals, the remaining 80 per cent (Category Three lands) in effect was handed over to Quebec's James Bay Development Corporation. Map 4.3 shows not only the meager extent of Category One lands but also the fact that the land settlement effectively separated the different Cree bands from each other. Our international panel found such a situation completely inadequate.

In effect the Cree agreed to the project in the 1970s in return for a degree of political self-sufficiency at the expense of maintaining control over the development of their homeland. Our panel found, for example, that neither the federal government nor Quebec Province had lived up to what they had promised the Cree under the Agreement. Furthermore, the James Bay Development Corporation (JBDC) had largely ignored the Cree in planning and implementing development projects in Category Three lands. Tourist and other facilities along the north-south access road, which fell under JBDC jurisdiction were almost exclusively run by outsiders with minimal Cree involvement, including employment.

Map 4.3 Cree Homeland in 1981 Showing Category One and
Two Land

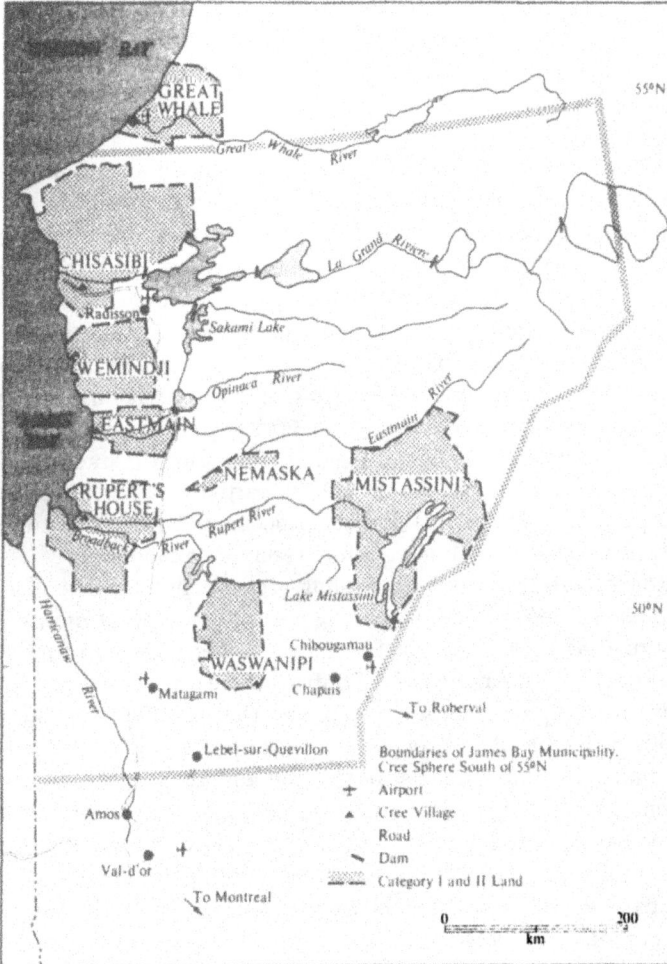

Source: Salisbury, 1986

Roads

While the Agreement opened up the Cree homeland for hydro-power and other development, it was the road system serving the project that gave outsiders and Cree alike greater access to the former homeland. During Phase 1 (La Grande) of the Project, over 1,000 km of roads were constructed north and south through the southern and central areas, and east and west through the central portion. Should Phase 2 (Grande-Baleine) proceed, 685 km of roads will be added, which will cross 21 of the 37 Cree traplines north of the La Grande river system.

Roads, of course, can bring people out as well as into an area. They also tend to benefit those who can acquire and maintain transport. In the Cree case, however, the overall impact has been negative. Project-facilitated roads, for example, have sped up timber extraction by outsiders in the BNR areas. According to Feit, such logging has proved to be extremely destructive to Cree interests, with the then Grand Chief of the Cree, Billy Diamond, estimating that clear-cutting has been destroying at least one family trap-line (averaging 600 square km in that area) per year. I personally believe that the increased number of logging concessions granted by the provincial government in that area is partially in anticipation of Phase 3 of the James Bay Project proceeding, with clear cutting removing commercial timber before reservoir creation.

Roads have also increased hunting pressure, including poaching, by outsiders and Cree alike. A significant decrease of moose, so important as a Cree food source, in the better vegetated southern area is one effect. Another is the impact of the sheer number of outsiders entering the area of Cree culture. During 1991, for example, 26,500 people in 10,850 vehicles traveled up the road to La Grande. In regard to other impacts, both Cree and Inuit in the Grande-Baleine contact area blame different perspectives concerning the James Bay Agreement for the widening gulf between members of the two ethnic groups. As for implementation of the La Grande Phase, this has had two quite different types of impact. One is the mercury contamination of reservoir fish (with inundation increasing the release of methyl mercury) to the extent that mercury contamination of Cree, for whom fish are an all-important dietary component, significantly exceeds World Health Organisation standards. Causality there can rather easily be ascertained. Such is not the case with the other type of impact, which includes a high incidence of sexually transmitted diseases (STDs) and such social pathologies as increasing spousal abuse and suicide, especially among young women. Unlike the situation on reservations in both Canada and the United States, government assistance such as unemployment insurance and aid to dependent children makes up a relatively small proportion of Cree income: only 6 per cent in 1985, for example. Can the increasing rates of STDs and social pathologies be associated with the project-related, accelerated rates of contact with outsiders and outside ideas, which Cree elders and leaders also tend to associate with an erosion of cultural values? I believe they can.

Botswana's Southern Okavango Integrated Water Development Project (SOIWDP)

Rising in Angola, the Okavango River is one of the largest in central and southern Africa and the eleventh largest on the continent. Shortly after entering Botswana, the river flows into the Okavango Delta from which less than 5 per cent of its annual flow escapes. The largest oasis in the world, the Delta includes over 15,000 square km of perennial and seasonal swamp and seasonal grassland inter-spersed with dryland tongues and hundreds of islands. Supporting a rich flora and fauna, it is this mosaic of wetlands and drylands which makes the Delta one of the natural wonders of the world. It is not a pristine wilderness, however, having been utilised by river bushmen for thousands of years and by a number of Bantu-speaking peoples for hundreds of years. Concentrated along the southern and western margins of the Delta and along the exiting Boteti river, the current population that is dependent on the Okavango's land and water resources numbers approximately 100,000 people. The Okavango is also host to a growing tourism industry, which is in the process of surpassing agriculture (including livestock production) as the country's second most important source of foreign exchange (diamond mining, which provides approximately 80 per cent of foreign exchange earnings, is the most important).

Following a joint study with U.N. agencies in the 1970s on the 'Okavango Delta as a Primary Water Resource for Botswana', the government of Botswana (GoB) formed in 1982 an inter-ministerial Okavango Water Development Committee, chaired by the Director of Water Affairs. From the start, attention was focused on one of the sixteen possible schemes that the U.N.-financed study had identi-fied. Subsequently known as the Southern Okavango Integrated Water Development Project (SOIWDP), terms of reference for the necessary feasibility studies were drawn up in the mid-1980s and awarded to Australia's Snowy Mountains Engineering Corporation, which also completed design studies and was the major organisation involved in carrying out an ecological survey and environmental impact assessments.

GoB's selection of the SOIWDP option was in part due to its being one of the more 'environmentally friendly' of the sixteen options. The major stated goal of SOIWDP, however, was to stimulate development. As enunciated in the draft terms of reference, project implementation would increase food production and living standards among approximately 50,000 people living in the southern portion of the Delta by developing 10,000 hectares of commercial irrigation and improving the productivity of 5,000 hectares of existing flood recession agriculture. Water supplies for villagers and their livestock would also be improved. While the emphasis was on raising living standards of the low-income majority (over 80 per cent of the population in the Okavango region fell below the government's poverty datum line), other goals included improving water supplies for the rapidly growing regional centre of Maun and for the Orapa-Lehlakane diamond mines, which contributed approximately 50 per cent of Botswana's diamond production. Benefiting some 50,000 people, such commendable goals would be obtained at the expense of a minimal number of relocatees and hosts, the project works requiring the physical relocation of fewer than 100 people (Scudder with Manley et al. 1993: Appendix III).

Implementing the SOIWDP would involve the completion of two phases of major engineering works (Map 4.4). During the first phase, channelisation of the lower 42 km of the major tributary currently draining the Okavango was designed to increase the flow of water into a major reservoir to be created by a dam approximately 10 km downstream from where the Boteti exits the Delta. Control structures would be built at either end of the wing-shaped reservoir to achieve improved natural resource management and flood recession agriculture. The second phase would involve a second dam and major reservoir lower down the Boteti at Sukwane, from which pipelines would distribute water to the mines and the subdistrict centre of Rakops.

The Cabinet approved SOIWDP implementation in late 1988. When the contractor selected to undertake construction began to mobilise equipment in Maun in late 1989, strong objections to the project were expressed that December and in January 1990 when perhaps 1,000 citizens demanded, at a public meeting, that the project be stopped. Though convinced that objections were based on misinformation, with Safari firms and international conservationists rousing the public in support of their own interests, to its credit the GoB agreed to suspend the project while carrying out further review.

Map 4.4 Okavango River System and the Southern Okavango
Integrated Water Development Project

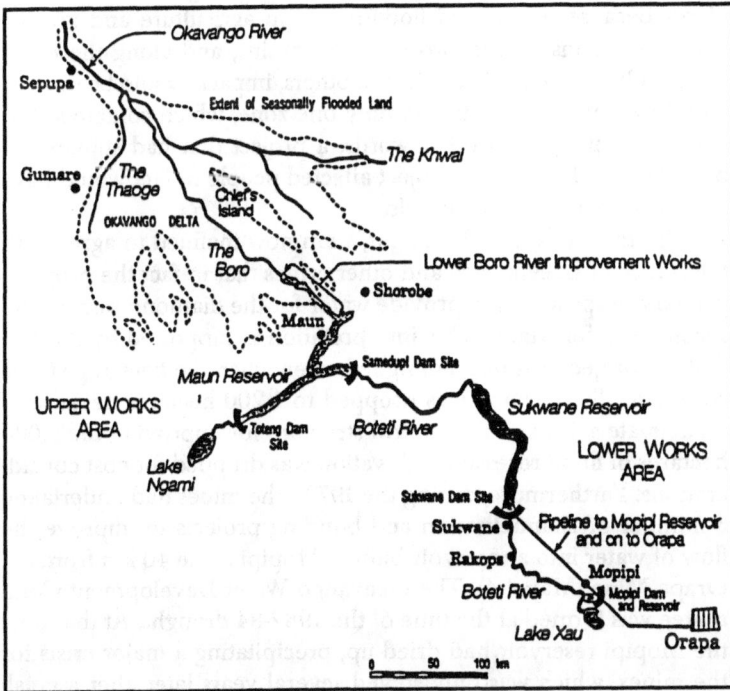

Source: American Society of Civil Engineers, 1993

Even more noteworthy, the government sought international review, asking the Swiss-based International Union for the Conservation of Nature and Natural Resources (IUCN/the World Conservation Union) to undertake a much more detailed scientific re-assessment. IUCN responded by fielding an interdisciplinary team of thirteen scientists who carried out field studies between October 1991 and June 1992, with a final report submitted in October 1992 (ibid.).

In that final report, IUCN recommended that SOIWDP be terminated once and for all. While that recommendation was based on a number of major project flaws, analysis of which need not concern us here, a major one was IUCN's conclusion that contrary to its major goal, SOIWDP would disbenefit rather than benefit a majority of the area's low-income population. The IUCN report also emphasised that local people were correct in their informed opposition to SOIWDP – opposition that the IUCN team found was much stronger than the government had realised. In reaching their conclusion, IUCN had divided the project area into nine zones. In six of these, SOIWDP's economic impacts would be negative on local residents because of reduced flood-recession agriculture and grazing below the dams, in the two reservoir basins, and along the channelised Okavango tributary. In two others, impacts would be neutral, and they would be positive in only one zone, which contained less than 1,000 people. In other words, a project that had supposedly been designed to benefit project-affected people in fact would have worsened their living standards.

With the wisdom of hindsight, I am now inclined to agree with the stance of Greenpeace and other critics that in fact the project's primary purpose was to provide water for the diamond mines, and secondarily for Maun. This interpretation is supported by the fact that the project was not redesigned, even when the hectarage to be commercially irrigated was dropped to 1,200 hectares because of inadequate soils, and the control structure for improving the 5,000 hectares of flood recession cultivation was dropped for cost considerations. Furthermore, during the 1970s, the mines had undertaken a number of channelisation and bunding projects to improve the flow of water into a reservoir built at Mopipi some 40 km from the Orapa Mine (Map 4.4). The Okavango Water Development Committee was formed at the time of the 1982-84 drought. At that time the Mopipi reservoir had dried up, precipitating a major crisis for the mines, which was only solved several years later after a crash ground-water development programme had tapped into sufficient supplies. Taking the initial goals set for SOIWDP seriously, IUCN then suggested an alternative that would better meet them at a much lower cost and without the construction of any major engineering works.

Downstream Project-Affected People

Introduction

Very few detailed studies have been made of the impacts of river-basin development projects on people living below dams, the assumption being that flood-control benefits would more than compensate for any disbenefits. Worldwide, informed people are beginning to realise, for several reasons, just how wrong such an assumption is. As in the Mississippi and Rhine river-basins, such previous development initiatives as levees and other flood control mechanisms have, in fact, led to increased flooding by reducing water-absorptive wetlands and channeling more and more water into a river's primary channel. That is one reason. Another is the growing realisation of the very high productivity of riverine habitats, wetlands in particular (IUCN ongoing), and the need to enhance rather than reduce their extent and productivity. Related to this reason, a third – with which we are primarily concerned in this chapter – is the fact that millions upon millions of contemporary people are dependent on the productivity of those wetlands and flood plains. Where dams, irrigation canals and embankments reduce them, local people are impoverished, and developers and donors do not take this into consideration. If they had in the past, and the necessary broader feasibility studies had been carried out, many completed projects would have been shown to be uneconomical.

Flood-plain utilisation has played a major role in the formation of city states and of civilisation in Africa, Asia, the Middle East and the Americas as shown by archaeological studies. Granted population increase, such utilisation may well support more people today than at any time in the past. The flood plains of the Bramaputra-Ganges system in Bangladesh is one Asian example. Others are the flood plains of the Mekong in Vietnam and of the Yangtze in China. In Africa, the flood plains of all the major rivers are of crucial importance to millions of people, whether the Nile, the Zambezi or the Niger.

Oddly, few socio-economic studies have dealt in detail with the contemporary utilisation of flood plains. Those that have emphasise the extent to which flood plains constitute by far the most important resource in local production systems (Scudder 1962, 1991; Horowitz, Salem-Murdock et al. 1990). Annual flooding is not only critical for maintaining that resource, but for the survival of dependent communities. As floods recede, for example, communities throughout the arid and semi-arid lands of Africa practice flood-recession agriculture. As the dry season progresses, the much higher carrying capacity of flood-plain grazing allows cattle and small ruminants to survive until the coming of the rains, while the flood cycle itself is necessary for sustaining productive fisheries.

Dam construction is apt to impoverish downstream riverine communities in two ways. One is through alteration of the annual regime of dammed rivers. The other, fortunately less frequent, is due to attempts by immigrants to displace resident households and communities from their land.

Dams and Flood Regularisation

Aside from run of the river installations, a major function of dam construction is to regularise a river's annual regime by augmenting low-flow periods and greatly reducing periods of flooding in order to make available a more constant water supply for hydro-power generation, navigation and commercial irrigation. Though few detailed studies have been completed on the impacts of such regularisation, those that exist have show them to have a devastating effect on millions of people (Scudder 1994).

The topic has been best researched in west Africa in connection with mainstream dams on the Senegal River and a number of dams in Nigeria.

After three years of studies, an Institute for Development Anthropology team showed that the Manantali Dam as managed by the trinational Organisation for the Development of the Senegal River Valley (OMVS) was adversely affecting up to 500,000 people below the dam (Horowitz 1993; Salem-Murdock et al. 1989). In his 1994 analysis of the Kainji Dam project on the Niger, Roder notes that adverse downstream impacts include an estimated 60-70 per cent reduction in the riverine fishery, and a 30 per cent reduction of seasonally flooded (*fadama*) land that has lowered swamp rice production by 18 per cent. Though I have seen no confirmation of his figures, in a 1979 FAO technical paper Awachie stated that Kainji had also been responsible for a 100,000-ton reduction in yam production further downriver, in which case we can assume that the dam's impoverishing effects involved hundreds of thousands of people. On a Niger tributary further upriver, Adams estimates (1992) that the costs of the Bakolori Dam to downstream villagers in terms of reduced crop, livestock and fisheries production actually exceeds the benefits realised from the project.

Elsewhere in Nigeria, dams constructed mainly for irrigation purposes in the Hadejia-Jama'are system have significantly reduced downstream flood plains – once again at the expense of local producers. Indeed, in at least one major case, evidence suggests another project-related loss, with Barbier *et al.* demonstrating that the net economic benefits of flood plains that have been significantly reduced by river control mechanisms were at least U.S.$32 per 1,000 cubic metres of water versus only US$0.0026 for the irrigated Kano Project when all costs (including operational costs) are included (referenced in Acreman *et al.*, forthcoming). The discrepancy was so great that Nigerian officials at a 1993 meeting agreed unanimously that 'flooding in the wetlands made possible by artificial releases from the dams in the wet season should be maintained to make possible the production of rice, dry-season agriculture, fuelwood, timber, fish, wildlife, as well as biodiversity and groundwater recharge' (HNWCP/NIPSS 1993). All sustained by natural flooding, the productivity of all those resources has been reduced by dam-induced impoverishment of the flood plains habitat, and by extension, of the dependent human population. While artificial releases would certainly improve the situation, as hypothesised by Scudder (1980) and as Horowitz, Salem Murdock *et al.* have conclusively shown for the Manantali Dam, this engineering approach is not without difficulty (Scudder 1991a; Adams 1993). In most cases the economies of those concerned would be better served by the natural flood regime (Scudder 1991a).

The Unequal Struggle - Immigrant versus Local Residents

I have already noted that immigrants tend to be the main beneficiaries of dam construction at project sites, in reservoir basins and elsewhere in the immediate vicinity. In the process, they are apt to utilise resources including job opportunities at the expense of the local population, although their entrepreneurial activities (as with the Lake Kariba sardine fishery or commercial irrigation schemes) can also provide additional employment opportunities. Relationships below dams may be still more exploitative, especially where a major purpose of dam construction is downstream elite-dominated commercial irrigation, or where the scheme provides a greater opportunity for realising political goals at the expense of the local population. Two of the three cases that follow have also involved either genocide or ethnocide.

Construction of the Manantali Dam increased the downstream potential for commercial irrigation in both Mauritania and Senegal at the same time that a period of drought was adversely affecting the rural economies of those living outside the river-basin. In Mauritania, riparian residents were distinct, culturally and racially, from the Bidan (White Moor) elite who dominated the government. After passing a land registration act that supported individual land ownership at the expense of customary tenure, the Bidan expelled riverine villagers from their land, killing hundreds and driving thousands into Senegal as refugees (Horowitz 1991), where they remain to this day.

A similar land grab began in Somalia after a decision was made to build the Bardheera Dam on the Juba River (Besterman and Roth 1988). There too, it occurred on communally farmed lands below the dam after the government passed a similar land registration act. In this case the incentive for a land grab by elite outsiders was also the potential for commercial pump irrigation in a drought-affected nation. Though the interclan warfare that followed the fall of the Siad Barre government stopped the project cycle before dam construction, this land grab may well have figured in the clan warfare that subsequently erupted in the Middle Juba Valley (communication to the author from Peter Little).

Moving now to Sri Lanka, one member of a cabal within the Mahaweli Authority of Sri Lanka has written a book on the cabal's efforts to use a multi-billion dollar river-basin development project as a mechanism for splitting the Tamil-speaking population of northern and eastern Sri Lanka in half, either by driving the downstream Tamil-speaking Hindu and Muslim majority off their lands or by rendering them a minority through a massive land invasion and land settlement of Singala-speaking Buddhists (Gunaratna 1988; Scudder 1994).

Notwithstanding major international funding in all three cases, in none of the cases did donors try to intervene. Though quite willing to insist on the implementation of guidelines for relocatees and hosts, no systematic effort was made, or has been made in other downstream locales, to protect the interests of such adversely affected citizens.

Resistance Movements

Introduction

In analysing movements of resistance to river-basin development projects, it is important to retain a long-term perspective. There are many examples where projects have been 'suspended' or 'cancelled', Quebec's suspension of the Grand-Baliene project on 19 November 1994 being the most recent, but such statements by the authorities do not necessarily mean the project is cancelled for all time. As my colleague Peter Rogers has pointed out, river-basin development projects are like vampires. They continually rise up again and again. The 'golden stake' that terminates them for good requires implementation of an alternative which precludes resurrection. Few implemented examples come to mind.

For a resistance movement to succeed, a number of distinguishing features seem to be required. In addition to the capacity of local leaders to mobilise and institutionalise local support, other requirements are, in my opinion, NGO and multilateral and/or bilateral donor assistance. National or provincial governments must also be amenable to strong economic and political arguments and pressures and characterised by a judiciary to which project-affected people have access. As India's Sardar Sarovar case indicates, even the existence of all of these requirements does not ensure success.

Downstream Residents

Turning now to project-affected people who are neither relocatees nor hosts, I am aware of no effective resistance movements among riparian communities living downstream from dams. Their strung-out nature along many kilometres (hundreds, in quite a few cases as below the Jebba Dam on the Niger and Cahora Bassa on the Zambezi) makes institutionalising local opposition difficult. Also important is the tendency of academics, NGOs, governments and donors to ignore the existence of such people as a category at risk of project-induced impoverishment. There are exceptions, of course, although they are few.

One example concerns over 40,000 peasants (*caboclos*) living on islands between Brazil's Tucurui Dam on the Tocantins River and the delta several hundred kilometres downstream. After the dam was sealed in the mid-1980s, the local production systems of all were adversely affected (Magee, 1989). In that case both the Catholic Church and the Rural Worker's Union became involved in representing local interests. In neither case, however, did involvement commence before the completion of dam construction. The Church's involvement was an extension to downstream residents of previous work carried out on behalf of relocatees. The Union became actively involved only after the peasants gained control following elections in 1985 (Ibid.). Such involvement, however, had little effect on the government parastatal responsible for dam construction, Magee noting that as of 1989 no 'promised' assistance had yet materialised.

Where cancellation is improbable, perhaps the best option for political action available to downstream residents is to influence how a dam is operated once complete. Controlled flood releases at strategic times are the best alternative. In some cases they can be negotiated after construction. However, since dam design may preclude such releases (as in the case of Kariba), the best approach is an attempt to influence policy during the planning and design stage.

Controlled flooding is a relatively new concept primarily initiated by researchers and planners. Where involved, local residents have been highly supportive. Government responses have been mixed, while donors have largely ignored such an option, except for some individuals within the World Bank whose understanding of the developmental possibilities is due primarily to the arguments of researchers and consultants (Cernea 1994). Controlled flooding is not a panacea, however. It involves trade-offs with hydro-power generation, for example, and those floods that are released may be ill-timed or insufficient to offset dam-induced downstream costs.

Project-Vicinity Affected People

The most successful resistance movements among PAPs have occurred in the vicinity of projects – not surprising granted greater ease for mobilising people and greater involvement of supportive organisations. Though the two cases discussed illustrate quite different strategies, they share two major characteristics. First, each involves a relatively unified resistance movement on the part of those involved. Second, in each case that movement has not necessarily stopped a project as opposed to either delaying it or leading to further negotiations.

Hydro-Quebec, James Bay and the Cree

Hydro-Quebec's plans for the James Bay Project encompassed the entire homeland of the Cree (Maps 4.1 and 4.2). As is so frequently the case, though most at risk from the project as PAPs, the Cree were not involved in its conceptualisation; Billy Diamond and other Cree leaders first heard about it on the radio in April 1971. Nor were the Cree involved when the James Bay Development Corporation was established a few months later. Mobilising quickly, however, leaders from the various Cree bands met, for the first time ever, in June 1991 to state their opposition to the project. Unified and able leadership greatly increased the effectiveness of resistance.

During 1974 a Grand Council of the Cree was incorporated, becoming the Cree's political arm. It represented Cree interests during the negotiations that led to the 1975 James Bay and Northern Quebec Agreement, and it has continued to critique the failure of the government of Canada and the Quebec provincial government to carry out their responsibilities under that agreement. When Quebec decided in the 1980s to go ahead with Phase 2 of the Project, it was the Grand Council which withdrew from further negotiations in 1988 to express its opposition to Grand-Baliene.

Strong leadership has charactersed the Grand Council up until the present. The first Grand Chief, Billy Diamond, proved an effective negotiator not just with Canadian government agencies, but also in the international arena, arguing the Cree case before the relevant UN agencies in Geneva. He also arranged an audience with the Pope, who – on a subsequent visit to Canada – emphasised on several occasions the importance of self-government for indigenous peoples.

Cree opposition also attracted other external support, including the ongoing support of McGill University's Anthropology of Development Programme. Alerted by students carrying out Cree research that the recently announced James Bay Project would have major impacts on the people, the then Director Richard Salisbury not only urged the Quebec government to consult with the Cree, but also received government support for a social-impact assessment. Today, faculty members such as Colin Scott continue to serve as consultants to the Cree as do other non-Cree professionals including lawyers and environmentalists.

The Cree have also received the ongoing support of the International Rivers Network which, with the Environment Defence Fund, is the main NGO in the U.S. mobilising opposition to large-scale dams and other major river-basin engineering works. When the Grand Baliene feasibility study was submitted in 1993, an elaborate review process was set in motion at federal and provincial levels. Hydro-Quebec also provided the funds for the Cree to undertake their own assessment and to recruit, in June 1994, its own six-member international panel of which I was a member. The results of this elaborate review process, plus the long history of Cree opposition, presumably influenced the government's decision not to proceed with the Grand Baliene-Project at that time.

Reasons given in the press were reduced demand for hydro-power generation rather than Cree opposition. On the other hand, should the project proceed at some future time, the strength of past opposition would suggest that Hydro-Quebec has been convinced of the need to negotiate directly with the Cree. In the opinion of the international panel, such negotiations should lead to an enlarged Cree land base and revenue sharing from hydro-power generation for financing a carefully designed participatory development plan. As in the Okavango case that follows, however, the final outcome remains uncertain.

Botswana's Southern Okavango Integrated Development Project

As in the Cree case, effective local resistance has been a major factor in delaying, but not necessarily stopping, project implementation. When construction of the Southern Okavango Integrated Water Development Project (SOIWDP) was tendered in 1988, subsequent bids significantly exceeded the government's expectations. As a result, those opposed to the project assumed that it would be cancelled, an assumption that grew when no further information about implementation was received as time went by. Far from cancelling SOIWDP, however, government was looking for ways to reduce costs, one of which was to eliminate that portion of the project that had been designed to increase the productivity of local flood-recession agriculture.

The main opponents to SOIWDP were the local people, whose opposition to channelisation was close to unanimous. Local people included the low-income village majority, Maun residents and the tourist-dependent safari industry, all of whom assumed – correctly as the IUCN studies subsequently showed – that implementation would have an adverse effect on the habitat, local economies and tourism. All were taken by surprise in late 1990 when the government-selected contractor began to mobilise equipment in Maun. Local opposition mobilised rapidly, facilitated by the efforts of the Maun branch of the Kalahari Conservation Society (KCS). The KCS was Botswana's main conservation-oriented NGO. Started by a key diamond-mining official who continues to this day as chairman, its elitist membership included citizens and expatriates alike. Though concerned about certain aspects of SOIWDP, the central office in Botswana's capital did not take a stand in opposition to the project. The Maun branch did. Also in opposition was a new NGO, Tshomarelo, which had been founded in late1990 by Maun's elite (again including citizens and expatriates alike) for the express purpose of opposing SOIWDP.

As opposition increased with local residents insisting that the Minister of Mineral Resources and Water Affairs hear their complaints, the government called, through the local chief, a public meeting (*khotla*) in January 1991. Up to 1,000 people attended, the large majority of whom were local villagers. According to researchers, the extent to which the Minister was insulted and shouted down by those present was a unique event in the history of Botswana since independence. Though convinced that the low-income citizenry had been led astray by the expatriate community, including the safari operators, some of whose transport was used to take villagers to the January meeting, the government was sufficiently taken back to suspend SOIWDP in order to allow further assessment to take place.

For reasons yet to be explained, simply because the outcome should have been obvious, the government first agreed to Greenpeace making a brief visit. While that resulted in a relatively moderate report recommending cancellation, this was backed up by the possibility of Greenpeace launching a major campaign against SOIWDP, should implementation proceed, which would coalesce around the theme 'diamonds are for death' – death referring to the project's assumed adverse effect on the Okavango's habitat and wildlife. The diamond mines, run by a parastatal owned jointly by the government of Botswana and DeBeers, immediately announced that SOIWDP was not their suggestion and that furthermore, the mines could meet their needs for the life of the mines by using groundwater.

Though ecological and social science investigations and public consultation had been inadequate, SOIWDP had been carefully planned for nearly a decade by competent engineers and hydrologists. I suspect that one reason why the government was willing to allow a Greenpeace visit was the conviction that the project was both environmentally and economically sound. After the Greenpeace report was received, IUCN was asked to carry out a much more detailed review. Unexpectedly (from the government's point of view), the thirteen member IUCN SOIWDP Review Team also recommended cancellation.

In addition to discussing other serious flaws, the IUCN Review Team stated in their May 1992 Draft Final Report that the opposition of the low-income majority was far stronger than government realised and was based on people's experiences with the adverse effects of past efforts to manipulate waters through dredging and bunding activities, rather than on the concerns of the safari industry. Furthermore, the IUCN report emphasised that local opposition was well founded since SOIWDP implementation would, indeed, make the majority of project-affected people worse off, contrary to the Project's goals.

In the week that the IUCN Draft Report was released, indeed several hours before the IUCN team gave a KCS public lecture reporting their findings, the government announced on the radio that SOIWDP had been cancelled. That was in May 1992. One would have thought that granted the apparent unanimity of local opposition, coupled with a very negative report by a highly qualified IUCN team, this combination would have been sufficient to ensure SOIWDP's demise once and for all. Such is not necessarily the case. Though recently the government has financed a major contract for exploring the IUCN assumption that conjunctive use of ground and surface water would eliminate the need for major engineering works, both Botswana's President and Vice-President continue favouring the Southern Okavango Integrated Water Development Project.

Toward the end of 1993, Botswana's President stated in a Maun speech that within the next twenty-five years the people would see SOIWDP implemented. Various news articles followed, stating that the President wanted the project to go forward, although one also noted that he feared Greenpeace. In March 1994 he invited Zimbabwe's President to come to Botswana and to Maun, where he gave a speech urging the people to take control of the Okavango from the international conservation movement by implementing the large-scale cultivation of such plantation crops as cotton, rice and wheat. His speech completely misrepresented the facts in a number of ways. For example, the government consultant's own reports had rejected large-scale commercial irrigation because of inadequate hectarage of appropriate soils or unfavourable investment returns, while the IUCN report had noted technical, managerial and marketing constraints. The next month, again with no scientific justification, Botswana's Vice-President called the IUCN alternative for meeting Maun's water-supply needs 'nonsense'. More recently, in June 1995, the Vice-President was quoted in the 30 June edition of the *Okavango Observer* as saying, 'I have always had a vision for Maun, a dream of Maun, which like Gabarone would have a dam... In the future, if we have a problem, I hope that we can discuss it amongst ourselves, before we call in foreigners.'

SOIWDP is a defective project actively resisted by the local people. Its continual support by Botswana's national leadership is an example of what Waterbury refers to as 'hydropolitics' – in this case the hydropolitics of the Okavango and Zambezi River systems. No treaty relates to the Zambezi river system, even though that system is the major water resource for a number of drought-prone countries. Currently each is attempting to meet its needs through unilateral off-takes. Botswana and Zimbabwe are middle-Zambezi basin countries. My interpretation of a major purpose for the Zimbabwe president's visit to Maun was to promote an understanding, whereby Zimbabwe would support Botswana's 'development' of the Okavango, and perhaps future extraction of Zambezi waters, in return for Botswana's support for Zimbabwe's unilateral offtakes from the Zambezi.

Conclusion

Before project-induced impoverishment can be reduced, let alone prevented, its extent must be better understood as must the rationale behind those projects that impoverish. As the cases described illustrate, adverse impacts of river-basin development projects tend to affect a much larger number of people, other than relocatees and hosts, than is acknowledged by researchers, government planners and donors. Furthermore, resistance movements involving those people seldom result in the *permanent* cancellation of such projects. Granted the extent of impoverishment that often results, the persistence of such projects remains to be explained, as does the inadequacy of environmental and social-impact assessments and the failure of the World Bank, as the major multilateral donor, to complete post-implementation audits of costs and benefits.

River-basin development projects are sponsored by a powerful coalition including heads of state, multinational corporations of consulting engineers, contractors and suppliers, and multilateral and bilateral donors. Whether as personal monuments or as means for implementing visions of the future, the names of heads of state are intricately associated with large-scale river-basin development projects. Examples have already been given. As Ribeiro explains, to remain competitive multinational corporations must move smoothly from one project to another; indeed, 'they stimulate the market for them by indicating and proposing new works' (1994:50). Their involvement is facilitated by bilateral donors linking favourable credit arrangements (as through export-import banks) to contracts for nationally based firms and by the World Bank's insistence on International Competitive Bidding.

Regardless of the rhetoric, seldom is the major purpose of such projects the development of the rural riverine population. Even in the case of TVA, 85 per cent of flood-control benefits went to the urban-industrial sector building on the Chattanooga flood plain (Chandler 1984), while farm families and labourers displaced by over twenty dams gave way to urban seekers of recreation and second, lake-side, homes. Designed to benefit the rural population, according to the IUCN review (1993), the Southern Okavango Integrated Water Development Project would have had exactly the opposite effect if implemented.

Heads of state such as Roosevelt and Nkrumah at least had visions, based on political ideologies and capital-intensive technology, of 'their' projects stimulating regional development. This political component Waterbury (1979) has labeled 'hydropolitics'. According to the World Bank's Fredericksen, 'the conditions encountered in a country's water sector reflect the political demands and the wisdom and leadership in these matters more than any other factor' (1992:4). In regard to specific cases, Waterbury's assessment of the Aswan High Dam concludes that 'the history of this project is testimony to the primacy of political considerations determining virtually all technical choices with the predicted result that a host of unanticipated technical and ecological crises have emerged that now entail more political decisions'.

Also using the phrase 'hydropolitics' in the title of his analysis of the binational (Argentina/Paraguay) Yacyreta High Dam, Ribeiro notes statements by Argentine specialists of better alternatives to Yacyreta in the form of smaller dams, better sites for high dams and use of natural gas (an alternative equally applicable to Quebec's James Bay project). He emphasises several other factors supporting the decision to proceed with Yacyreta. One is project specific, involving competition between Argentina and Brazil (with its binational Itaipu High Dam) for 'regional hegemony'. The other can be generalised to other national political economies. Rejecting the word 'development', Ribeiro sees large-scale projects, like Yacyreta, as 'a form of production linked to economic expansion' into 'outpost' areas (Ibid. 163).

Ribeiro's interpretation would also appear to be applicable to both the James Bay Project and the Southern Okavango Integrated Water Development Project. In addition to economic expansion, the former project gives the Province of Quebec increased control over indigenous lands of ambiguous legal status as far as that province is concerned. SOIWDP would not only channel more water to the diamond mines (and hence to the advantage of both the government and the DeBeers/Anglo-American multinational corporation), but also provide increased access for the Botswanan elite from the more densely populated eastern region to Okavangan resources in the form of water for irrigation and grazing and water for cattle. Rhetoric aside, intended beneficiaries of neither project, in my assessment, are supposed to be local people. Impacts on such people are ignored or played down – to the extent possible – throughout the project cycle, in the same way that the arena in which environmental impacts are assessed is kept as small as possible. Appropriate assessment of those impacts, because they are widespread, is expensive, which is another reason why they are under-assessed.

Granted our increasing understanding of the extent of project induced impoverishment, those engaged in research have a responsibility to ensure not just that World Bank-type guidelines for relocatees are extended to all project-affected people, but that the horizon of Environment and Social-Impact Assessments be expanded to include all habitats and human populations that are likely to be affected. Should that be done, in many cases I suspect that other alternatives to major engineering works will be seen as preferable. Furthermore, where major engineering works continue to be the 'least-cost alternative' I suspect that such major changes in design and operation such as controlled flooding will be called for.

PART TWO
RESISTING IMPOVERISHMENT

5

Fighting for a Place

THE POLICY IMPLICATIONS OF RESISTANCE TO DEVELOPMENT-INDUCED RESETTLEMENT

Anthony Oliver-Smith

Introduction

In Goethe's *Faust*, in the conflict between the protagonist and
Philemon and Baucis, an aged couple who refuse to be relocated
to make way for Faust's triumphant final project, the author evokes
the modern images of the developer and the 'people in the way'
who must be moved for the greater glory of the projects that will supposedly benefit humankind (Berman 1982:68). To entice them to
move from their coastal homesite so that he can build an observation
tower for people to gaze out into the new world he has made, Faust
offers the aged couple a cash settlement or resettlement to a new
home, but they refuse his offers, preferring to remain where they can
continue to live meaningful lives, providing service to shipwrecked
sailors and wanderers. To this persistent resistance and refusal to be
moved, Faust ultimately says: 'Resistance and such stubbornness/
Thwart the most glorious success,/ Till in the end, to one's disgust,/
One soon grows tired of being just.' (11,269-72) (Berman 1982:67) In
the end, the power of the developer is served, the resistance of the
elderly couple is overcome and they are destroyed.

There is an undeniable Faustian quality in development projects
that transform environments and overwhelm people's lives for the
benefit of 'society'. In my lectures in anthropology courses I have
often, in part facetiously, referred to political power as 'the ability to

move people and things about the landscape in any way you see fit'. When one considers the whole phenomenon of development-induced resettlement, that perspective, all facetiousness aside, is remarkably apt. Development-induced resettlement is, in many ways, the ultimate expression of a state with its monopoly on the management of violence and its ambitious engineering projects, freed from all other non-political power or institutions of social self-management, and able to exert ultimate control over the location of people and things within its territory (Bauman 1989:xiii). Conversely, to be resettled is one of the most acute expressions of powerlessness because it constitutes a loss of control over one's physical space. The only thing left is the loss of the body. As Margaret Rodman so cogently notes, 'The most powerless people have no place at all' (1992:650).

Resistance to Development-Induced Resettlement

As resistance to development-induced resettlement essentially challenges the state and its hegemony over the territory and people within its borders, it may have profound implications for policy at local, national and international levels. In the sense that involuntary migration and resettlement are part of the means or outcomes of intentional, usually state-driven development projects and strategies, the phenomenon of resettlement is, therefore, fundamentally a political one, a clash of contesting interests involving the use of power by one party to relocate another. Reigning development models, promoting large-scale infrastructure projects, transform social and physical environments and espouse the concept of 'the greatest good for the greatest number' rather than the rights of the less numerous and the less powerful. Although the record does not reflect it entirely, such a position assumes that the less powerful will benefit eventually, through the project itself or through a well-designed and implemented resettlement programme. For some, within the framework of current economic structures and conditions, realism dictates acceptance of this development ideology. The opposing view tends to emphasise the rights of the less powerful and the significance of cultural diversity over what they consider to be ecologically risky and economically questionable projects. When communities embrace such a position within a local context, specific resistance movements can broaden the agenda and become more general movements of cultural resistance to hegemonic forms of discourse, debating fundamental questions of cultural identity and human rights. When local communities propose alternative models of development, based on less environmentally disruptive, smaller-scale forms of 'sustainable development', respecting human rights of self-determination and cultural diversity, they convert their discourse of resistance into development strategies in and of themselves.

The negative impacts of development were the topic of a conversation I once had with an agricultural economist during which he employed the old, but quintessentially modernist (and indeed Faustian), saying, 'If you want to make an omelette, you have to break some eggs'. My retort was something to the effect that it was a shame that those with the fewest eggs too frequently saw them get broken for the development omelette. The conversation had little place else to go after that. But I began to think about that old saying he used in terms of what kind of eggs get broken for the development omelette. The disruption and trauma which involuntary migration and resettlement inflict upon people may be profound, an unintentional result of development projects, perhaps, but one that has been considered an acceptable risk or cost, whether or not efforts are made to mitigate it. Resettlement imposes forces and conditions on people that may completely transform their lives, evoking profound changes in environment, productive activities, social organisation and interaction, in leadership and political structure, and in worldview and ideology. Under these circumstances, it is not surprising that resistance or hostility to the idea of resettlement has been characterised as 'normal and ... expected', indeed, virtually inevitable (Cernea 1988a:15).

Resettlement means uprooting people from the environments in which the vast majority of their meaningful activities have taken place and on which much of their understanding of life is based. They may be relocated in a new place, where they may have little first-hand knowledge and experience. Anthropological research has recently demonstrated the role that a sense of place plays in individual and collective identity formation, in the way time and history are encoded and contextualised, and in interpersonal, community and intercultural relations (Low and Altman 1992; Malkki 1992; Rodman 1992). Place and space are the central concepts in the entire problematic of resettlement.

Resistance to resettlement reveals how important a sense of place is in the creation of an 'environment of trust' in which space, kin relations, local communities, cosmology and tradition are linked (Giddens as cited in Rodman 1992:648). The human need for 'environment of trust' is fundamental to the sense of order and predictability implied by culture, and threats of removal from these spatial and symbolic environments have generally elicited some form of resistance.

Resettlement not only removes a people from their home ground, it also remakes them. When a community is relocated, it is not simply lifted up and set down whole in a new site. In most cases the community is reconfigured in specific ways. Most development projects, especially those that occasion the large-scale resettlement of populations particularly in rural areas, directly or indirectly further two fundamental processes, the expansion of the state and integration into regional and national market systems. Neither of these processes of inclusion is particularly simple or straightforward, but, in most instances, provokes a restructuring of social, economic and political relationships toward the priorities of the larger society. In many respects, the process of resettlement, insofar as it is oriented by development goals, is designed to change local cultures. In that sense, resettlement will not necessarily destroy 'local cultures', but it will appropriate them and restructure them in terms of values and goals often originating from far beyond the local context. Such a process of development must involve the reduction of local culture, society and economy from all their variegated expressions to a narrow set of institutions and activities that make them compatible with the purposes of the larger society (Garcia Canclini 1993).[1]

Moreover, implementation of poorly designed resettlement projects imposed on people may exacerbate the stresses occasioned by uprooting from the geographical location of 'environments of trust'. Most mandated resettlement projects deprive people of control over fundamental features of their lives and have generally been derelict in providing affected populations with the kinds of information necessary to reassert satisfactory control and understanding over the resettlement process or the changed circumstances of their lives. Understanding of and control over circumstances are fundamental for human beings to deal productively and positively with the forces of change. Therefore, if people find that their understanding and control are diminished, change will be characterised by conflict, tension and, perhaps, active resistance. The often extremely negative concrete impacts of resettlement projects on affected peoples compound the disorientation generated by the loss of control and understanding as motivations for resistance. Resistance is a reassertion of both a logic and a sense of control. Thus, when we consider what is at stake for people threatened with resettlement, the picture of small

---

1. I am grateful to Jacquelyn Jeffrey for bringing the relevance of Garcia Canclini's analysis of the restructuring effects of capitalism on traditional societies to an understanding of resettlement to my attention.

local communities confronting the power of the state and multi-lateral institutions becomes more comprehensible (Alvares and Billorey 1987). What is perhaps less understood but extremely important is that the actions and organisation of resistance have profound implications for both resistors and those resisted (Oliver-Smith 1991a).

Development-Induced Resettlement, Resistance and Change

Since resistance to resettlement, in some form, is to be found frequently, a literature documenting its occurrence has emerged from a wide variety of examples and cases of population removal and resettlement. Population removal has been a common strategy of conquest, pacification and territorial appropriation throughout history, and there is a large historical literature ranging from antiquity to relatively modern times pertaining to resettlement and resistance. For example, much of the history of Native American-White contact and interaction deals with white land appropriation and resettlement schemes of violent and non-violent nature and subsequent Native American responses to these efforts (Fixico 1990; Levine and Lurie 1968). Currently, resistance to development projects requiring the resettlement of populations has generated considerable interest because it tends to be frequent, attract more attention and be better documented both because of the scale at which it is often undertaken and its relationship to publicly defined goals.

The form and development of resistance will be shaped in part by the nature of the force or forces threatening a population with resettlement. Some forces are clearly resistible, others permit the possibility of resistance and still others preclude resistance altogether. For example, forced removal by wartime military forces is difficult, if not impossible, to resist for unarmed populations. Many environmental conditions triggered by natural disasters result in conditions that require relocation through sheer destruction or because the environment has been made more hazardous. Development projects, while frequently massive in scale and formidable in political support, however, present more variable contexts for the possibility of resistance. Development projects are not forces of nature and, at least initially, tend not to resort to military force and violence to achieve their goals of resettling a population. Tribal and peasant peoples are generally interpreting development projects as products of a larger society that is the source of a series of broad-scale problems with which they have had to cope or resist for some time. In effect, development projects present as a form of gradual onset disaster that offers both time and space for contestation.

Thus, while local populations may resist resettlement purely on its own grounds, their resistance may be intensified by alternative views on both increasing economic integration and changed relationships with the nation-state to be effected by the project. Where the market and particularly the state have not been important in setting local agendas historically, a resettlement project that increases their centrality and compromises local autonomy, particularly over territory and cultural identity, may be resisted tenaciously. The resistance and insurgency of tribal peoples in Bangladesh (Zaman 1982), Brazil (Fisher 1994) and the Philippines (Drucker 1985) to such encroachments demonstrate clearly that resistance constitutes a rejection of the state's right to change local agendas.

However, by the same token, the decision to resist a development project that includes resettlement embarks a community on a journey that, even if successful, entails significant changes for that community both internally and externally. It is fundamentally through the conflict forged by confrontation and resistance that communities subject themselves to forces of change, regardless of how conservative their motivations for resistance may be. Conflict can be an important organising principle of human behaviour. Friends and enemies and good and evil are more clearly defined in conditions of conflict. In conflict, clarifying the ambiguity of changing conditions and events becomes easier, and people can articulate their sense of identity and their positions on issues more exactly (Marris 1975:159). Resistance requires action, and consciousness is generated in and changed by social action (Marshall 1983 as quoted in Fantasia 1988:8). In this sense, society is constantly in the process of reconstituting itself through actions of alignment and disengagement, along the axes of individual-group, ethnicity, age, gender, class, etc., activating a process of continual contestation and interpretation of culture, that is, therefore, also constantly 'in production'. The threat of resettlement constitutes a crisis of enormous proportions for many communities. Crises are those moments when customary practices of daily life are suspended and new repertoires of behaviour, associational ties and valuations are created (Fantasia 1988:14). When communities are confronted with the threat of forced resettlement, rather than acquiesce to the disruption and changes they will be subjected to, they resist, and in so doing become subject to a different set of changes that will come about in their resistance. The initial steps taken in resisting resettlement may have a galvanising effect on people as they become aware of not only their own resources and capabilities, but the vulnerability of their opponents as well. Undertaking resistance to the Grand Rapids Dam by the Swampy River Cree of Manitoba, Canada, began a process of political socialisation that has enhanced their capabilities for future negotiations with the government (Waldram 1980). The actions of resistance groups, as well as the changes in groups set in motion by the requirement of action in resistance, produce the kinds of alignments and coalitions that may gather sufficient strength and resources to influence policy throughout local, national and international systems.

Thus, it is in the social action required by resistance that consciousness becomes changed. From a cultural standpoint, in the conflict of resistance more precise definitions of cultural identity are worked out, and conceptions of the community in broader national and global contexts are developed. From the standpoint of social organisation, resistance efforts often initiate a process of redefinition of a variety of internal and external relationships and institutions. The need to organise for resistance will exert a new form of pressure on the internal organisation of a community. The organisation of a resistance movement may sharpen both internal and external pre-existing conflicts. The existence of patterns of internal differentiation based on ethnicity, caste or class in a community may constitute obstacles to the formation of the necessary levels of solidarity and cooperation for effective resistance, and may require efforts to alter local social structural patterns to enable the formation of an organised movement by isolating or banishing dissidents (Lawrence 1986). On the other hand, a successful record in defending local interests, usually based on a long history of internal coherence and solidarity, effective political structure, leadership and previously existing community organisations which may backstop a resistance movement, may also affect the community's ability to mount and ultimately institutionalise serious resistance efforts (Bartolomé 1992; Wali 1989; Waldram 1980). In terms of external relationships, resistance, on one hand, requires the intensification of relationships with traditional allies and, on the other hand, the development of new relationships with others, often completely foreign to the local context. The downstream *caboclos* affected by the Tucurui Dam in Brazil acquired significant allies in a rural workers union and church organisations, articulating them with the larger community of Amazonian peasants and enabling them to assume new political roles (Magee 1989).

Today, many resettlement projects are taking place in situations of extreme asymmetry in social structure and power, in which elites are the most capable of expressing their interests and needs. Basically, particular groups, whether defined by class, race, ethnicity, religion or another differentiating factor, may find their interests furthered by certain features of a resettlement project while other groups will see themselves suffering great disadvantage. Land compensation may be seen by some to be an economic opportunity, while formal sector housing, particularly in urban resettlement, may draw interested people into a project area. Differential costs and benefits from resettlement projects may vary according to land and labour factor markets, social differentiation or other local features, predisposing some groups to favour resettlement and others to oppose it. Therefore, some caution must be exercised in ascertaining whose interests are indeed being represented in resistance movements (Partridge 1993:9; Nachowitz 1988). Communities threatened with resettlement cannot be assumed to be homogeneous. In resistance movements all players have specific agendas which they attempt to further.

Economically, resistance requires the mobilisation and expenditure of labour and other resources in novel ways, diverting time and energy from other important tasks and stressing communities that may already be pressured to meet normal needs. However, the acquisition of allies may make available other resource pools, injecting new skills, technology and access to specialised economic resources into the local context. Politically, the established leaders of the community, if they favour resistance, are chosen to lead the movement, but, if they prove unsatisfactory or unequal to the task, new leadership may emerge in the context of the conflict. Furthermore, the enhanced contact with others brought about by resistance, combined with more precise definitions of community or ethnic identity, lead to more sophisticated understanding of local power, particularly that based in ethnicity, class, gender or religion in relationship to that of the group controlling state power. The Kayapo in Brazil have been particularly astute in their understanding and use of local, national and international sources of power for resisting the Tucurui Dam and other Brazilian government and private initiatives affecting their land (see Posey in this volume and Fisher 1994). However, it must also be understood that the internal changes in communities set in motion by the decision, organisation and actions of resistance do not inevitably bring about changes in policy in the sense of establishment of new public goals at any but the local level. Indeed, depending on the reigning political climate, mobilisation for resistance at the local level may provoke a hardening of some policies at the regional or state level.

Since resistance in effect constitutes a challenge to the state, the politics of state-local relations in all their complexity come to the fore.

This sort of challenge constitutes 'news' and attracts the attention of the power structure as well as the media (and, I might add, the academic community) quickly. When brought into broader public contexts, resettlement of this type becomes then the forcing ground for basic policy questions of development and the extension of state hegemony over territory and population as well as majority-minority relations, state versus local determination, national development priorities and human-rights issues, not to mention important questions of practice and ethics for the social, behavioural and policy sciences.

Development projects involving large-scale infrastructure construction and/or environmental changes currently provide the most conflictive context of resettlement cases. Hydro-electric complexes, irrigation projects and major transport systems bring about the wholesale removal and relocation of populations. As the scale of these projects tends to be vast, informing the people to be relocated has generally had a fairly low priority. Usually, the projects are already underway by the time the people to be resettled are informed. When people decide to resist resettlement, they must decide whether to resist the specific project, which may be backed by the state and multilateral financial institutions, or to accept the project and to resist an unjust and poorly designed resettlement project. Individuals and communities must assess both the odds of success and failure, as well as the stakes that are involved in either eventuality, both in the short and long term and in terms of the implications of their strategies and goals at local, regional, national and international levels.

If people as a community decide to resist the development project itself, confronting the state and its ambitions, they are choosing a course of action that challenges both the specific project and, in essence, the development models that include such massive projects. In this case, resistors challenge a global political economic structure reinforced by a deep ideological tradition and philosophy of progress. Conversely, people may decide to accept the development project as a fait accompli and concentrate on improving the resettlement project. Although the degree of 'informed consent' afforded the Kuna affected by the Bayano Dam in Panama is questionable, once the project was initiated, resistance efforts were directed at both defending their culture and influencing the resettlement process (Wali 1989:63).

Policy Implications of Resistance to Resettlement

To assess the implications of resistance movements for public policies, I chose a broad approach to the concept of policy that emphasises as much the political positions of all the participants in resettlement disputes as the formally defined strategies of governments and multilateral agencies. This approach is based on a changing climate in world politics, due in large measure to the expansion of the human-rights movement, which has created the opportunity for former recipients or objects of policy to now adopt policies of their own in their relations and interactions with larger national and international entities. In this approach, then, policies are the intentions and goals of public entities and the means and strategies to achieve them.

Policy thus involves public interests in which the public may be formally defined by statute or legislation, or informally defined by social and cultural organisation. It is clear today that a number of groups and communities, many of them relatively small, are engaging in the establishment of policies regarding group goals and relations with other groups, communities or entities of various sorts. In effect, small cultural groups, when they organise for resistance, acquire information and perspectives, often from newly found allies, that result in the alteration of long-held positions (or implicit policies) recasting their relations with neighbours, local government or the state. Indeed, the current political climate allows for a commonality of interests between large public or non-governmental multilateral organisations and small communities of resisters against the previously sacrosanct sovereignty of the state.

Therefore, when we speak of policy implications of resistance movements we refer to the impacts of resistance movements on the definition of goals and strategies in various institutional contexts and levels in which policies are formulated and activated. Such implications are felt throughout an interactive system, but these impacts will be different and will affect the various elements of the system differently. Furthermore, by 'implications for policy' there is an implicit focus on change, and more specifically, change and improvement in policy. In this case, given the theme of this volume, it is clear that policy changes which reduce impoverishment and enhance the material, socio-cultural and political well-being of the affected population are the issue at hand. In many respects, the extent to which at least state-level policies are impacted by resistance movements is linked to its receptivity and the democratic or authoritarian character of the regime. Similarly, just as communities cannot be assumed to be homogeneous, the state often displays considerable internal differentiation, with competing factions, agencies and ministries with widely differing agendas. Nor do policy makers, planners, and implementers constitute a homogeneous group, often coming from different class and ethnic backgrounds. This internal differentiation offers resisters the opportunity to play one set of state actors against another in achieving both immediate gains and long-term policy changes.

At first glance resistance movements seem to display similar motivations, strategies and tactics, as well as levels of institutional support. Scrutiny of these similarities, however, often reveals only a superficial resemblance among resistance movements, since they emerge in response to extremely different events, projects, cultural contexts and institutional frameworks. As resistance movements in general evolve over time, they trace unique paths, evolving as systems in interaction with both inputs and outputs with other systems. Such is the variety of forms, strategies and tactics available to resistance movements that a 'natural history of resistance movements' is probably less fruitful than developing a set of levels of analysis or contexts of action in which resistance movements operate and variables that influence the evolution of structure and behaviour of a movement (Oliver-Smith 1995).

As a resistance movement emerges and develops, it interacts with processes and variables operating in at least four contexts: the local context of the affected community or region, the design and implementation of the project, the national political economic context and international political economy and political culture. Clearly such contexts are composed of different elements which must be understood as separate, often internally contradictory or opposing, but also interacting. In addition, in many instances the project becomes a means by which local interests can communicate with national institutions in clear and unmistakable ways. Particularly important for resistance movements are those factors which develop the level of organisation and capacity to operate effectively in both local and national level contexts (McAdam et al. 1988:697).

The Local Context of Action

Most resistance movements have an initial local expression in response to a specific project. In many cases, people simply do not believe that they will be resettled (Scudder and Colson 1982:271-272; Wali 1989:74). The idea that such an act would be contemplated simply strains their credulity. Their astonishment at the idea of resettlement may be a measure of the nature and quality of interaction between the community and the state. As communication becomes more frequent and intense between communities and the state, we can expect that people's credulity at the institutional operations and ambitions of the state will no longer be strained.

The threat of resettlement, once fully recognised, is often perceived as such a total threat to socio-cultural and physical survival that it galvanises action as few other threats can. As previously noted, the decision to resist resettlement almost invariably involves people in innovative behaviour, resulting in changes in social relations and organisation, as well as altered relationships with external individuals and entities. When the decision to resist is taken, such action often evolves into the formation of grassroots organisations, in many instances initiating efforts that result in changes in the way that the local community interacts with power structures at various levels in the hierarchy of state institutions (Ghai and Vivian 1992). Furthermore, the speed and intensity of communications in previously remote areas have enabled local resistance movements to establish contact with similar efforts in other parts of the nation or indeed the world, resulting in the insertion of local communities into larger networks of resistance. Insertion in these larger networks can markedly change the resource base and strategic orientation of local resistance movements, ultimately perhaps creating pressure for policy adjustments at various levels. The experience of those expropriated by the Itaipu Dam had considerable influence on the formation of a successful resistance movement by farmers to be affected by the Santo Capanema project in Brazil (Bartolomé 1992:10). There is no question that the sharing of these experiences and others by people threatened with resettlement or those actually already resettled resulted in the formation of CRAB (Regional Commission Against Large Dams, in Brazil. CRAB, through the political acumen of its leaders, many of them originally small farmers, and its networking skills with regionally and culturally diverse populations threatened with resettlement, has developed a power base that enables it to negotiate effectively with Electrobas, the national power company of Brazil and its regional subcontracting affiliates (Bartolomé 1992; Serra 1993).

Even when resistance is framed in highly traditional terms, the need to resist and its consequent expression may alter the ways a community interacts with planners and policy makers. Resistance may be catalysed or conditioned by the flexibility of a group's vital mythological symbols and the ability of the people to interpret and recontextualise the threat of resettlement in terms of those symbols. The threat of resettlement was recontextualised into mythological terms by both Chinantecs and Mazatecs in Mexico, generating a resistance movement expressed largely in messianic form (Bartolomé and Barabas 1990:76-77; see also this volume). As such the messianic resistance movement strengthened traditional culture and produced an activist stance toward regional and national authorities. The 'incipient messianic movement accomplished what politicians, engineers, businessmen, and false mediators have tried to prevent: the unity of the Chinantec people'(Bartolomé and Barabas 1973:15). The achievement of local unity in opposition to the state and its allies also implies both an alteration of traditional relationships and pressure for adjustment of policies on both sides of the conflict. Local expressions of regional levels of social and institutional development will impact the action and organisation of resistance movements. The structure of local leadership and its relationship to similar structures at the regional level are important. The degree of local integration with the state and its operating procedures and goals will impact on the articulation of the resistance movement with external resources and choice of strategies and tactics. If, for example, resisters are aware of and can affiliate with a national union, they may choose to form a local chapter whose main agenda is resistance to resettlement, thereby tapping into a larger resource pool for their efforts as well as acquiring an expanded agenda of goals (Wali 1989:85).

The Project Level of Action

The choice to resist or accept resettlement may be mediated by the quality of the resettlement project itself (Chambers 1970). Where national resettlement policy has been inadequate or non-existent, resistance to a project becomes a means to affect or create appropriate policies at a national level, particularly when international allies support the case (Cernea 1993b:32). The project is, in effect, the projection of the state onto the local context, reframing it in its own terms and for its own ends.

A project that is poorly designed and/or implemented may generate resistance in the local context, producing not only rejection of the project, but also the right of the state to redefine local agendas and terrain. In other cases, particularly where local interests predominate, the goal of resistance is less to improve policy than it is to improve the project. In this instance, resistance to resettlement is resistance to a bad resettlement project and implies a strategy of negotiation in which varying tactics are used to acquire bargaining chips in the effort to secure better terms and conditions for resettlement such as improved replacement land, compensation for losses or housing allowances.

Resistance to specific projects also constitutes an important corrective not only for the project, but, where administrators are astute, for revising inadequate policy as well. Resistance has contributed in major ways to improvements in resettlement policies and procedures, both in specific projects as well as at national policy levels. Indeed, it can be fairly argued that protest over and resistance to specific projects stimulated in large part the increased attention by social scientists to the deficiencies in national resettlement policy, leading to the adoption of specific policy and practice guidelines for resettlement projects at the World Bank and other international organisations and institutions (Morse and Berger 1992; Gibson 1993, Cernea 1993b; Serra 1993; Guggenheim 1993). However, a clear distinction must be drawn between resistance movements that result in policy and project improvements and the conflicts that emerge during consultation with relocatees during implementation. For example, while there was considerable resistance to government plans to resettle communities for the Aguamilpa and Zimapan projects in Mexico, altered national policies, in part the result of international pressure, created a context in which a form of participatory planning of resettlement took place. However, numerous problems and conflicts, some of which involve improvements in the planning process, may emerge in the context of the participation of community members. (Guggenheim 1993)

A project which does not empower relocatees with significant roles in design and implementation, enhancing both their understanding and control over their lives, will not inspire much confidence in a community threatened with resettlement. A resettlement plan which is vague or obtuse or does not demonstrate sensitivity to crucial issues in local economics, social organisation, politics and culture will likewise be unconvincing.

Regardless of the quality of the plan, resistance will often be provoked once resettlement is underway, by manifestly inferior aspects of implementation (Serra 1993). Indeed, sound policy and solid planning can be completely undone by poor implementation. This is where resistance can serve as an important corrective indicator for both specific projects and general policies for design and implementation. Broken promises, unfulfilled plans, negative environmental impacts, inadequate or inappropriate compensation, inferior replacement land or cultural unacceptability of settlement or residential patterns in the new community have all been known to trigger resistance movements after resettlement has taken place (Wali 1989; Serra 1993). Often, specific elements of resettlement schemes, particularly those requiring major adjustments by people in culturally important dimensions of their lives, will elicit the greatest opposition. Ultimately, a relocation project must not only be well designed and entirely adequate to the task, but also well presented and communicated in terms which permit comprehension and stimulate discussion among the target population (Cernea 1988a:15). Again, as mentioned earlier, the record of resettlement projects in these areas has been generally poor, and responsible, at least in some measure, for the frequency of resistance to planned resettlement. Indeed, there are some who argue convincingly that positive, productive resettlement schemes are not only extremely difficult to achieve, even under the best of circumstance, but inevitably promote cultural disintegration (Chernela 1988:20).

The National Level of Action

When local communities mount resistance to resettlement movements, their efforts have been shown to have policy implications at the level of the state and national political organisation and political culture. In development projects the impelling force for resettlement today increasingly is the nation-state. Frequently, ethnic differences between those in control of the state apparatus and those subjected to its authority complicate the relationship between local contexts and the state in resettlement contexts (Colson 1971; Zaman 1982; Wali 1989; Bartolomé and Barabas 1990; Oliver-Smith 1991a). In some cases, the control and integration of ethnic minorities is a secondary goal, although somewhat covert, of development-project resettlement, and resistance will be expressed in terms of defence of ethnicity as well as territory (Zaman 1982).

Clearly, the general political climate of a nation will condition the way a resistance movement develops and operates. The democratic or authoritarian character of the state will provide a more or less fruitful terrain for resistance and its possible effects on policies (Magee 1989; Bartolomé 1992; Robinson 1992). For example, in Brazil in the 1960s a repressive military regime provided little space for either resistance or policy reformulation during the construction of the Sobradinho and Itaipu projects. However, during the late 1970s and 1980s with the Brazilian political 'abertura', strong national-level resistance movements emerged, acquiring significant political power that enabled them to negotiate at the national level and to force the national-level relocation authorities to address the possibilities of alternatives or cancellation of resettlement projects as well as other issues of concern to them (Bartolomé 1992:21; Fisher 1994). Indeed, the organised resistance of individual communities and in concert through the efforts of CRAB has contributed to an entire reconsideration of Brazilian national resettlement policy, designed to create an 'Environmental Master Plan' involving new relationships between the power sector companies, the local line agencies and affected populations. In many senses, the resistance movement at the local and national level both stimulated and constituted one of a variety of pressures on the Brazilian power sector, including legislation requiring more rigorous environmental scrutiny, more stringent requirements from international funding agencies and national and international environmental and human-rights activists and academics. The new relationships established in the master plan are to recognise previously unperceived 'costs' of a socio-cultural and socio-economic nature to an affected population in the design of projects. Forums and formats under the new plan must provide for adequate information on project content and implementation schedules as well as formal representation of all interest groups (Serra 1993:68-71).

Furthermore, resistance movements in Brazil, in coordination with national and international allies, have actually directed a significant critique at the nation's overall development policy, calling for more sustainable alternatives (Turner, T. 1991; Fisher 1994). Similar efforts in India have linked resistance to resettlement to the lack of sustainability of urban culture, questioning the entire nature of the development process in that nation (Bandyopadhyay 1992:276). Popular resistance to resettlement has become part of a linked array of human-rights issues that exerts pressure on the state to alter civil and political-rights policies. Emerging resistance and negotiation efforts among different groups facing resettlement in Mexico have initiated a national dialogue on the power sector's relocation of peasant communities. These debates provoked by the resistance movements are both a partial cause and an effect, along with other issues such as the 1992 election results, that have produced popular pressures for greater governmental accountability and increasing governmental responsiveness (Robinson 1992). On the other hand, the authoritarian regime of Ferdinand Marcos in the Philippines made it almost inevitable that resistance to the Chico Dam would ultimately become framed in violent terms and in alliance with sectors dedicated to the larger goal of overthrowing the state (Drucker 1985).

The International Context of Action

The role resistance movements have played in international contexts has contributed to key changes in policy in very specific institutions, as well as to what can only be described as a fundamental transition in the terms of global political discourse. In some senses, the changes in specific institutional contexts have also become part of the larger discourse. The principle institution in which resistance movements achieved major impact in policy formulation was the World Bank.

For many years, within the World Bank and in other development institutions financing large infrastructure projects involving resettlement, policy makers and planners had little use for social science information on either project development or impact. Costs of such projects were calculated basically in economic terms, and the resettlement dimensions of the projects were generally underfunded, poorly staffed and haphazardly planned in the borrower nations constructing the projects. Social impacts of such projects were deemed to be negligible or unavoidable. However, in the 1970s the difficulties created by poor planning and implementation as well as staunch local resistance in the Bank-assisted Sobradinho project in Brazil and the Chico Dam in the Philippines underscored the need for increasing use of social science knowledge and perspectives for the formulation of explicit resettlement policies within the Bank (Cernea 1993b:19-20).

This emerging position paralleled an overall interest on the part of the Bank in projects that addressed rural poverty in general (Shihata 1993). This interest, as Escobar notes, was due more to rural protest and resistance and the failure of modernisation theories than any transformation in the Bank's thinking (1991:664). However, as Autumn cogently points out, since institutions are rarely gifted with 'either superhuman prescience or unalloyed altruism', changes in institutional policy are usually responses to changes in the real world (Autumn 1994:34). The increasing media attention to and public recognition of resistance by local peoples to large development projects, coupled with sharp criticism of Bank financing of these efforts by NGOs and other organisations on human-rights and environmental grounds, constituted just such real-world changes and stimulated efforts to formulate a set of resettlement policy guidelines within the Bank. The result of such efforts was Operational Directive 4.30: *Involuntary Resettlement* (World Bank 1990). O.D. 4.30 calls for minimising resettlement, an improvement or restoration of living standards, earning capacity and production levels, resettler participation in project activities, a resettlement plan and valuation and compensation for assets lost (Ibid.:1-2).

However, the Bank soon found that resettlement policy guidelines within the Bank constituted little guarantee of their application by borrower nations undertaking resettlement projects. Consequently, the Bank has advocated the formulation and implementation of resettlement legislation in borrower nations, resulting in significant policy changes in several developing nations, most notably Brazil, Colombia and Mexico, as well as other development agencies such as the OECD and the IDB (Cernea 1993b:32; Shihata 1993). However, a number of nations have seen the guidelines contained in O.D. 4.30, as well as pressure to adopt them or some version of them as national policy, as a distinct infringement on national sovereignty. Others see the guidelines as written for large-scale hydro-power projects and have questioned the appropriateness of, for example, certain forms of compensation called for in the guidelines for urban resettlement projects. Furthermore, adoption of formal policies, either by the World Bank or borrower nations, is not assurance of adequate implementation. The World Bank-commissioned independent report on the Narmada Sardar Sarovar project in India (Morse et al. 1992b), recommending cessation of the project pending major improvements, resulted in rejection of further World Bank funding by the government of India.

The impact of resistance movements in the broader contexts of political discourse begins at the local level, but may well be part of an overall process creating a climate for major policy changes of which the World Bank's resettlement guidelines are only the beginning. When a population threatened with resettlement employs resistance to gain a bargaining position to improve the conditions and terms of the resettlement project, a potential conflict may ensue between the threatened community and its actual and potential allies at local, national and international levels who may have much broader, more systemic goals, reaching beyond the local context. While the community threatened with resettlement may choose to view the struggle in local terms, limiting goals and action to their local context, the allies frequently acquired at the national and international levels may conceptualise the struggle in terms of dominant models of national development (Nachowitz 1988; International Dams Newsletter 1985; World Rivers Review 1988). The strategies and tactics preferred by these allies commonly reflect the goal of combatting models and policies of development that call for major alterations of natural and social environments. For local communities involved in resistance, embracing such far-reaching goals requires the realisation of a coincidence of interests and the construction of a shared or common ideological basis of motivation with others often distant socio-culturally and economically, as well as geographically, from them. It is in this context that local resistance dramas 'in the shadow land ... at the outer edge of the realm of politics ...' are internationalised with the potential for changing the character of political culture on the world stage (Falk 1983:25 as quoted in Wilmer 1993:39; Fisher 1994).

When local dramas of resistance to resettlement are cast in national debates and attract the attention of national and international non-governmental organisations and institutions, they become active participants in a larger global dialogue. The entrance of local resistance movements on to national and international stages as significant participants has contributed to a variety of debates of issues with broad policy relevance internationally. In effect, resistance to resettlement has helped to frame the entire contemporary debate on development, the environment and human rights, a debate that shows considerable signs of expanding and of gaining increasing relevance to both national development and human-rights policy as well as international standards.

The linkage of two global movements, environmentalism and human rights, with the resistance of people threatened with relocation or suffering from poorly implemented resettlement, has begun a rethinking of the relationship between human beings and places on the earth and the rights that pertain thereto. This re-examination entails a critique not only of the model of development that accepts the necessity of relocating people for national priorities, but also a questioning of the scale of development interventions that create major disruption for both people and environment. As Adam Curle in discussing the removal of the Chakmas for Kaptai Dam in Bangladesh so succinctly puts it, there is '... a moral problem. How much suffering for how many can be justified by how much good for how many?' (1971:105). Further, the discourse that addresses these issues implicitly and explicitly has drawn into debate a reassessment of the extent of state sovereignty (Downing and Kushner 1988).

Conclusion

The centre of the discussion on the environment has shifted from an exclusive focus on the destruction wrought by human beings on the natural world to an exploration of a sustainable relationship between human needs and the earth's resources (Redclift 1987). In this discussion the industrialised world is portrayed as developing through an unsustainable, environmentally destructive relationship with the environment, consuming non-renewable resources, creating non-absorbable toxic by-products and intervening in non-reversible ways in the various systems and cycles that ensure the renewability of the ecosystem. In the discussion of sustainable forms of human intervention, certain local economies in the non-industrialised world have been explored as examples of low-impact systems on the ecosystem at the same time that greater credence has begun to be given to indigenous voices in the development dialogue. This emerging discussion has found abundant material among the communities that are threatened with or have been subjected to resettlement. The construction of a large hydro-electric project in a rural area juxtaposes dramatically the two approaches to resource use and their constituents.

Although at some risk of romanticising local communities into 'ecologically noble savages'(Redford 1991), the debate on local knowledge and approaches to resource use has linked the sustainability issue to questions of local human rights (Redclift 1992). Among these human rights are those defined as environmental rights, pertaining to the right to live in a healthy, non-degraded environment (Johnson 1994). Notwithstanding the fact that local people are not always free from responsibility in the degradation of their own environments, their participation at the grassroots is seen as essential for the return to or maintenance of a sustainable relationship with the ecosystem (Ghai and Vivian 1992). In this fashion, not only the participation but also the empowerment of local communities becomes a key dimension (Redclift 1992). One dimension of empowerment is gaining a voice and not only being heard, but also being listened to.

If voices from the 'shadowland' of indigenous and peasant communities resisting resettlement as only one of a myriad of incursions upon their lives and resources are being heard increasingly by elites, it may be indicative of important changes in global political culture. These voices, questioning the entire model of development of the industrialised world, are insisting that territory not only consists of resources, but is also the basis of a particular way of life that people have a right to maintain. Such a position is consonant with a shift in world politics perceived by some, away from struggles over power and wealth toward struggles over normative issues (Wilmer 1993:40). Such a shift toward normative issues in international political culture has significant implications for the definition of the state as a political community with rights over both territory and people. When local communities resist the state's efforts to resettle them to make way for development projects, they call into question not only reigning models of development and resource exploitation, but also the state's right to define local terrain and priorities.

While there is little question that long-standing development strategies are undergoing some scrutiny in international fora, the actual practice of development continues to be realised in policies favouring infrastructural expansion and economic growth over ecological and cultural concerns. On average, 300 large dams enter into construction every year, displacing more than four million people, while urban development and transportation projects uproot an estimated six million more (World Bank 1994a:i). Most of these projects are not constrained or influenced by World Bank or other, similar guidelines in the resettlement of uprooted people. Although undoubtedly many, if not most, of these projects will produce benefits for the societies and people they affect, realistic attempts to mitigate the high costs they present to uprooted people and impacted environments are only beginning. However, the fact that we are increasingly hearing serious discussions favouring international normative standards in issues of human and environmental rights over the power of the sovereign state places people who resist development-induced resettlement in the crucible of global policy change.

6

Indigenous Resistance
to Involuntary Relocation

Andrew Gray

Involuntary relocation, as detailed in a number of chapters in this volume, causes countless problems for local communities. Economies are destroyed and production activities disrupted, giving rise to impoverishment, while social and cultural disintegration along with psychological stress lead to sickness and even death (Hallward 1992:44). Those who work with involuntary resettlement programmes testify to their deleterious effects: 'From the perspective of the displaced people, forced resettlement is always a disaster' (Partridge 1989:375).

Even though well-documented evidence demonstrates the harm caused to the victims of resettlement, enormous numbers of people continue to be relocated every year to make way for development projects. The 1994 World Bank review of projects involving involuntary resettlement (World Bank 1994a:i) puts the current figure as high as four million people. Particularly problematic in this context is resettlement as a result of the construction of dams. According to Cernea (1990b:332), each year between 1.2 and 2.1 million people are relocated involuntarily as result of hydro-electric dam projects.

Dams have long been the subject of criticism on both environmental and social grounds (Goldsmith and Hildyard 1984). Non-governmental organisations, such as the International Rivers Network and their publication *World Rivers Review*, the *Ecologist*, the Environmental Defense Fund and countless other institutions keep abreast of developments through active monitoring and campaigning. Meanwhile, local organisations representing those affected by dams have gradually joined with the environmental movement over the last fifteen years to mobilise large international campaigns against dams, several of which have been highly successful. This resistance has become particularly effective through the politicisation of victims of forced resettlement (Oliver-Smith 1991a:135).

In contrast to campaigns and direct action against projects, agencies such as the World Bank have carried out research on the consequences of relocation. The Bank has established an Operational Directive aiming to minimise the destruction wrought on the victims of involuntary resettlement (Cernea 1988a; Escudero 1988; World Bank 1990). By responding to the criticisms of its policies and practices on dam construction and forced resettlement, the World Bank has tried to establish criteria and principles whereby economic development can take place with minimal harm to the victims. In spite of all the attempts to ameliorate the social and environmental damage caused by relocation, forced relocation is still a major problem facing local peoples throughout the world. After thirty-seven years working on the subject, Scudder says of his experience in Africa and elsewhere: 'My conclusion [is] that dam-induced displacement more often than not leaves the majority worse off [in other words, transforms that majority into refugees]' (1993:148).

This chapter looks at the consequences of large-scale dams and in particular the resistance of those targeted for forced resettlement. An opposing perspective arises from those interests which are eager to establish hydro-electric schemes, particularly governments caught up in international debt and the World Bank, which acts as a midwife for up to 10 per cent of all large-scale dams. The strategies of resistance by the victims and the attempts by the World Bank to ameliorate the effects of their projects provide a gulf between two perspectives on development which have rarely, if ever, been bridged.

Of all the victims of dam-induced resettlement, this chapter focuses specifically on the effects of hydro-electric and irrigation construction on indigenous peoples, because they illustrate this clash of perspectives particularly clearly. There are over 300 million indigenous people in the world, ranging from the native peoples of the Americas, the Inuit of the Arctic and Saami of Scandinavia to the mainland and island tribal peoples of Asia, the Bushmen, Pygmies and pastoralists of Africa and the Aboriginal peoples of Australia, the Maori of New Zealand and the colonised peoples of the Pacific.

Over the last twenty years, the position of indigenous peoples has become increasingly prominent in the discussion of human rights and development (IWGIA 1988:5-9; Gray 1995). Whereas no single defi-

nition exists for indigenous peoples, several criteria provide a poly-
thetic orientation to its meaning: they are the inhabitants of a territory
which was invaded prior to, or during, the establishment of a nation-
state; they are peoples whose economic, social, political and cultural
characteristics distinguish them from those of the dominant national
society; they are discriminated against and unable to exercise their collective and individual rights and freedoms; and finally they recognise
themselves as indigenous (Burger 1987:5; ICIHI 1987:5-6).

Indigenous peoples are particularly affected by the construction of
dams because they are frequently found in more isolated areas and
because of their special sacred ties to their territories and cultures. Relocation is a traumatic experience for indigenous peoples not only personally but because of the threats on their lands, lives and cultures.
However, this is not to say that indigenous peoples suffer any more than
other 'oustees', rather that their specific characteristics are sufficiently
prominent to draw attention to factors other than the economic, social
and individual traumas discussed frequently in studies of relocation.

The main question concerning the rights of indigenous 'oustees' is
whether, after ascertaining the environmental and social consequences of large-scale development projects, there is really any justification for imposing initiatives with only a short-term economic
benefit for a few interested parties. Increasingly, commentators agree
that the costs of large-scale dams should not only be calculated in
terms of construction, but include the economic, social and cultural
impoverishment arising from implementation.

The Kaptai Lake – Long-Term Effects of
Dam Construction

In December 1990, while accompanying the Chittagong Hill Tracts
Commission to Bangladesh, I was driven through Rangamati and in
the early-morning haze saw the massive pale blue waters of the Kaptai
Lake, stretching out to the horizon. The Bangladeshi driver remarked
how the lake reminded him of Matthew Arnold's 'Dover Beach' ...

> ... for the world, which seems
>
> To lie before us like a land of dreams,
> So various, so beautiful, so new,
> Hath really neither joy, nor love, nor light,
> Nor certitude, nor peace, nor help for pain;
> And we are here as on a darkling plain,
> Swept with confused alarms of struggle and flight,
> Where ignorant armies clash by night.

Beneath the Kaptai Lake lies a history of suffering from relocation and resettlement which has since provided conditions throughout the Hill Tracts for a prolonged period of military oppression leaving the area 'swept with confused alarms of struggle and flight'.

Hidden beneath the depths of Kaptai are countless lost temples, villages and communities which were submerged when the dam was completed in 1963. Funded by a bilateral loan from the United States Agency for International Development (USAID), 250 square miles were flooded, destroying 40 per cent of all the cultivable land in the Chittagong Hill Tracts (ASI 1984:32). The electricity was used to generate industrialisation for the Plains areas of Bangladesh, outside of the Hill Tracts, while the navigation facilities encouraged exploitation of the scarce forest resources of the hill areas (Mey 1984:26).

The human suffering and unrest caused by the dam was on a massive scale. One hundred thousand Jumma hill people, constituting one-sixth of the total indigenous population, were relocated. Even though they were promised financial compensation and new lands for those lost, sixty thousand received nothing whatsoever. Forty thousand people migrated to Arunchal Pradesh in India, where they currently live without Indian citizenship for themselves or their children born after the move. Inter-ethnic conflicts still occur between the hill peoples of Arunchal Pradesh and the migrants of thirty years ago. In addition to those moving to India as a result of the Kaptai Dam, twenty thousand Hill Tracts people migrated to Arakan in Burma. The remaining forty thousand dispersed throughout the dwindling resources of the Chittagong Hill Tracts, leaving 'a deep legacy of bitterness and distrust' (CHT Commission 1991:13).

With eight thousand Jumma families seeking new lands within the Hill Tracts, the pressure on the remaining resources became more severe. Those people who had previously farmed in the valley areas submerged by the lake had to move to higher ground where they survive by means of swidden agriculture. Those who gained compensation received three acres instead of the six they had owned on average before the dam was built, while of the U.S.$51 million set aside by the Pakistan government for rehabilitation, only U.S.$2.6 million was used (ASI 1984:33).

The environmental effects of the dam were compounded by a proposal by a Canadian firm, Forestal Incorporated, to convert large areas of the Hill Tracts into plantations for fruit trees. The local Jumma people found that their subsistence economy was undermined as they were increasingly forced into working for commercial agriculture. The strain on the environment was aggravated by the Pakistan government's policy, later compounded by the Bangladesh government, to encourage Bengali settlers from the overcrowded Plains to move into the Hill Tracts to seek a new life. The consequent shortage of land was a major contributing factor to the social conflict which has erupted in the Chittagong Hill Tracts since the late 1970s, causing the deaths of an estimated 200,000 people from torture, forced relocation and massacre. Furthermore, the silting of the Kaptai Lake as a result of the dam and increased deforestation means that the original 78 megawatts of power generated envisaged when the dam was constructed has decreased considerably (CHT Commission 1991: 114).

A survey completed in 1979 of the Jumma people who had been affected by the dam provided the following information:

> 69 per cent felt the dam created food and financial problems for them, 89 per cent said that they had to change residence, 69 per cent complained of inadequate government help for resettlement, 58 per cent were distressed that they had no scope for employment on the Kaptai hydro-electric project and 93 per cent felt that the economic condition of tribal people had been better before the Kaptai Dam (ASI 1984:36).

Writers on Kaptai are agreed that whereas the dam itself did not cause the genocide which subsequently inundated the Jumma people of the Chittagong Hill Tracts, it provided a context within which unrest, brutality and consequently genocide took place. The severe social problems, shortage of land and misguided economic initiatives, along with the massive invasion of Bengali settlers, created the conditions for the destruction which led to the mass killings which have plagued the Jummas for the last twenty years (Oliver-Smith 1991a).

The Social and Environmental Effects of Large Dams

The experience of the Chittagong Hill Tracts is by no means unique, and although the genocidal consequences which arose out of the construction of the Kaptai Dam were particularly horrific, a familiar pattern of incompetence and unnecessary suffering can be traced throughout the world whenever large-scale dams threaten the lives of indigenous peoples. The pattern follows a trail of environmental degradation and social disruption which poses serious questions as to the viability of large dams within a framework of sustainable development.

The construction of dams has always been an aspect of human and animal activity. However, unlike beavers and our ancestors, current construction has, over the last fifty years, grown to enormous proportions. Rivers are blocked by dams which tower hundreds of feet high, creating floods and lakes stretching for enormous distances. Many thousands of people are relocated and obliged to move to areas where land is not available and where, often without compensation, they try to start their lives afresh against insuperable odds. The destruction wrought by dams clearly varies from case to case depending on the people affected and the environment where the development takes place, but when construction takes place on the lands of indigenous peoples, the consequences are often severe.

Attracted by the possibility of cheap energy, governments of poorer countries often see dams as providing the means of salvation from their economic problems and huge external debts. The benefits gained from dams range from hydro-electricity and cheap power to potable water and irrigation useful for stimulating food production (Goldsmith and Hildyard 1984:14). Dams are considered by governments and those with financial interests as an unavoidable and ultimately beneficial contribution to the development process. Yet when looking at dams in more detail, the life span of a large-scale dam, particularly in tropical areas, can be quite short. The electricity generated decreases rapidly, as has occurred with the Kaptai Dam, and in some cases the life of a dam can be thirty years or even less (Ibid.: 221), while the supposed production benefits of irrigation works do not necessarily reach the poor (Ibid.:179).

In spite of the criticisms against dams, there are proponents who argue that nation-states have to develop, and that the benefits from projects should be positively weighed against the social and environmental costs: 'There are many cases where societies must balance the cost of resettlement with benefits such as safe water supplies, efficient transportation systems or irrigated agriculture' (Cernea and Guggenheim 1993:2).

In this way, development is part of a process where the advantages for the state as a whole have to outweigh the desires of the minority. The background to this argument rests in the legal concept of 'eminent domain', which consists of a state's right to expropriate property in certain circumstances (Escudero 1988; Shihata 1991a:190). According to this perspective, the aims of a project often require unpleasant means, but that when looked at from a broad perspective, the disadvantages of large dams and the consequent involuntary resettlement are both politically and economically justifiable in terms of the 'greater good'.

However, this greater good depends on who is considering the broader perspective. If the state is taken as the starting point of the discussion, then the broader perspective begins and ends with the desires and goals of the governing elite. However, from another perspective, a 'broader view' looks at the long-term environmental effects of dams and the social costs of involuntary resettlement which in most cases are ignored by those in authority who are so eager to install dams on indigenous territory. From this perspective, the justification of large dams on economic and political criteria is certainly questionable.

The environmental effects of dams can be very serious (Goldsmith and Hildyard 1984). Upstream, apart from the loss of fertile agricultural areas from flooding, species of wildlife and forest areas are destroyed and fish migrations affected, while the increase in evaporation loss from the new lake and its gradual silting slow down the river flow and lead to an ever-decreasing production of electricity. Downstream, the problems are different. Silt reduction leads to a loss of soil fertility and the disappearance of fish stocks, while in irrigated areas, problems range from the rise of the water table and salinisation through the evaporation of salt, to an increase in parasites from stagnant pools and canals. In addition to all of these environmental problems, dams are also thought to contribute to the frequency of earthquakes (Ibid.:118).

When turning to the consequences of dams on the people living in the targeted areas, several themes recur throughout the world. Scudder and Colson have organised the effects of involuntary resettlement into a general framework. Scudder (1973:51) describes resettlement as a 'multidimensional insult with psychological, physiological and socio-cultural components.' All involuntary relocation is opposed by definition, which means that when removal takes place political leaders are undermined and the community undergoes a sense of failure (Scudder 1993:126).

As people are wrenched from their homelands against their will, psychological stress arises from the trauma of moving, guilt at the impotence of resistance, grief at the loss of a home and anxiety for the future. Socio-cultural stress arises from the failure to pay attention to the need for communities to remain together, the lack of economic sustainability after resettlement and the disruption of cultural activities as a result of dislocation or interference by outside interests. A physiological aspect of resettlement stress results from the increase in morbidity and mortality rates following removal arising both from disease and depression (Scudder and Colson 1982:268ff). This is particularly problematic in the case of large dams, where mosquitos in irrigation schemes are sources of malaria, the flat worms in freshwater snails can cause schistosomiasis and blackfly worms can cause onchocerciaias or river blindness.

In addition to analysing the different aspects of stress, Scudder and Colson have also developed a four-part scheme (1982:274) (also presented in a five part format [Scudder 1993:126]) to explain the process of relocation:

1. Recruitment stage. This is the period when a government makes plans for establishing a development project, usually without informing the local inhabitants that their future is threatened.
2. Site preparation. This is the point after which the project has been approved that the victims are aware that something is happening and the local people learn of the plans to remove them.
3. Transition stage. During this period people learn that they have to move and the stress discussed earlier becomes marked. This is usually the time when 'consultation' begins, although the whole process has already been planned.
4. Potential development and community formation. After the trauma of removal, the people, with adequate support, begin to reconstruct their economy and organise their social and cultural life. This often involves trying to establish relationships with 'host populations' who already live in the new area.
5. The consolidation stage. This is the point at which a long-term integration into the new social and economic environment has been achieved and the people overcome the period of stress. The relocation is complete.

This ideal type covers the way in which, in the best of all worlds, a resettlement could take place providing the means are available for a people to overcome the trauma and establish a positive new life for themselves. However, as Scudder and Colson explain (1982), most of the involuntary relocations which take place remain fixed in the transition stage of maximum stress and during which there is neither innovation or revitalisation within the relocated community. In cases involving indigenous peoples, however, stages four and five are, more often than not, wishful thinking.

For indigenous peoples the factors of land and culture provide a consistent theme which gives rise to serious consequences in any example of involuntary resettlement. Indigenous peoples who have not already been thrown off their lands are the owners of territories which they have lived on, used and held for centuries. In many countries, such as India, indigenous peoples are 'landless' according to the law because their territory has no official recognition or else has been titled in the name of one person.

Almost all indigenous peoples hold their land collectively and exercise territorial rights to their resources. The legitimisation of indigenous peoples' ownership of land is guaranteed through the sacred aspect of land and resources. This is often impossible to explain to non-indigenous peoples who consider areas where indigenous peoples live as 'empty'.

For indigenous peoples, cultural perspectives of the universe are bound up with an understanding of the land as part of indigenous territorial identity. This makes an anthropological approach to the position of indigenous peoples involved in involuntary resettlement particularly pertinent regarding rights to land and culture because understanding from the natives' point of view (Cernea and Guggenheim 1993:6) frequently questions the whole enterprise of constructing a large-scale dam.

Indigenous peoples bring into focus a particular aspect of the problems of involuntary resettlement because of their specific cultural connection linking the invisible world and the environment. Although each culture articulates its relationship with the environment in a different way, several factors constantly recur which orient us towards a perspective of indigenous peoples and their territories.

Indigenous peoples regularly refer to the collective relationship they have with their lands. This often takes the form of ownership at a community or ethnic level which is converted into personal property by use and through acceptance by the rest of the people. This collectivity is bounded by a holistic view of the environment which links together economic resources, political control, historical contiguity and spiritual presence. For non-indigenous people these elements of the environment are frequently separated into concepts such as land, territory, landscape and the earth, but for indigenous peoples they are usually inter-twined. Another common element which indigenous peoples describe when talking of their relationship with the environment arises from inalienability. Land cannot be given away because it is held in trust from ancestral times for future generations, which means that it is usually non-negotiable as a commodity.

These aspects of indigenous peoples' relationships to their environment are extremely important when discussing involuntary resettlement, because opposition which arises is not simply based on one factor but encompasses and incorporates economic, political, historical and religious aspects of life. What often appears to outsiders as a two-dimensional problem of environmental and social effects of large-scale dams, becomes, from an indigenous perspective, one dimension where the social and environmental effects are culturally drawn together through the invisible world which guarantees ownership, mediates resource allocation and endows meaning and identity on both collective and personal levels (Gray, forthcoming).

In spite of a constant stream of criticism about the effects of large dams, construction continues to be promoted throughout the world. African heads of state have considered them 'symbols of national development' (Scudder 1973:45) while in Asia, Nehru heralded them as 'the temples of modern India' (Colchester 1987:284). In spite of all the well-documented devastation which results from these projects, they continue to be encouraged, not only by governments of poor countries, but also by institutions and governments of the industrialised world.

Large-scale dams are attractive because they stand for more than simply material advantage: they are physical manifestations of the power of the state. In order to construct dams, the environment has to be changed completely, and through the exercise of 'eminent domain' the state forcibly obliges people to move from lands and territories which they consider to be their own property. This is particularly sensitive in the context of indigenous peoples, whose territorial rights rest on principles stemming from a period prior to the formation of the nation-state.

The writer Karl Wittfogel (1963) has produced a controversial thesis that Marx's 'Asiatic mode of production' is based on the control of irrigation networks by the ruling despotic elites of pre-capitalist states. This thesis takes an interesting twist when looking at the political economy of large dams. Construction attracts foreign currency into a country while at the same time the dam provides a symbolic manifestation of the assertion of progress in development. Politically, this means demonstrating state control over the environment and the people living on the margins of national society. Large-scale dams provide elites with economic benefits and the state with an excuse to exercise political power over people and the environment, while operating an ideological symbol of integration into the march of progress.

The conflicts which arise between indigenous peoples and those who promote large dams are part of a power struggle between the nation state as a homogenous all-embracing oppressive entity consisting of government and economic elites, and the peoples whose ties to the land pre-date the formation of the national society. This chapter will now address the conflict between those interested in promoting dams and those who resist the whole phenomenon.

Ameliorating the Inevitable – the World Bank

Proponents of dams argue that blanket criticisms of hydro-electric projects ignore the variations which occur in different parts of the world. Dams outside of tropical areas, in high mountains, for example, frequently do not affect so many people and are less plagued by silting. Furthermore, most of the forced relocation takes place with projects where irrigation networks are included in the programme (World Bank 1994b:38).

In addition, proponents of hydro-power argue that without dams more emphasis would be placed on coal and nuclear power, causing even more environmental and social damage (Ibid.). According to this perspective, dams are inevitable, and some element of forced relocation is going to be necessary; although an evil, its harmful effects should be ameliorated through better planning and clear policies.

Although the OECD and the Interamerican Development Bank have both produced guidelines for involuntary resettlement in development projects, the World Bank has most experience in policy formation on both involuntary resettlement and indigenous peoples, through its Operational Directives on Involuntary Resettlement (4.30) and Indigenous Peoples (4.20). The World Bank currently supports between 3 and 10 per cent of the large dams currently under construction, which covers a small but significant proportion of peoples being involuntarily resettled.

The first guidelines on involuntary resettlement were drawn up in 1979 and 1980, when Operational Manual Statement (OMS) 2.33 was formulated. Between 1985 and 1986 an in-house policy analysis recommended the publication of two papers (Cernea 1988a and Escudero 1988) which provided the basis for Operational Directive 4.30 of 1990. In April 1994 the Bank produced a review of projects involving involuntary resettlement from 1986 to 1993.

The World Bank takes the position that large dams are inevitable and that unless they can be stopped when they are incipient, the only way to manage the difficult task of involuntary resettlement is through planning. This involves understanding what each project needs, preparing to counter-act the detrimental aspects of the relocation and compensating the victims as far as possible. The solution is not seen in political terms, but primarily through technical provisions and careful planning.

The technical paper on involuntary resettlement (Cernea 1988a) is probably the most thoughtful exposition by the World Bank of this perspective. The report comments: 'Throughout the world, involuntary resettlement has probably been the most unsatisfactory component associated with dam construction, whether in nationally or in internationally financed projects' (Ibid.:9). The paper advocates a policy to minimise and reverse the negative effects of compulsory relocation. One of the main difficulties the Bank has to face is the task of engaging local governments in taking responsibility for the problems of involuntary resettlement and incorporating development objectives into what would otherwise be seen as a salvage and welfare operation. Acknowledging the profound disruption caused by relocation, the report advocates that planning begin at the preparation stage of the project and recommends that the resettlers are involved at every stage of their project so that they participate in their own removal. The aim of the policy is that resettlers regain their previous standard of living and integrate into the new host community which can only take place with a land-for-land compensation scheme (Ibid.:24).

The legal introduction (Escudero 1988) draws attention to the importance of adequate compensation and the right of resettlers to be rehabilitated. Furthermore, it emphasises how the special relationship between indigenous peoples and their territories should be taken into account in resettlement plans. The report also discusses the 'eminent domain' of states and leaves the settlement of the problem in the technical hands of those carrying out the planning.

The Operational Directive in 1990 on Involuntary Resettlement contained five main points: a) involuntary resettlement should be minimised; b) means should be provided to improve and restore the former living standards of those being resettled; c) resettlers and hosts in the new areas should both be involved in resettlement activities; d) the resettlement plan should follow a strict time schedule; e) all losses should be valued and compensated.

The provisions in the Operational Directive reflect many of the concerns raised about involuntary resettlement and consist of ways to ameliorate the problems without actually preventing the implementation of the project. In the Review of 1994, the Bank expresses this in terms of an opposition between those who oppose all involuntary resettlement and those governments who wish to push ahead with development projects without taking the needs of the victims of relocation into account. The aim of the Bank's approach is to avoid the problem: 'good resettlement can prevent impoverishment and even reduce poverty by rebuilding sustainable livelihoods' (World Bank 1994a:vi). The review looked at 192 projects involving forced resettlement primarily in India, China, Indonesia and Brazil. Sixty-three per cent of the projects involved dams, and these constituted the largest cause of displacement.

In spite of claiming that performance in Bank projects has improved, the report says that 'though fragmentary, the weight of available evidence points to unsatisfactory income restoration more frequently than to satisfactory outcomes' (Ibid.:x). The main obstacles to preventing impoverishment are a lack of resources for compensation, particularly land; poor planning, whereby finances run out before resettlers receive their compensation; inexperienced institutions that lack legal knowledge carrying out the relocation; and programmes that are top-down without sufficient participation or use of local knowledge.

The report recommends that borrower governments be encouraged to become committed to ensuring adequate provisions for resettlement; that the World Bank enhance the borrowers' institutional capacity to carry out resettlement; that project designs be improved, participation be promoted and financing be adequate; and that development provisions be made available for those being relocated. A crucial proposal of the report is that borrowing governments must accept responsibility for the welfare of people who are to be involuntarily resettled.

The NGO response to the Bank review was critical. Oxfam (1994) said that the 'latest Bank report, though it tried to put a brave face on it, is a dismal catalogue of failure'. Resettlement is more difficult, expensive and time consuming than has hitherto been assumed. The critique continues: 'Although the data are weak, projects appear often not to have succeeded in reestablishing resettlers at a better or equal living standard and that unsatisfactory performance still persists on a wide scale.' The World Bank review could not document one case where a population which had been displaced had regained its standard of living. Another NGO comment on the report says: 'However, rather than attempting to avoid or minimise resettlement or to limit future lending for resettlement, the review concludes that the World Bank should put more money and resources into resettlement, with the danger of possibly creating a resettlement industry' (NGO, 1994).

The significance of the theoretical approach of the World Bank and its Operational Directive is that it has been the first international institution to establish a policy on involuntary resettlement which constitutes the strongest existing set of provisions. However, the theoretical policy position which allows projects to take place provided that measures are taken to ameliorate and mitigate threats to the victims of resettlement is questionable in practice because, according to the review, implementation of the involuntary resettlement Operational Directive has been a failure.

In November 1994 the World Bank produced a Status Report looking at the remedial action planning for involuntary resettlement. It points out that fifteen projects which had been looked at by the review had been cancelled or modified to avoid involuntary resettlement. Out of the ninety-seven projects reviewed, at least one-third had some remedial treatment during the year, which is certainly an improvement on the situation prior to the report. However, over 50 per cent of the projects still require some fundamental adjustment to ensure that the resettlement factor conforms to the Bank's policy on involuntary resettlement.

A similar phenomenon can be seen when looking at the Operational Directive on Indigenous Peoples. The first World Bank policy on indigenous peoples arose from a document published in 1982 and encounters a tension which runs through the whole policy:

> The Bank's policy is, therefore, to assist with development projects that do not involve unnecessary or avoidable encroachment onto territories used or occupied by tribal groups. Similarly, the Bank will not support projects on tribal lands, or that will affect tribal lands, unless the tribal society is in agreement with the objectives of the project, as they affect the tribe, and unless it is assured that the borrower has the capability of implementing effective measures to safeguard tribal populations and their lands against any harmful side effects resulting from the project (World Bank 1982:3).

The statement on the one hand supports the right of indigenous peoples to veto projects on their territories which are imposed without their consent, yet at the same time it accepts that if the borrower gives certain assurances the project can still go ahead. The 1982 Operational Manual Statement 2.34 which came out at the same time as this policy paper was internal to the Bank and more cautious, omitting any reference to the right of veto.

The most recent modification of the World Bank's policy on indigenous peoples is in Operational Directive 4.20. The current policy (which is under further revision) supports the protection of indigenous peoples from the harmful effects of projects and advocates their participation in the development process. Although an improvement on OMS 2.34, the current OD 4.20 still lacks the strength of the original policy document of 1982 which supported the indigenous veto on projects and respected their right to self-determination.

Even though neither the involuntary resettlement nor the indigenous peoples' operational directives are perfect, in these the World Bank acknowledges that there exists a serious problem which is crucial to address when undertaking projects. Even though the results of applying the policies would not remove all problems, the implementation of these guidelines would certainly alleviate and mitigate many of the injustices which are currently taking place. However, unfortunately, implementation is extremely weak (Colchester 1993; Gray 1994).

Indigenous Resistance

Although indigenous organisations have existed for hundreds of years in many countries, only since the 1960s has an indigenous movement begun to take root on a worldwide basis. A fluorescence of indigenous organisations numbering in the thousands has taken root locally throughout the world. Communities have formed local federations while national indigenous organisations and institutions have been established, representing indigenous interests at the level of the nation-state. At the same time, indigenous peoples have coordinated themselves on regional and international levels, taking indigenous concerns to agencies such as the United Nations and the International Labour Organisation.

The indigenous movement arose during the post-war period of decolonisation when civil-rights questions were prominent and at a time when financial support was available for popular organisations. The industrialised countries of North America, Scandinavia, Australia and New Zealand were some of the first to be mobilised nationally in the late 1960s. Throughout the 1970s the movement spread throughout Latin America, while in the 1980s it took a solid foothold in Asia and the Pacific. During the 1990s the indigenous movement has spread to the former Soviet Union and throughout Africa, where peoples such as the Bushmen, Pygmies and pastoralists of East Africa are supporting its goals. These demands include rights to lands and territories, social and cultural freedom of expression, freedom from discrimination, the right to be represented by their own institutions and the right to consent and control over development. All of these concepts are bound up in the over-arching right to the recognition of self-determination for indigenous peoples, which means the capacity of a people to make decisions which affect them and control their own lives.

The rise of the indigenous movement has occurred within the context of a political mobilisation in the face of countless problems. Throughout the world, indigenous peoples suffer from discrimination, the invasion of their territories and the extraction of their resources. The awareness of the injustices which surround them has been a key factor in the mobilisation of the indigenous movement. Among these factors has been the effect of the prospect of involuntary resettlement as a consequence of the construction of large dams. As Oliver-Smith says: 'In effect, the threat or enactment of resettlement presents so stark a challenge to survival that political mobilisation and empowerment may follow closely' (1991a:132).

Indigenous peoples have been resisting dams continuously over the last twenty years. The next section of this chapter looks at several examples of resistance movements to see the extent to which they have been successful. The aims of different campaigns vary widely; some seek to change a project, some to ensure that compensation is provided to the displaced people, while others try to stop a dam altogether. The cases reviewed below are well-known examples of indigenous resistance which have concentrated on cancelling the construction of dams.

Successful Campaigns of Resistance

Two successful campaigns of resistance against dams have taken place in the Philippines and in Brazil. The Chico dams were planned at the beginning of the 1970s, when the Philippines became a target for World Bank development support (Bello et al. n.d.). The dams were to be built in Luzon on the lands of the indigenous Kalinga and Bontoc peoples, flooding 2,753 hectares of rice terraces and affecting 90,000 indigenous peoples (AST 1983; Drucker 1988).

In 1974 the government ignored protests against the dams and sent survey teams into the area. Within a year, 150 indigenous leaders had signed the 'Bodong' Peace Pact, expressing solidarity against the dam and prohibiting any support for its activities. The government responded by sending in forces which clashed with local peoples to the extent that by 1976 the whole area was militarised and the armed guerilla movement, the New People's Army (NPA), offered the Kalinga and Bontoc peoples its support.

In 1977 at the International Monetary Fund conference in Manila, massive demonstrations took place and the President of the World Bank was forced to say that no projects would be approved which were opposed by local people. The conflict continued until 1980, when the Chico Valley had become a war zone (Drucker 1988:158), and within a year the government postponed indefinitely the Chico River Dam Project.

The Chico dams were stopped because of a long-term campaign by local peoples seeking solidarity from indigenous peoples throughout the Philippines, an international campaign and above all the constant fear of violence within the area concerned. The resistance was local and, through the experience of the Chico Dam, resistance and political mobilisation in the Philippines became strengthened by means of the Bodong pact which united the Cordillera of Luzon in a way which had never previously occurred.

In 1981, a review of indigenous areas threatened by hydro-electric projects in Brazil (Aspelin and Coelho dos Santos 1981:104) expressed concern about a possible dam project on the Xingu river basin under consideration by the Brazilian state company, Electrobras, for some nine or ten dams to flood 6,000 square kilometres and affect 4,000 indigenous people in forty-two villages from at least six groups. By 1986 the plan had been included in a programme called Plan 2010 to construct and complete hydro-electric projects throughout the country: 136 dams over twenty years with seventy-eight in the rainforest affecting 124 communities (Leonel et al. 1992:16).

The Kayapó, a fiercely independent people, strongly resisted the Kararao and Babaquara dams on their lands and mobilised in their own defence, travelling to Washington to protest to the World Bank about the power-sector loan for U.S.$500 million then under discussion. In 1987, after an intense campaign, the Bank sent a staff member to carry out an environmental assessment of the project and eventually agreed to pay regard to its policy and suspended the loan and postponed the dam. However, the Brazilian government still planned to continue with the scheme. The campaign, which involved an alliance of environmental non-government organisations in Washington, indigenous-rights organisations, local institutions and indigenous organisations turned its focus from the World Bank to the Brazilian government.

This alliance had been in operation for several years, campaigning against World Bank projects as far apart as Brazil, Paraguay, Indonesia and India. A meeting was planned at the town of Altamira in 1989 where organisations from the Developed and the Developing World joined forces to oppose the dams. The protests against the dams succeeded in forcing the Brazilian government to shelve the projected development schemes on the Xingu River.

The Brazilian protest was different to that of the Philippines. The campaign involved a more developed alliance between NGOs from the Developed and the Developing World, which succeeded in alerting the World Bank to the situation and causing it to suspend its loan which would have funded the dams. Moreover, the massive meeting at Altamira which gained publicity throughout the world succeeded in finally convincing the Brazilian government of the hostility to their plan (Hildyard 1989).

These two successful strategies were respectively local mobilisation with a violent uprising and a massive publicity campaign linking non-government organisations from all over the world. In both cases indigenous leaders risked threats to their lives by asserting their rights in the face of government opposition. The two targets for both campaigns were the World Bank and the national government. The first to recognise the problem was the World Bank, although its influence was not sufficient to stop the project; yet in both cases the dams were 'postponed indefinitely' at the moment that the national government decided that continuing was no longer worthwhile.

Unsuccessful Campaigns of Resistance

In October 1987 the waters began to rise behind the Balbina Dam on the Uatuma River, north of the city of Manaus in Brazil. Flooding an area of 2,346 square kilometres, the dam destroyed a large portion of the reserve of the Waimiri-Atroari people (Cummings 1990:44). At the turn of the century the Waimiri-Atroari numbered about six thousand people living in an area of about eight million hectares. By 1981 their population had been reduced to 600, and they had only 15 per cent of their lands remaining.

For several years there was both local and national resistance to the dam, with the combined support of Church and labour organisations. While the power-sector loan was under discussion with the World Bank, the international alliance also made protests. Nevertheless the loan went ahead in June 1986 when U.S.$500 million was used for projects including support for the completion of the Balbina Dam.

In spite of the warnings and protests, by 1987, when the sluice gates of the Balbina were closed, no preparations had been made for relocating two Waimiri-Atroari communities of Taquari and Tapupuna amounting to one-third of their population. Eventually they were settled in government posts near to the BR-174 highway: 'The Waimiri-Atroari are now dependent on government provisions for their food, clothing and health care, unable themselves to provide for their basic needs' (Cummings 1990:51). According to Hallward, within a few years the population of the relocated people had been reduced by one half (1992:44).

Another massive dam, the Tucurui, on the Toncantins River, was completed at the same time, affecting the Parakanan Indians (already relocated twice previously). Flooding 216,000 hectares, a total of forty thousand people were affected in spite of a resistance campaign of the Church and unions parallel to that of the Balbina (Oliver-Smith 1991a).

The reason that the Balbina and Tucurui dams were not stopped is that they had been planned and executed by the Brazilian government prior to the World Bank's entry into the discussion. The Bank was unwilling or unable to change the Brazilian government's intransigent position that the dams should go ahead, and the international campaign encountered an obstacle too powerful to shift.

Another case where a dam affecting indigenous peoples was not stopped in spite of a massive campaign was in Norway in the Alta region. From 1970 the company, Norwegian Hydro, announced that it intended to construct a dam on the River Alta on land which was to flood not only part of the protected the Masi heritage area of northern Norway but also principal reindeer herding areas of the indigenous Saami. Considerable opposition was raised against the proposal (Kleivan 1978). In spite of this concern and a huge campaign, the Saami lost the appeal to stop the dam in the courts (Solem 1982). The resistance campaign involved Saami chaining themselves in the paths of the bulldozers as the police and army carried out the largest military operation in Norway since the Second World War. The dam went ahead: 'all in all, the question of what the project will [or may] mean to reindeer pastoralism was seriously neglected' (Paine 1982:92).

Although the area affected by the Alta Dam was not large in comparison with some of the tropical forest reservoirs, the swelling of the river was such that the reindeer herds could only ford the water with difficulty, limiting some to the coastal areas of the north. Some herders have felt the pressure on land which has led to conflicts between different Saami groups in Finland and Sweden for access to grazing lands (IWGIA personal communication). Although the effect of the Alta Dam has not meant the physical destruction of the Saami people, as, for example in Brazil, the consequences have been to threaten the livelihood and culture of a people struggling to assert their identity in an increasingly hostile world.

The case of the Alta Dam demonstrates clearly the way in which a government, even one renowned for its humanitarian and democratic principles such as Norway, can ignore the concerns and wishes of local people and push ahead with large-scale development projects. These examples illustrate the need for several factors to be operating simultaneously before a government or multilateral development bank will change its mind:

1. The local campaign of resistance has to be effective and with strong international backing.
2. The government has to demonstrate willingness to listen to the concerns of the protestors.
3. If the World Bank is involved, an influential sector within the organisation has to be opposed to the project and against the plans of the borrowing government.

'Success' and 'Failure'

Most campaigns of resistance against dams contain elements of success and failure, and a long-running campaign which illustrates this is the case of the Narmada Dam in India. The Narmada Valley lies in the states of Gujarat, Madhya Pradesh and Maharashtra, and the whole scheme plans to include thirty large and three thousand small dams flooding 350,000 hectares of forest.[1]

Whereas two million tribal people in India risk being displaced by hydro-power projects, the whole Narmada valley project threatens one million with relocation (Colchester 1987:286-287). The largest dam in the Narmada project is the Sardar Sarovar which, at 155 metres in height and with a 210 kilometre reservoir, threatens 230 communities consisting of 100,000 people, 60,000 of whom are tribal Tadavi, Vasava, Dunghari Bhil, Rathwas, Naika and Goval.

In spite of a campaign against the dam which started internationally in 1984, a year later the World Bank provided a U.S.$450 million contribution to the U.S.$6 billion needed for the construction. The loans were approved with neither the required social studies nor the incorporation of the recommendations by the Bank's consultants (Colchester 1987:288). As the dam grew in size, so did the campaign. It was raised at the International Labour Organisation in Geneva as a violation of Convention 107 on indigenous peoples and since 1988, thousands of local people have stated that they are prepared to die rather than be flooded out (Esteva and Prakesh 1992:46).

In 1989 local resistance grew to an unprecedented scale with the Narmada Bachao Andolan (Save Narmada Movement), which under its two inspiring leaders Medha Paktar and Baba Amte, held a demonstration of 50,000 people at the dam site. The following year a long march throughout the affected area drew thousands of people to the site of the dam in protest. Hearings at the U.S. Congress and the European Parliament all put pressure on the World Bank which in 1991 established the 'Morse Commission' to conduct an independent review of the Sardar Sarovar Dam. The report (Morse *et al.* 1992b) provided a damning critique of the project. The number of people affected had been seriously underestimated in the project (the real figure was 240,000 rather than 100,000), and there was a failure to provide basic data and appraise their circumstances. The conclusion was that: 'The Sardar Sarovar Projects as they stand are flawed, that resettlement and rehabilitation of all those displaced by

---

1. The case study of the Chico, Altamira and Narmada dams have been discussed in a parallel article which looks at the World Bank and indigenous peoples (Gray forthcoming).

the projects is not possible under prevailing circumstances, and that the environmental impacts of the projects have not been properly considered or adequately addressed' (Ibid.:xii).

The resistance against the Narmada Dam was successful in that, like the Altamira example, it combined local protest with international campaigning, bringing together human-rights, indigenous-rights and environmental organisations through an alliance which reached governments and the World Bank. The Morse Commission and its report was a major breakthrough, although the initial reaction of the Bank was to reject its findings and ignore its recommendations. Eventually, however, the Indian government officially requested the Bank to withdraw in 1993. In spite of the World Bank's withdrawal however, the Indian government has not stopped its commitment to the dam and the scheme in the valley as a whole. Thus, the resistance was successful but the results came too late: the dam was completed and on 23 February 1994, the sluice gates were closed. The local people refused to move and resistance continues with victims willing to sacrifice their lives for their lands and communities.

Nevertheless, the Morse Report had several repercussions within the Bank. It was partially responsible for the review which the Bank carried out on involuntary resettlement which came out in 1994 and the establishment of an Inspection Panel which queried the controversial Arun III Dam in Nepal at the end of 1994. In India, according to campaigners, the withdrawal of the Bank has left open a political space for lobbying which did not previously exist. The legitimation which the Bank gave to the project has been removed, and the potential for legal redress for the victims has increased. India, perhaps, is the example which shows that the presence of the Bank does not always ensure that victims face the 'least bad' options.

Conclusion

This chapter has looked at the problems arising from the involuntary resettlement of indigenous peoples as a result of the construction of large dams. Two approaches have been compared in the discussion.

The first takes as its starting point the fact that development projects are inevitable and that the only way to help indigenous peoples faced with involuntary resettlement is to carry out the process as smoothly, efficiently and fairly as possible. In this way the effects will be mitigated and impoverishment avoided. This is the position of the World Bank analysts who see their approach as a reasonable position, midway between those (usually NGOs) who argue that dams should be cancelled if they interfere with the rights of local peoples and those of borrower governments who consider that the right of 'eminent domain' does not include any responsibilities to those being moved.

In contrast, the position of indigenous peoples is that they have the power of 'eminent domain' over their territories where they have lived since time immemorial. They point to the original World Bank policy paper on indigenous peoples in 1982 which recognises their right to veto projects on their lands and take this right as the starting point for their resistance. To indigenous peoples, the approach of the World Bank, which starts the discussion from the position of mitigating factors, is fundamentally supportive of the borrowers and does not respect their indigenous rights. To them the balance is not between a project which might or might not provide support for indigenous peoples, but between project or no project.

In order to defend themselves, indigenous peoples have resisted in increasingly more organised ways during the last fifteen years. Local, national and international ties have been created connecting Developed and Developing World interest groups and organisations, while alliances have been forged connecting environmental and peoples' organisations with human-rights bodies. Together they have had remarkable success in making institutions such as the World Bank rethink some of its projects. The effect of resistance to development projects has itself aided the mobilisation of non-governmental popular organisations. However, as was noted in the Narmada case, not every protest is successful, and yet the successful aspects, although not ultimately capable of resolving problems, can at least ensure that the rights of local peoples are never completely ignored.

While each hydro-electric project should be viewed on its merits, no argument can justify the forced relocation of indigenous people for hydro-power projects. On the contrary, solutions should arise from two areas. All projects, if agreed to by the local population, should be constructed on a scale appropriate to the local social and environmental conditions. Meanwhile, investment should be encouraged into alternative sources of power without harmful effects.

Information on the long-term effects of involuntary relocation is not always available, but on the data which is available it is clear that indigenous peoples constantly have had to make do and reconstruct their lives as best they can after the trauma of failed rehabilitation. The impoverishment and suffering caused by involuntary resettlement can only be mitigated by ensuring that the only relocations which are acceptable are those sanctioned by the local peoples and that they are ensured a standard of living and territory equal to their loss. Conditions should be considerably more stringent before any relocation occurs, which means that resettlement should not be involuntary.

Rather than, like the World Bank, assume that large-scale dam projects are in most cases inevitable, it would be more sensible to look realistically at the consequences of a project before it is initiated. Indigenous peoples should be informed about the prospect of large-scale development projects on their lands at the very beginning of the planning and preparation stage, with completely open fora where they can freely express their opinions. In this way they will be in a position to debate fairly whether they wish to provide the consent necessary to go ahead with the project. If the project is against their wishes, it should be abandoned. However, in between these positions there will be situations where detailed discussions and negotiations will be necessary to reach an acceptance or refusal. Only if there is free and informed consent can the parties begin to look at the real costs of the mitigating factors which can be analysed and subsequently incorporated ('internalised') into the project.

The social and environmental costs of large dams are rarely included in the initial costing, and certainly not in the calculation of the benefits. Yet impoverishment can be most easily prevented if anticipated well in advance. Indeed, if indigenous peoples were really to be compensated in full and the environmental effects were taken into consideration, the cost of large dams would be far higher than currently assumed.

In conclusion we can consider two elements which should, as a matter of an imperative, be incorporated into any planning framework involving projects on the lands of indigenous peoples.

1. A project should only go ahead after obtaining the free and informed consent of the peoples affected. This means that information should be freely available and the processes of decision-making are transparent and democratic to those affected. They must be in a position to understand clearly what is proposed and agree with the criteria on which the project is to go ahead. On this basis consent can really take place.

2. Providing that free and informed consent has been obtained, accurate planning and preparation can take place which must recognise the right of local peoples to control over their development. This means that national laws have to recognise legal rights, and the territorial rights of the peoples concerned are fully recognised before the project takes place. Should the people agree to move or receive compensation, an independent means agreed by the victims should be available to settle dis-

putes. At any moment the project should be stopped until agreements are made. Any financial planning should be agreed and guaranteed before the project begins.

This double-faceted approach to projects and involuntary relocation consisting of consent, then control over their resettlement, fits into the frameworks mentioned in this chapter. The first is the World Bank's policy which should accept that these points effectively consist of a pre-preparation stage of the project cycle, taking place prior to its acceptance. The second framework which has been examined has been the five-phase description by Scudder and Colson outlining the effects of relocation. If the two elements outlined in this conclusion were incorporated in the initial recruitment phase which establishes a project, many of the problems connected with forced relocation would be eliminated, and maybe more projects could move beyond the tragic impasse of stage three.

The effect of this would be to reduce considerably the number of large-scale hydro-electric projects and convert forced relocation into voluntary resettlement. The reduced number of dams would not be a serious problem, considering that they are in many cases ideologically and politically motivated rather than initiated for economic, social or environmental benefit. Rather than being the victims on the periphery of development, indigenous peoples should be respected as the controllers of their own lives and resources with the right to determine what happens on their territories.

7

The Kayapó Indian Protests against Amazonian Dams

SUCCESSES, ALLIANCES, AND
UN-ENDING BATTLES

Darrell A. Posey

Indians in Brazil have historically been considered, at best, as 'relatively incapable' human beings that must be 'protected' as wards of the federal government. The Brazilian Indian Foundation (Fundação Nacional do Indio-FUNAI) serves as the official organ responsible for Indian affairs. Under past national constitutions, FUNAI was considered the only legal institution that could represent or defend native peoples. Land demarcation, sales of mineral rights and lumber, judicial proceedings, even labour contracts and agricultural sales were all conducted by – and legally only by – FUNAI officials.

With decrees such as those made in 1985 by Brazil's ex-President Figueiredo authorising the sale of mineral and other natural resource rights even within legally protected Indian reserves, FUNAI and other government officials came under increased pressure to 'help make the heads' of indigenous leaders so they would consent to mining and lumbering on their lands. In many cases, however, the Indian leaders were not even consulted on decisions to exploit their natural resources.

Claims of corruption within FUNAI have swollen to a level equal to accusations against its predecessor, SPI (Sociedade para Proteção do Indio), which was extinguished in 1967 due to scandalous dealings. As Manuela Carneiro da Cunha (1987:13) points out, 'the Indian question today is centred around disputes over mineral and natural resources on Indian soils and sub-soils'. Those who lobby for the exploitation of these resources have the entire capitalist machine in their favour and, consequently, are very powerful. Native peoples, by virtue of their low numbers (approximately 1 per cent of the Brazilian population) and cultural, social and political differences – as well as being marginalised by a system that officially considers them 'relatively incapable' – are markedly disadvantaged in this deadly serious battle.

Much of the general strategy to dominate the 'Indian question' depends upon the maintanence of traditional stereotypes of Indians as 'primitive' and 'incapable'. In a country where paternalism is as much of the national fabric as Carnaval, it has been all too easy to mask attempts to thwart native independence movements with rhetoric about 'helping' Indians to make decisions about 'what is best for them'. Rarely have Indian leaders been heard, because, it is said, they could not possibly know enough about white man's society to make good judgements. Thus, 'indigenistas' (non-Indians who supposedly represent Indian interests) are called upon to advise on government decisions. Even FUNAI, the government organ specifically in charge of indigenous affairs, has shockingly few Indians in any of its ranks, but especially few are involved at decision-making levels. This means, of course, that native leaders have been, and continue to be, denied valuable decision-making opportunities as well as the experience of working in the governmental system. This conveniently prepetuates the 'incapable' Indian myth, since government decison-makers must be persons 'with experience'.

It is equally important for the strategy of those who wish to exploit Indian lands – especially in Amazonia, which is the refuge of over two-thirds of Brazil's remaining aborigines – to say that such lands are unproductive and/or unoccupied. The whole of the Amazon Basin, for example, is considered empty (Moran 1981:5) – one great frontier where only a few 'primitive' Indians and 'cultureless' *caboclos* (peasants) struggle to survive. 'Indian lands are, in reality, treated as "no-man lands": always considered as the first option for mining, hydro-electric projects, land reform, and development projects in general' (Carneiro da Cunha 1987:14). This strategy has been relatively easy to maintain over the years because of the difficulties of native peoples and *caboclos* to organise and represent themselves in a dominant society where minority rights were traditionally never even considered an issue.

Despite major victories by tenacious and energetic Indian-support and defence groups such as CPI (Commission for the Indian), CEDI (Ecumenical Center for Documentation and Information), CIMI (Indigenous Mission Council), and others such as the Brazilian Anthropological Association, the relatively unified voice for indigenous protection was faint in the halls of power. The ecological/conservationist movement, with growing politicial and economic influence in the Developed World as well as Brazil, had – until very recently – managed to divorce ecological issues from Indian/human rights. Thus these two major movements to 'preserve' the human and biological richness of the planet were at best disunited, and often at loggerheads.

During the last decades, however, major changes have occurred. Most indigenous organisations have taken strong stands on environmental issues, while conservationists have realised that 98 per cent of the entire biodiversity of the planet is still being preserved by the few remaining native peoples who struggle to populate it. Luckily, human- and minority-rights issues were also becoming more and more of an international cause embraced by those nations in economic and cultural vogue. Even the scientific community began to realise that indigenous knowledge is an invaluable human treasure that offers knowledge of plants, animals and alternative resource managment models that can provide solutions to disastrous planetary ecological homogenisation.

One significant advance for indigenous and ecological rights came with the proclamation of the new Brazilian Constitution on 5 October 1988. The Articles that treat Indian peoples represent a considerable improvement and are the results of perseverence by anthropologists, religious Indian rights groups and Indian leaders, like Kayapó chiefs Paiakan and Kube-i, who led no less than four 'invasions' by Kayapó warriors of the Constitutional Convention at critical lobbying and voting times.

Even though Indians continue to be legally considered 'relatively incapable', they at least gained the right to seek legal representation and take legal action independent of FUNAI. Furthermore, exploration of sub-soil resources can only be authorised with consent of the National Congress. Surface resources are protected by equally progressive Articles protecting the environment that call for stiff penalities for careless destruction of natural resources. One of the major tests of the 1988 Constitution was a court case by the Brazilian Justice Ministry against two Kayapó chiefs, myself and our lawyer, José Carlos Castro.

Initial charges stemmed from a trip to Miami, Florida in January, 1988 by Paiakan, Kube-i and myself to participate in an international symposium on 'Wise Management of Tropical Forest' organised at the Florida International University by the university and a number of national and international ecological conservation groups. I delivered a scholarly paper on my ethnobiological research into indigenous natural-resource management systems and chaired a symposium session on the practical application of scientific research. I also translated for the Kayapó chiefs as they spoke to the general assembly.

Participation of the Kayapó leaders in the international symposium was a logical extension of the philosophy of a twelve-year multidisciplinary 'Kayapó Project' to study traditional ethnobiological knowledge. The Project had already taken Paiakan and Kube-i, as well as other Indian leaders, to a number of national scientific meetings and symposia. Both Paiakan and Kube-i had accompanied the research teams' investigations of plant, animal and ecological knowledge of the Kayapó; both had served as consultants about native strategies of resource management; and both were fluent in the ecological terms that are used in Portuguese to discuss maintenence of biodiversity, conservation of nature and sustained development of renewable resources.

The two Kayapó leaders explained how indigenous peoples preserve biological and ecological diversity, while utilising the renewable resources available to them in their Amazon homes. They also emphasised the threats from outside forces that they must face daily: mining and mercury pollution, erosion, massive burning of the rainforest, logging roads that penetrate deep into their forests and megaprojects, such as those that call for the construction of huge hydroelectric projects.

Specifically, they voiced their concerns about the 'Altamira-Xingu Complex' that, if approved, would innundate 7.6 million hectares (approximately 15 million acres) of rich river-bottom land – almost all of which belongs to various Indian groups. The U.S.$ 10.6 billion project, the world's largest, would displace thousands of Indians from eleven different nations, all of which are already reduced to a dangerously low number of individuals.

Equally disastrous would be the loss of knowledge about the natural diversity of the ecosystems that each group preserves in its oral tradition. Since equivalent ecosystems outside the Xingu River basin do not exist, there would be no reason to continue the rich oral lore about useful plants and animals of that region. Thousands of years of accumulated knowledge – from eleven very different folk scientific systems – would be lost forever.

Members of the assembly urged Paiakan and Kube-i to take their protests to the World Bank. Representatives of the National Wildlife

Federation and the Environmental Defence Fund present at the meeting even offered to pay the expenses to Washington and to organise the visit. The two Kayapó chiefs accepted the invitation, and plans immediately got underway for their trip during the first week of February. During the chiefs' exhausting blitz of Washington, they visited four Executive Directors (ED) of the World Bank and the Bank's technical staff for Brazil. Although met with defensive hostility by the technical staff, the leaders were heard with great interest by the directors. The directors for the United States, Britain, the Netherlands and West Germany seemed disturbed that the Bank's progressive-to-liberal policy on native peoples was not being respected by Bank-supported projects. The policy demands that native peoples be consulted and their decisions respected in order to get World Bank funding. Paiakan and Kube-i assured the directors that neither they, nor any of the indigenous leaders of the Xingu, had ever been consulted or informed about the proposed hydro-electric project. The American ED assured the chiefs that he would continue to vote against the 'Power-Sector Loan' to Brazil that would be destined for the Xingu Dam construction. Other EDs were less committal, but assured the Indians they would investigate infringements of Bank rules protecting native peoples and the natural diversity upon which they depend.

Paiakan and Kube-i also met with State Department and Finance Secretary representatives – as well as members of Congress. Congressman John Porter, chairman of the Congressional Human Rights Caucas, listened with great interest as the two spoke of their frustration within Brazil at not being heard – and their inability to get facts about mega-projects that uproot native cultures and remove Indians from their lands without their consent.

The Kayapó spoke of personal acquaintances from other indigenous groups such as the Parakana, Gaviäo and the Atrori-Waimi, all of whom had been expelled from their lands without due compensation – and even without guaranteed land rights (Treece 1987). Everywhere the Kayapó leaders went they asked which countries were financing the disaster that native peoples and the Amazon were experiencing. There were many red faces, but few straight answers.

Paiakan and Kube-i also met with Native American leaders of the North American Indian Congress and Americans for Indian Opportunities, as well as indigenous lawyers that lobby for native rights and represent Indians in legal struggles over land and mineral rights. It appeared to me that they were beginning to see their struggle in a much larger context – and to realise that there exist international agreements and a legal infrastructure to support Brazilian Indians in their struggles.

Upon return to Brazil, we all faced repeated police interrogation. We learned that a special Brazilian ministerial delegation was in Washington at the same time as the Indians. They had gone to re-negotiate the Bank power-sector loans that Kube-i and Paiakan were trying to stop. The Brazilian delegation had charged that the loans had been paralysed because of our visit, which 'jeopardised Brazil's economic relations', thereby, 'provoking an economic crisis in Brazil'. This had, according to the federal police accusation, 'deni-grated Brazil's image abroad'.

I was specifically charged with having 'illegally taken Indians out of the country'. Not only this, but I had done so – according to the accusations – with premeditated maliciousness to 'use' the Indians to denigrate and jeopardise Brazil.

It became very clear through our evidence presented in the pre-liminary investigations that the Indians had been granted permission to leave the country by FUNAI, which is responsible for its 'wards'. Furthermore, I pointed out that the federal police itself controls the national frontiers and that no one – especially a foreigner – could have 'illegally taken' anyone out of or brought anyone into Brazil without consent and knowledge of the federal police itself.

I also produced documents proving that the invitation to go to Washington, as well as the financing and organisation of the visit, had been provided by the internationally respected non-govern-mental groups, National Wildlife Federation and Environmental Defence Fund. Paiakan repeated his denouncements made in Wash-ington and declared his responsibility for what he had said. He even produced newspaper articles from Brazil published well before our trip to the United States that quoted him saying exactly the same things as he had said in Washington.

However, such explanations were to no avail. As the federal police investigator told me in my second interrogation: 'Someone had to be behind those Indians. They would have never gone to Washington and said those things by themselves'. That logic is legally supported, since 'relatively incapable' wards of the state cannot be held respon-sible for 'crimes' committed in Washington. Worse still is that most people believe this outdated view of native peoples.

With no evidence, we were certain that the whole story would end with the preliminary investigations by the federal police. It seemed evident that my role had been as interpreter and that I had acted totally in a professional and ethical manner as a concerned sci-entist. The only 'crimes' that had been committed, therefore, were that the Kayapó chiefs had voiced the truth of their views and concerns in centres of international economic and political power.

The federal Justice Department, however, had other ideas. On 8 August 1988, Paulo Meira, the federal prosecutor in Belém, Pará, brought formal charges against me (Process Number 35340-1st Region of Pará State, 3rd Vara) in the federal District Court evoking the Law of Foreigners (the same articles as in the orginal police accusation). Much to everyone's surprise, the charges (evoking article 129 of the Penal Code) included the two Kayapó chiefs as accomplices to my 'crimes'. The specific charges were that I had taken Paiakan and Kube-i to Washington, where I had manipulated through my translations their testimonies with the 'intention of frustration the execution of Brazil's Energy Plan'. The 'denouncement' states that the Indians' testimonies were so effective that 'at the very least, credit negotiations were suspended until the Indians' charges could be investigated ... by the entities contacted'.

These charges shocked the national and international community. First and foremost because never before, in nearly five-hundred years of white-Indian relations in Brazil, had Amerindians been prosecuted as foreigners in their native land.

Shocking as well was the allegation that 'crimes' committed outside of Brazilian national territory could be prosecuted by Brazilian courts. The attempt to extend Brazilian authority outside the country, as well as to prosecute Ameridians under the Law of Foreigners, was formally protested by the Brazilian Legal Society, OAB (Ordem de Advogados do Brasil), Brazil's most powerful legal entity (reported in *O Globo*, 16 August 1988).

In a special despatch, OAB's influential Human Rights Commission called for national and international protests against the federal Justice Department, which was being manipulated by powerful economic interests from southern Brazil. According to José Carlos Castro, President of the Commission and legal representative for the accused, 'authoritarian measures were being forced upon the Amazon by powerful economic interests outside of the region wanting to exploit its natural resources at any cost'. One such measure, according to Castro, was to 'to use police investigations and judicial procedures to intimidate those trying to defend it from destruction'. He continued alleging that authoritarian decisions are the life line of mega-projects, such as the Altamira-Xingu Hydroelectric Complex, which are always decided in secret and without consulting the local people who will be most affected.

OAB's call for protests began a series of similar measures by the Brazilian Anthropological Association, the Brazilian Society for the

Advancement of Science, the International Society of Ethnobiology, Cultural Survival, Survival International, Amnesty International and literally hundreds of non-government groups concerned with ecological conservation, Indian and human rights and Amazonian issues. Thousands and thousands of irate letters have been sent to José Sarney, President of the Republic, and petitions of support have been circulated around the world. None of this seemed to have any effect on the determination of the government to continue its prosecution.

On 3 August 1989, Paiakan and I were called for the opening testimony for the trial. Nothing more could be said than had been given as testimony in the previous federal police interrogations. In the official dossier of prosecution, we were amazed to learn that the only evidence against us was newspaper clippings from Brazilian newspapers reporting the Indians' visit to Washington. It became even clearer that the entire case was, as José Carlos Castro had already pointed out, 'a politically motivated manoeuvre to silence the scientific community and native leaders' so as not to speak out against mega-projects supported by the authoritarian government.

Despite lack of evidence and much public opposition, the case continued on 14 October 1988, when Kube-i was summoned to give his testimony. What was unexpected and unprecedented was that Kube-i did indeed arrive at the court building for the testimony – but with over four hundred Kayapó warriors to accompany him. Brazil had never seen such a well-organised show of force by indigenous peoples.

As the amassed warriors blocked one of Belém's busiest avenues, Paiakan unveiled a large map that he had acquired during his trip to Washington. It was a map, never before seen in public in Brazil, showing the nine dams that were planned for the Xingu River Basin. Paiakan repeated the charges he and Kube-i had made in Washington. This time, their outrages were being reported by journalists and filmed for broadcast not only in Brazil, but around the world.

Inside the courthouse the judge, Ivan Velasco Nascimento, announced that he would refuse to hear Kube-i's testimony if the Indian leader did not appear in 'proper dress' (shirt and trousers). Kube-i was wearing only shorts and sandals, but was otherwise – by his cultural standards – dressed for the most solemn occasion in parrot-feather headress and black and red body paint.

The judge, however, insisted that Kube-i was 'semi-nude and in costume', thereby showing 'disrespect' for the court. Kube-i was given twenty minutes to appear in proper dress. If he did not do so, declared Judge Nascimento, his testimony would not be heard and his actions considered as refusal to testify. Kube-i refused to dress as the White Man – and announced his refusal to the assembled press.

The judge and federal prosecutor called a special session of the court to formalise their decision. Our lawyer protested that denial to hear the chief in his traditional dress was contrary to the newly approved Brazilian Constitution that prohibits racism and considers as a crime the denial of minority rights. The spectators in the Court Room, which included representatives of the OAB Human Rights Commission and the international press, were jolted by what was to follow. The judge, echoed by the federal prosecuter, stated that their position was the only defensible one because 'Indians must become acculturated'.

The justice officials also ordered that psychological, psychiatric and anthropological tests be administered to Kube-i and Paiakan to 'determine their level of acculturation ... and to what extent they were aware of their complicitity in the "crimes" committed'.

The following day, front-page headlines in Brazil read 'Indians Offer Solidarity to Their Chief: Testimony of Kube-i Attracts International Press' (*Correio Braziliense*), 'Kube-i Stopped From Testifying Because Not Dressed as Whiteman' (*O Liberal*), 'Indians Protest Against Government' (*The State of São Paulo*), and 'Kayapó Protest Takes 400 Indians to the Tribunal' (*O Globo*). International headlines were reported in most European and North and Latin American countries. National and international television carried the story for days.

The struggle of the native peoples in Brazil to preserve their lands and natural resources was suddenly on the lips of even average citizens around the world. If the Kayapó in their protests in Washington against hydro-electric projects had 'denigrated the image of Brazil', the government's insistence to prosecute such 'crimes' was eradicating all vestiges of Brazil as a major world democracy that respects human rights and ecological issues.

On 18 October, our lawyer, José Carlos Castro, filed formal charges against the judge under Article 5/Paragraph 41 of the Brazilian Constitution that prohibits racial discrimination. The judge's refusal to hear Kube-i in traditional dress, as well as his public declarations that Indians must be acculturated, were cited as evidence. Anthropological and legal experts had been consulted, all of whom agreed that the judge's statements were not only racist, but a clear call for 'cultural genocide'.

Interestingly, under the Constitution, racism is considered a crime for which the accused can be jailed without bond if sufficient evidence is presented. Given that the witnesses were official representatives of OAB and the international press, the situation provoked an amazing stand-off. Castro also filed a formal petition protesting the administration of psychological, psychiatric and anthropological tests to the Indians. From a procedural point, if such tests were to be considered necessary, they should be requested by the defence, not the prosecution. Furthermore, he stated, such tests are completely unviable since 'acculturation' has never been legally defined – nor even recognised as possible to define by the scientific community.

Castro specifically charged the justice officials with racism and incompetency. The judge responded by formally charging Castro with 'injúria' (disrespect and defamation), thereby provoking yet another judicial case linked to the original. This charge provoked strong reactions in favour of Castro, who is a character beloved throughout Brazil for his fearless defence of popular causes.

In November Paiakan undertook a trip to eight countries in Europe and North America. The purpose of the Indian leader's trip was to make citizens in the Developed World aware of the case and the devastating effects on native peoples and their environments that are provoked by projects financed by the banks and governments of their countries.

Paiakan's trip publicised even further the absurdity of the case and the urgency for protection of the rain forest and its peoples against hydro-electric and other mega-projects. His eloquent speech and charismatic manner won many to his side – and showed with unquestionable clarity that he was perfectly capable of speaking for himself. It was not necessary for anyone to 'be behind' a 'relatively incapable' native to tell him what to say, as had been alleged in the indictment.

Despite much national and international pressure, the federal Supreme Court refused in December 1988, to 'deactivate' or suspend the case. Continuation of the trial was set for 6 March to hear witnesses for the prosecution: the two Brazilian journalists who covered the Indians' visit to Washington (Roberto Garcia of *Journal do Brasil,* and Moisés Rabinovich of *O Estado do São Paulo*), the regional superintendent of FUNAI, and the vice-director of the Museu Paraense Emilio Goeldi (where, according to the original indictment, the two Indians and I are employed. In fact, I was a researcher at the museum, but the Indians have never had any official ties with the museum whatsoever).

Defence witnesses were named as: Robert Keating, United States Executive Director of the World Bank; Hon. Representative John Porter, Member of the U.S. Congress and Chairman of its Human Rights Caucas; Bruce Rich, Environmental Defence Fund; Barbara Bramble, Director of International Programs, National Wildlife Federation; Dr Nelson Papavero, Museum of Zoology of the University of São Paulo; and Dr Elaine Elisabetsky, Director, Laboratory for Ethnopharmacology, Federal University of Pará.

Most observers felt that the trial would never reach the point of such embarrassing hearings. The general feeling was that the police investigation and the federal prosecution were primarily intended to intimidate scientists who opposed financially important mega-projects and to weaken indigenous leadership. Therefore, since both objectives had horrendously backfired, the case would be 'quietly closed'.

On 12 February 1989, in the wake of Carnaval, a favourable decision by the Brazilian Supreme Tribunal was handed down based on the *habaes corpus* request. Since this whole complex of cases was profoundly political, the outcome may have been something of a measure of the rapidly changing politics of a presidental election year – the first direct popular elections for a president Brazil had held in more than two decades. It may also have been an index of the degree to which the military and government leaders were finding it increasingly difficult to convince the Brazilian people that the move to 'save the Amazon and its peoples' was nothing more than an international plot to steal national territory. In this view, Indians are simply being manipulated by internationally motivated powers to weaken their strategic defence of Brazilian 'patrimony'. This 'conspiracy' apparently includes Indians, human-rights groups, environmentalists, drug traffickers and ethnobiologists.

Interestingly, during Paiakan's trip to Europe and North America, he was able to raise money for a project that he and Kube-i have dreamt about for many months: a meeting of indigenous leaders from the Xingu River basin, along with Indian leaders from all over Brazil and even other countries, to force public debate over proposed hydro-electric projects.

That meeting, 'The First Encounter of Native Peoples in the Xingu', took place from February 20 to 25 1989 in the tiny Amazon town of Altamira, the centre of the proposed dam project. Over six hundred indigenous leaders from throughout the Americas participated. Non-Indian leaders met in parallel sessions to consolidate their network and to give solidarity to the Indians. Together with indigenous leaders they elaborated an historic document to guide this new alliance of forces. This document's title was: 'A Unified Strategy for the Preservation of the Amazon and its Peoples'.

The 'encounter' in Altamira was the end of a long, tiring and tedious struggle to bring together native peoples and conservationists to preserve the rapidly disappearing bio-, eco-, and ethno-diversity of the Amazon – and the planet. The 'encounter' was historic for another reason: it was organised by the Indians themselves, who – instead of being represented by non-Indians – had the unusual experience of having to limit time for the non-Indian leaders to express their views. Brazil, despite the efforts of its government and justice department, had suddenly become the centre of an indigenous-led movement to fight ecologically and socially damaging forces that threaten the Amazon.

The Kayapó protest against the Xingu Hydro-electric project has been one of the great successes in the environmental and human-rights movement. Not only were the Altamira dams stopped, but the entire hydro-electric project was dropped by the World Bank. Funding from other sources has been impossible, and civil resistance against such mega-projects within Brazil makes such plans politically unviable. The alliance between indigenous peoples and environmentalists continues, although solidarity is difficult due to differing social, cultural and economic conditions.

The environmental community in general holds romantic notions about the nature of indigenous peoples. Thus, when economic conditions necessitate that indigenous groups sell timber or take up ranching, they are 'dropped' by their allies for not being 'real Indians'.

A classic example of this attitude occurred during the Earth Summit (the United Nations Conference on Environment and Development) in 1992. Brazilian magazines and newspapers splashed the photo of Paulinho Paiakan across their covers, alleging that he had raped the seventeen-year-old tutor of his daughters, then tried to murder her after ritually drinking her blood. 'The Savage' was the headline across Paiakan's face in Brazil's major weekly, *Veja*. Roberto Smeralti, President of Friends of the Earth Italy, gave an interview saying that neither he nor his group had anything to do with Paiakan because he had been responsible for selling mahogany from his reserve. 'That's what happens', Smeralti is quoted as saying to a reporter of *O Globo*, 'when Indians leave the forest'. He had, interestingly enough, been responsible for organising, a year or so earlier, a European trip for Paiakan to speak on environmental issues. Steven Cory, Director General of Survial International, went even further. In an interview to *Folha de Sao Paulo* he related the alleged rape to a general disorientation of the Kayapó due to outside trade forces linked to a Body Shop project.

Perhaps the most remarkable feature in this high-profile event is that none of the environmental or human-rights NGOs that had been responsible for Paiakan's various trips to North America, Europe and Japan even bothered to obtain the facts in Paiakan's case. The alleged victim was twenty-three, had never tutored anyone's children and was seen alive and well minutes after the alleged rape in the house of friends. Furthermore, the physician that examined her was being prosecuted by Paiakan because he had sterilised

Paiakan's wife without her consent, and the arresting officer is now in jail for extortion. None of these facts, however, have interested the press, nor most environmentalists.

It seems more crucial to ask why Paiakan was 'set up' in this manner. Brazil has a long history of using press scandals for political ends. A few weeks after the accusations against Paiakan, Kube-i was charged by the police with murder of a farm worker. The fact that Kube-i was not even in the vicinity of the murder when it occurred did not stop the flow of 'facts' about his guilt in the press.

One might ask: but why Paiakan and Kube-i? There are many other Indian leaders to be silenced. Perhaps the collective memory in Brazil is better than we think. It may be no coincidence that the two Kayapó leaders who dealt the Brazilian government one of its most painful stings are not suffering the famous Latin *vinganca* (vengence). There is an old Kayapó saying: 'When you win a battle, become even more prepared; the enemy will always return and always better armed than before!'

Post-Script: In November 1994, Paiakan was acquitted of all accusations due to lack of evidence.

PART THREE
THE IMPOVERISHMENT PROCESS

8

Unrecognised, Unnecessary and Unjust Displacement

CASE STUDIES FROM GUJARAT, INDIA

Gautam Appa and *Girish Patel*

Introduction

This chapter defines three arguably new categories of involuntary displacement induced by economic development activity. It attempts to show through case studies[1] from Gujarat, India, that displacement due to development can be indirect (and hence hidden and unrecognised), unnecessary and manifestly unjust, although legal. Unrecognised displacement, as Scudder describes in an earlier chapter, is a poorly understood category which needs to be properly defined and documented. Most unnecessary displacement and some unjust displacement can be tackled with simple policy changes, which are outlined. The need for a national policy on development-induced displacement is highlighted.

It is now known that about ten million people annually enter the cycle of forced displacement and relocation through dam construction and urban/transportation projects alone. Cernea earlier pointed out that this is a partial figure because it does not include populations

---

1. Six of the seven cases presented in this chapter are based on cases filed in the Gujarat High Court on behalf of project-affected people in which Girish Patel, one of the authors, acted as advocate.

displaced from projects involving forestry, mining, transportation corridors, urban growth and environmental infrastructure, and resettlement caused by structural adjustment programmes. Case studies presented at the Oxford Conference (January 1995) from all around the world showed that a vast majority of these directly project-displaced people either get no compensation or get little and inadequate compensation which is often too late (see Mathur [1995] for a harrowing case study).

Alas, however, the full story of the horrors of involuntary displacement is even bleaker. Almost every major project creates a vast number of indirectly affected people who do not even get a mention in any official statistics. For example, it is well known that all large dam projects lead to displacement of people in populated submergence zones by direct impact. What is not so well known is the involuntary displacement due to indirect impact, most notably in the downstream areas. Thus, even in the case of the Sardar Sarovar Projects – arguably the world's most controversial, and hence the most heavily researched irrigation project – on River Narmada in India, no estimates are available for the number of fisherfolk and their families downstream who will be displaced because they will lose their livelihood.

The seven cases outlined below highlight aspects of involuntary displacement not readily found in the literature on the subject. In each case the starting point is the obvious fact that development projects entail change of use of scarce natural resources, especially land and water. In India, as in other developing countries, this often means transfer of land and water from poor and unorganised people to projects designed by the powerful industrial and urban elite. Some development projects, such as railway lines, do benefit many, but there are others, illustrated by some of the cases below, which produce dubious benefit. Some entail indirect loss of agricultural land or water resources which remains unrecognised and uncompensated. Some are imposed in a particular place even though viable and less costly alternatives are available. If mistakes are made in land acquisition for a project, the land is not returned to the dispossessed and displaced owners. The common procedure in India is for the central or state governments to decide what is in the 'public interest' and to hear and compensate only those with a legal interest in land, home or other immovable property to be acquired for the purpose of development under the antiquated Land Acquisition Act (LAA) of 1894. Progressive government officials (see Ghosal 1995) as well as non-government organisations recognise the limitations of this approach. This Chapter is an attempt to tease out further limitations by looking at some cases from Gujarat, India. In particular we show how unrecognised, unnecessary and unjust displacement occurs and discuss what can be done to stop it.

Case One – North Gujarat University Campus

In 1988, when the government of Gujarat issued Section 4 notices under the LAA to acquire land for the North Gujarat University Campus near Patan in Gujarat, Sipai Memdoobhai Dadubhai and thirty-nine other small farmers from the villages of Matarwadi and Samalpati of Mehasana district filed a petition in the Gujarat High Court on the grounds that their land was very fertile while seven to eight kilometres away wasteland was available. The *Gram Panchayats* (village councils) and local MLAs (members of the state legislative assembly) were prepared to give evidence on behalf of the petitioners. However, they were not heard because under the LAA only 'persons legally interested in the lands' can and need be heard. Courts interpret this to mean a party whose land is to be acquired. Although in theory 'public purpose' is challengeable, in reality the courts accept the judgement of the government on public purpose as final and regard it as almost unjustifiable. The petition was rejected by the High Court in 1992 – leading to a clear case of unjust but legal acquisition in which interested parties with knowledge of the local situation were not even heard.

Case Two – Gujarat Mineral Development Corporation

In 1992 this public-sector company wanted to start a copper plant near Ambaji in Gujarat with the help of international finance. This plant would need about 900,000 litres of water per day, for which the local source was in a nearby forest. As this required the construction of expensive new roads and permission under the Indian Forest Act, the company decided to dig two French wells about one kilometre away. This tribal area has very little ground water and surface water is available in the local river only for one month of the year. Tribal people dig holes in the river bed and obtain water for the rest of the year. French wells draw water horizontally and the planned extraction of 900,000 litres per day aroused fears that little would be left for human and animal consumption for the fifty tribal villages in the area. A petition was filed in the Gujarat High Court by Uttar Gujarat Adivasi Samaj Sudhara Kalpanadip Trust (Kalpanadip Trust for the

Improvement of North Gujarat Tribal Society) and sixteen tribal people, to stop the company digging French wells in order to avoid the adverse effects on 35,000 tribal people in fifty tribal villages of Danta Taluka of Banaskantha district and Khedbrahma Taluka of Sabarkantha district. A letter dated 20 January 1994 from the Project Administrator, Tribals Sub Plan, Khedbrahma, to the chairman of Gujarat Mineral Development Corporation justifies the fears of the tribals about deprivation of water. It recognised that these people will have to migrate if the plans go ahead. The villagers had pointed out alternative sites where the factory could be located. But the company, relying on its own surveyor's report that showed that 50 per cent of the water would still be available to the villagers, refused to concede that there was any problem.

The petition is still pending. If the company is allowed to go ahead, in the best circumstances it would require considerable extra effort for the villagers to get water. If the worst fears of villagers are realised, there is no provision in the law even to compensate them. Clearly therefore, this is a case of legal but unjust treatment with the potential to lead to unrecognised displacement.

Case Three – Adani Chemicals' Salt Works in Block Mundra, Kutch

The Mundra region of Kutch has most fertile land which sustains fruit gardens growing dates, coconuts, *chiku* fruit, etc., and earning foreign capital. Cargill, the infamous multi-national connected with the Bhopal gas leak tragedy, sought to start a salt works here but failed. Then Adani Chemicals, with the backing, it is said, of Siddharth (the son of Chiman Patel, the ex-chief minister of Gujarat), stepped in with similar plans. Adani Chemicals put in a bid to acquire fifteen acres of land, 4.5 acres of which is mangroves. The state government (of Gujarat) granted the required land. So confident were Adani of obtaining the land that even before the land was acquired they built a large guest house and decided to purchase the *Gochar* (common grazing) land of one village to start building Adani *Nagar* (city), in spite of opposition from local villagers. It is rumoured that the village *Punchayat* (the village council) was bribed. Adani Chemicals started work building a dam and spent hundreds of thousand of *rupees* in the certain belief that with high-level political backing they would be able to overcome local opposition. Late in 1993 during the hearing of a petition in the Gujarat High Court (by Kapil Devjibhai Kesaria, a social worker and the owner of a *wadi*, two other agriculturalists and one journalist) the government claimed that the petition should be dismissed because the decision regarding the permission for the salt works was far off and hence the petition was premature. Then in December 1993 the government granted the company's request. The villagers who cultivated fruit trees had petitioned because salt works increase the salinity in the sub-soil leading to the ruin of fruit *wadis* or gardens. If this were to happen without acquiring any land, migration would ensue due to unrecognised indirect impact of a 'development' project.

The company has also asked for and obtained permission from the Gujarat Maritime Board to start a private jetty. The road leading to this jetty passes through many creeks which provide a living for many fisherfolk and attract tourists. The very names of these creeks are based on the local communities. The road will destroy the creeks and the fisherfolk's livelihood, reducing them to work in the salt works under desperate conditions. Gujarat Jan Jagran Sangh (Association for the Awakening of the People of Gujarat) filed a petition in the Gujarat High Court on behalf of hundreds of fisherfolk and obtained a stay of execution. However, the company secured the acquiescence of some local fisherfolk who signed documents saying they had no objection to the jetty and the road. It is alleged by the local NGOs that some Muslim fisherfolk were blackmailed by entangling them in criminal cases, while bribes and pressure were used on others to obtain their signatures, eventually creating a division among the fisherfolk. Meanwhile the case came up for hearing in the court of a new, unsympathetic judge so that a compromise had to be accepted and the petition withdrawn.

The end result is deprivation and displacement without any compensation whatsoever. If the first petition is rejected by the High Court, unrecognised displacement will take place quite legally. The second petition was withdrawn because of unjust power games played successfully by people with economic and political clout against poor fisherfolk.

Case Four – Gujarat Ambuja Cement's Acquisition in Saurashtra

In Navagam, near Kodinar in the district of Amareli of Gujarat, Ambuja Cement planned to set up a plant in order to expand its infrastructure. The company acquired land by private agreement from people desperate for cash. Although voluntary, this was a suicidal act because the people were selling their means of livelihood.

The company subsequently applied to the government to acquire the remaining land, stating that it had made honest efforts to buy the land and failed. The government began the procedure for land acquisition, issuing Section 4 Notification on 16 December 1992 and Section 6 Notification on 26 December 1993. Eight small farmers, one of whom has been given the national title of *Krushi Pundit* (Agricultural Wizard) petitioned the High Court of Gujarat in 1994 not to allow change of use of this highly fertile land. A sympathetic Chief Justice suggested a compromise requiring the company to buy land privately and give land for land. But, once the case is heard and provided the legal procedure is followed, there is no legal case for compensating the farmers beyond what is required by the LAA. If the petition is lost this could be seen as another case of unjust acquisition.

Case Five – Ukai Kakarapara Dam on the River Tapi

This is the second largest dam on Tapi, the second largest river of Gujarat. About 80,600 people, 90 per cent of them tribal, lost their land and/or homes. A Gujarat government GR (Government Resolution) had promised three acres of land per family. Ukai Nav Nirman Samiti (Committee for the Regeneration of Ukai) fought against the dam under the leadership of Ramesh Desai, and a petition was filed in the Gujarat High Court in 1984 by the Lok Adhikar Sangh (Association for People's Rights). Only those displaced land-owning families with title deeds for their land were given three to four acres of land, the rest received nothing. The government and its apologists claimed that because of opposition to the dam there was a lack of proper co-operation which led to this outcome. However, even after finding that 10,000 out of the 74,000 acres of acquired land will not be submerged,[2] the government refused to return the land, keeping it instead for afforestation. In the command area of the dam marginal farmers are selling their land, but the government will not buy this for the oustees.

A proper study of the effect of Ukai Kakarapara dam would be very revealing.[3] Post-project analysis of costs and benefits are very rare, and

2. Some of this land is submerged for about one month in the year during heavy floods while the rest is totally out of the submergence zone. It is common practice to lease land that is subject to temporary submergence on an annual basis. In this case, however, the government insisted on keeping all land for 'afforestation'.

3. A direct result of the dam is increased sugar-cane farming. Jen Breman has studied the effect and commented that the 'trickle-down theory' does not work in sugar-cane production. New job opportunities in sugar-cane harvesting do exist, but the

this project provides an ideal opportunity to carry one out owing to the high involvement of NGOs in the struggle for compensation for the project-affected people at an early stage. Meanwhile, it can be seen clearly that this is a gross example of what we have termed unnecessary displacement of people using or living on 10,000 acres of land.

Case Six – Karjan Dam

Land was acquired in Juna Raj for this dam on the River Karjan in the district of Bharuch. However, the village is above the reservoir, and although surrounded on three sides by water, it is not submerged. The villagers want their land returned because the alternative land given to them has no access to the forest or other natural resources they used to have. The government refuses because it wants to keep the acquired land for afforestation. Here then, is yet another case of unnecessary acquisitions and displacement.

Case Seven – Sardar Sarovar Projects (SSP)

A study by Appa and Sridharan (1992) revealed that in the downstream area of the Sardar Sarovar Dam on the River Narmada in India, there are fisherfolk from Bihar who fish for prawns for four months in the year, local fisherfolk with their own land who fish for eight months in the year and hundreds of fisherfolk in the *Machhi Vas* (fisherfolks' residences) in the city of Bharuch who depend entirely on the river. It is universally accepted that the dam will alter the water regime in the downstream area leading to displacement of families totally dependent on fishing. Surprisingly, however, the deterioration of living standards for these communities does not feature in any government of Gujarat records.[4] The people are paying

---

conditions of work are so poor that it is the oustees, who have little choice but to take up such employment, rather than the locals who refuse. Medha Patkar's work among sugar-cane harvesters in Surat district in the early 1980s revealed that the sugar factories insist on round-the-clock harvesting by workers in unhygenic, malaria-infested swamps (witnessed by both authors), with no clean water or access to medical facilities or markets.

4. In December 1993, in an interview with C.B. Patel, the then Chairman of Narmada Nigam Ltd., revealed that there was one minor (sic) point on which the Independent Review was right to criticise the project authorities, namely, that he (C.B. Patel) had forgotten to look at the downstream impact. It seems that the unrecognised direct impact does not even enter the consciousness of the project authorities, leave alone any cost-benefit analysis or official statistics.

a personal price for the development of Gujarat without being recognised as losers, leave alone being compensated for the loss.

An important part of the Sardar Sarovar Projects is the largest canal network in the world, with an aggregate length of 75,000 kilometres. The right of way required for the main canal is 250 metres wide at its head and 100 metres at the Rajasthan border, which is at the tail end. The main canal and major branches are so wide that it is sometimes necessary to acquire whole farms, homes, communal land or amenities and even entire villages (such as Koliyari in Bharuch district). As detailed in Appa and Sridharan (1992) there are many ways in which severe hardship is caused by the construction of the canal to people who are not entitled to any compensation. Loss of commonly owned resources, bifurcation of land, damage due to ancillary works and serious danger of hardship in the future owing to poor quality of work are some of the causes. Some of the victims are already displaced and others could be in the future. The following are some examples of displacement.

Construction of a canal chokes up the natural drainage system in some places. To allow the natural flow of water, aqueducts are constructed, but these are expensive. To economise, engineers collect several flows at one point, leading to new water paths which cause heavy soil erosion. The eroded soil clogs up the new aqueducts, leading to severe flooding. Already, local papers in Baroda have reported cases of severe hardship to whole villages because of this. Moti Manekpur, Underam Gotri, Ankodia, Sevasi, Bajwa and Koyali in the District of Baroda have experienced such problems. In Dhawat the contractors extracted soil from the village tank for construction, but did not keep their promise to strengthen the tank's sides. Flooding is expected. In Allahadpura and many other villages of block Sankheda, villagers explained how the process of compacting, of building canal embankments with particular soil types, etc., was not adhered to, and open cracks in cement lining were visible in many places in the main canal, posing a serious threat of waterlogging and the attendant spread of diseases.

An often recurring problem is that of land left on the wrong side of the canal. Not only does such land fail to benefit from the new irrigation possibilities, but depending on the distance to the nearest bridge, it can become inaccessible and is as good as lost. Moreover, the canal can not only bifurcate a family's land, but sometimes it can deprive a whole village of important amenities. Marketplaces, schools, common grazing land, etc., can be, and in some cases have been, left on the other side. In such cases accessible bridges, constructed as soon as the canal is dug, are essential. Without them a whole community suffers unnecessarily. Yet in Dhawat the canal has been dug, but the promised bridge has not been built. Chandan and Songam have been fighting for a bridge near their village for years. Gadkoi and Kelania villagers held up construction work to get their demand for a bridge accepted. Over the entire canal network the siting and building of bridges can avoid hardship, sometimes severe, to the canal-affected communities. What is needed is consultation and a caring attitude. Instead, what has been on offer is one or more of the following: neglect, false promises, threats and coercion.

Another gross example of unnecessary displacement is the case of acquisitions for Kevadia colony, a luxury housing complex built to house government officers, engineers and visitors to the dam site. Six whole villages were acquired for the purpose long before permission had even been obtained for construction. A large number of houses constructed on the villagers' land remain empty because government officers prefer to commute from their city bases rather than be 'marooned' in the wilderness near the dam site. However, the villagers, many of whom now work as servants in the new housing colonies built on their farms or homes, are not given back the land which remains unused.

Thus Sardar Sarovar Projects, even though they have been in the public eye at the national and international level, are a catalogue of unrecognised, unnecessary and unjust hardship and displacement.

Policy Implications and Conclusions

In today's world we can rarely find a place where natural resources such as land, water, forests, etc., are not being used by some people. Modern economic development either directly or indirectly alters the pattern of use of these resources. As a result, all over the world and particularly in developing countries large numbers of people suddenly find themselves deprived of their resource base. Such development projects raise a number of complex problems, such as the justifiability of the projects (involving a challenge to the very concept of public purpose or eminent domain), the problem of compensation to the people affected, the question of resettlement and rehabilitation of such people.

Large development projects which involve the alteration in the use pattern or distribution of natural resources have two types of consequential displacement: (1) direct and unavoidable displacement which is directly visible, open and foreseeable, such as those people whose lands are submerged by dams or whose lands are taken away for a vast industrial complex; and (2) indirect and un-recognised displacement. Some of the cases cited above provide illustrations of such indirect displacement which, in a true sense, is a direct consequence of the development project. Examples of this are the people in the downstream area whose lands are not directly acquired for the dam and yet who suffer great deprivations; the people who may be called 'environmental refugees' – displaced as a result of the adverse environmental impact of projects such as the salt works or the cement works in our case studies, or the people who lose their livelihood because of the works connected with the development projects, such as the fisherfolk in Adani Chemicals case.

The resettlement and rehabilitation policies developed so far take cognisance of only some cases of direct displacement because the definition of directly project-affected people does not include all the directly affected people by adopting a narrow definition of 'oustees', such as the definition of 'oustees' in the Sardar Sarovar Projects which excludes the canal-affected people or the people affected by the construction of Kevadia colony.

In contrast to this, however, the resettlement and rehabilitation policy does not take into account cases of indirect displacement even in terms of principle or law or the Constitution. There is no real difference between the plight of people displaced by direct impact and those displaced by indirect impact. It is necessary, therefore, that the direct and indirect consequences of any project must be accurately examined in depth and the definition of affected people must include all such people whose deprivation of resources is traceable to the project. Law, equity and the Constitution demand this. Moreover, project-affected people themselves are increasingly aware of their rights, so that ignoring indirect impact will lead to more and more discontent and strife. Witness the fact that many cases demanding equal treatment for the canal-affected people and the Kevadia colony-affected people in relation to the Sardar Sarovar Projects are pending in the High Court of Gujarat.

Some of the case studies are examples of unnecessary displacement which is a result of careless planning of the project. The cases of over-acquisition of lands for projects are well known and numerous. They are justified on the grounds that such errors on the side of excess acquisition are better than errors on the side of deficit, with the result that the claims for acquisition are in many cases extravagant. After the projects are completed, the project authorities continue to remain the owners of these lands because under the Land Acquisition Act, once the acquisition is completed, the ownership of the acquired lands remains with the authority and the original owners do not have any claim whatsoever. The authority thereafter either diverts the purpose for utilising these excess lands or disposes of them at a profit. Here two things are absolutely essential. Careful and advanced planning is needed to determine precisely the areas of lands required, and secondly the resettlement and rehabilitation policy must include a provision that any excess lands should be handed back to the original owners. The latter provision is an easy-to-implement change in policy which will do away with unnecessary displacement in the long run.

In many cases, the displacement is also unjustified because the more suitable alternatives are not even considered. Though under the Land Acquisition Act the owner of the land to be acquired is permitted to point out viable alternatives to the authorities, the authorities usually remain firm on their proposal. As soon as the authorities state before the Court that they have considered all the alternatives, the Courts do not enter into the area and accept the authorities' stand. This is illustrated by the case of North Gujarat University, where people pointed out less fertile or useless lands as an alternative, but the University had made up its mind to acquire the lands of the petitioners. Other unbiased local people were willing to testify in favour of the various alternatives, but they had no right to be heard as per the existing law. Similarly, while the projects are being planned, even the people likely to be affected are not heard. It is only when the acquisition proceedings start – a long time after the acceptance and adoption of the project – that the directly affected people are heard. At that time, the people affected cannot successfully challenge a project on the ground of other efficacious and more economical alternatives.

All such difficulties arise because the hundred-year-old Land Acquisition Act does not provide a just, proper and adequate framework for large-scale acquisition of lands and for modern development projects. Land is a means of livelihood and not merely a marketable property, and where a community or a village is displaced, the total loss is more than the losses of individual properties of the members. What is necessary, therefore, is new and comprehensive legislation to provide for the modern development projects involving large-scale acquisition of such properties. Such legislation should provide for the participation of all the people likely to be affected from the very stage where the project is conceived and designed, and should also provide for detailed advance planning at every stage and monitoring at subsequent stages.

Displacement of people in a country such as India, where the Constitution guarantees right to life under Article 21, involves a clear violation of the right to life, including means of livelihood and the right to a support system, and it cannot be justified by reference to the principle of majoritarianism or utilitarianism. The law must ensure that the people likely to be affected consent to the project and its consequent displacement. This is possible only if displacement is considered to be a part of development, and the development project includes the very development of the victims as an integral part.

It is often argued that development projects by their very nature benefit some and harm others. There are no optimal solutions in which no one person becomes worse off in an attempt to make others better off. It is further argued that although it is always possible to question the priorities and particularities of a specific project, merely pointing out that some people are forcibly displaced is not enough, because even a well-designed project will displace some people. While this is true, our case studies clearly point out that what happens in practice is sub-optimal. A better policy framework and a political will to implement pro-poor policies can go a long way in mitigating real and often unnecessary hardships.

The most significant policy change required in India is an introduction of a national policy for rehabilitation and resettlement for all the people displaced directly or indirectly by development projects. This would do away with the need to fight for the same rights again and again for each project. A properly designed (and implemented) national policy could have taken care of all the cases presented here. The donor countries should insist on a national policy and thus assist NGOs and progressive forces within India to achieve a standard framework such as the one outlined by the National Working Group on Displacement in Fernandes and Ganguly-Thukral (1989).

Even with the best of intentions the existing legal framework is inadequate for preventing involuntary displacement. In fact the intentions of development-oriented bureaucrats and politicians are not always beyond reproach. Many regard uprooting of ancient communities as a process of modernising them. Local politicians work hand-in-glove with building contractors, giving scant attention to the needs of the unorganised and poor farmers. The existence of unrecognised, unnecessary and manifestly unjust displacement revealed by our case studies makes it even more important to adopt policy frameworks which can begin to remove these injustices.

9

Mediation or Self-Management
LARGE DAMS, SOCIAL MOVEMENTS
AND ETHNICITY

Alicia M. Barabas and *Miguel A. Bartolomé*

Tens of millions of people have been uprooted and resettled as a consequence of infrastructure development projects over the past decade. Mexico's own national development strategy includes huge hydro-power and dam-construction projects designed to increase the country's electricity-generating potential, whilst attracting international aid and investment and at the same time installing monuments to politicians in power. Such grandiose hydro-electric schemes are aimed, theoretically, at improving the conditions of life and opportunities of Mexican citizens. In reality, however, local populations usually do not receive tangible benefits from those works and quite often become the victims of progress.

The fact that the displacement of populations implies a critical social cost has been generally disregarded by state bodies in charge of national development. In Mexico this situation has generated interactive processes marked by structural conflicts between the agencies responsible for the works and the affected populations.

One of the most frequent outcomes of social conflict has been the emergence of protest movements opposing dam construction. Initially, resistance movements were regarded as part of a transitional process, played out against national interests by populations manipulated or patronised by parties or other political organisations. However, it is the persistence of resistance to certain planned developments that compels consideration within the general framework of social movements. In such a way, these movements and the wider implications have gradually become a genuine field for anthropological reflection and praxis.

Reflection must be aimed at analysing the nature of the social costs arising out of displacement in order to generate institutional practices towards their mitigation. This chapter, in examining the evolution of social movements in Mexico, contributes to this process of constructive reflection.

As in other countries, the building of most dams in Mexico has brought about structured protest movements. Because of the multi-ethnic character of Mexican society and the fact that indigenous populations live mainly in rural areas, the displaced are more often than not members of ethnic minorities. This presupposes additional problems so far as it implies a confrontation among cultural groups that sustain different kinds of socio-ecological rationalities, which are shown in their distinct ways of relating to the environment: one rationality seeks to coexist with the environment, while the other tries to transform it (Bartolomé, M. 1992).

At the same time that indigenous populations have different cultural and identity configurations in relation to the hegemonic one, they have traditionally played subordinated roles in regional and national political structures. That is why the social processes that result from the relocation of indigenous populations show cultural and political traits that differ from those of other populations within the national society. Consequently, the indigenous protest movements against relocation reflect the cultural singularity of their protagonists, giving particular modalities to their political responses.

It should be remarked that the evolution and development of those movements often come about as a result of damages caused to the affected people because of flawed planning and execution of resettlement programmes. Once the social movements have started, the consequences, in terms of the costs of the dam, can be critical when the affected people decide to stop the dam works. Thus both social actors involved in the interactive process of relocation have traditionally been affected by social movements.

Following these observations, we will analyse the causes, characteristics and consequences of two indigenous resistance movements against compulsory relocation. We shall explain the effects that these movements have on the native societies as well as the hydraulic institutions in charge of the dam works. First, the *chinantecos* in the state of Oxaca, affected by the *construction* of the Cerro de Oro Dam. Second, the *nahuas* of the Alto Balsas River in the state of Guerrero, affected by the *announcement* of the construction of the San Juan

Tetelcingo Dam. They represent dissimilar cases of social mobilisations, not only with regard to their outcomes but also to the ways in which those political responses were structured. This may seem to be a limited situation since we are only dealing with two cases, but they have involved more than 66,000 people and are good examples both of the national political behaviour and of the contrasting ways of indigenous political expression.

Let us hope, then, that this analysis becomes a contribution to the emerging field of 'dams' anthropology' and specifically to the issue of social movements that have resulted from them. Early works in this sub-field of anthropology would include Barabas (1977), which deals with a messianic response against Cerro de Oro Dam. More recent, and of a wider scope, is the essay by Scherer-Warren and Reis (1986) who studied a movement in Brazil within the theoretical perspective of the 'new social movements'.[1] Sigaud (1986), also Brazilian, understood them as expressions of the new forces resulting from the confrontation between the executive agencies and those affected by their policies.

Brazil has been one of the places where quite often such movements are highly structured. An excellent synthesis on the subject has been written by Bartolomé, L. (1992). A few years ago Cernea (1988) remarked that the emergence of social movements should be considered as recurrent phenomena within the processes of forced migration. Perhaps the most revealing contemporary reflection on the subject is that of Oliver-Smith (1991), who regards them as appropriate contexts for the political socialisation of groups traditionally marginalised by formal political structures. It should also be pointed out that several authors have treated this issue in the study of concrete cases.

The *Chinantecos* and Cerro de Oro Dam

The construction of the huge Cerro de Oro Dam hydro-electric project began in 1972 and was completed in 1989, having been interrupted several times. The dam consumed inundation of 26,000 hectares of some of the best riparian lands of Oaxaca state, land which is an important part of the ancestral territory of the *chinantec* ethnic group. As we have pointed out in a previous work (Bartolomé and Barabas 1990), this group was also affected by the resettlement of about 26,000 members of several communities in the municipalities of Ojitlan, Usila and Valle Nacional. Most of them

1. See, for example, Dalton and Kuechler 1992; Escobar and Alvarez 1992.

were relocated to various areas in the state of Veracruz, far from and ecologically different from their traditional habitat. The lack of effective participation mechanisms in the process and the previous political situation of the affected people brought about both religious and secular mobilisations. In spite of their different natures, both responses took place within the mediatory and fractionary structures pre-existent in the indigenous society, which got worse and were multiplied within the conflictive interactive context created by the hydro-electric works.

The redistribution of lands as a result of the 1940s agrarian reforms, by means of a common landholding system (the *ejido*: land that is held corporately by the group of people, the *ejidatarios*, constituting the *ejido*), brought about major transformations in the local economic and political structures. On one hand, the introduction of new agents (agrarian officials) impelled changes in the structure of traditional leadership, because the gerontocracy lost its central role in the internal resolution of territorial conflicts and adjudication on the use of communal lands. These decisions became a responsibility of the new indigenous and even *mestizo* authorities on common *ejido* lands which, thanks to alliances with the national society, became mediators between both sub-systems. This was the beginning of a new mediatory system.

On the other hand, domestic productive groups had very limited capacity for decision making in the development of commercial production aimed at big markets, because those decisions were made by a new group of economic mediators who became, in effect, an intermediary bourgeoisie. Thus, the moneylenders *(habilitador)*, or intermediary dealers, became mediators between the indigenous peasants and the market. The power of the *habilitador* was not based on territorial possession, but rather on the control of informal credit and the imposed use of *ejido* land. This was determined by the mediators according to their own interests and those of the market

The alliance between c*reole* and *mestizo* members was joined in 1970 by *chinantecos* who recruited customers, thanks both to their privileged economic position and, mainly, to alliances with kin groups that were established through godparents networks. This process of *cacique*[2] formation had repercussions in the political sphere because the economic mediators gradually usurped local political power, by first displacing and later depriving the indigenous system [or structure] of religious-political positions, which were for-

---

2. A rural intermediary bourgeoisie that acquires leadership on the basis of economic and political power by controlling a wide clientele.

merly headed by the Council of the Elders.[3] A *cacique*-like system was established which combined an economic and political control based on customised relations. This control depended on a greater efficacy in the articulation with the surrounding society. Traditional political structures based upon consensus, service, prestige and redistribution of goods stopped being efficient; the manageability of the roster-like communal functions was lost, and political roles ended up in the hands of the *caciques* or their representatives. The new system of national political party leadership, besides breaking the socio-political dynamics of consensus, removed vital positions in the reproduction of the traditional system (e.g., the *mayordomía*)[4] and marginalised the Elders from power. The new ways of adhesion and participation were created within a factionalised social field dependent on the various mediator *caciques*.

As we have seen, therefore, before the commencement of hydroelectric works in the 1970s, the indigenous society was factionalised and controlled by brokers of different class and ethnic affiliations which acted as inter-cultural brokers. The only sphere of power still available to the Elders by 1970 was the ideological control that they exercised by means of manipulating the sacred. The capacity of *nahualismo* (control of one's own and others' animal co-essences) was the only mechanism that still made possible some incidence of the old regime on the behaviour of the collectivity. The reason for this lies in the fact that through the practice of the traditional worldview, the Elders could control the behaviour of the *chinantecos*, by causing them spiritual damage and using sorcery if they had not followed the commandments.

When the Cerro de Oro project began in 1972, 50 or 60 per cent of the *chinanteco* population was monolingual. The population had very little, or no experience at all, of interacting with state institutions and the national society, because of its dependence on the *cacique*-like mediatorship and on the peasants' low migration indexes. The Papaloapan Commission, in charge of the development works, instituted an authoritarian administration which denied the local population access to crucial information and provided no room for participation over decision-making for the forthcoming relocation.

3. The Council of Elders is the highest decision-making level of the rotating system of political and religious offices (community duties), in which most men of each village participate. The 'cargo' system is the central institution that rules the political and ceremonial life of indigenous villages, where the elders are the central authority.

4. The '*mayordomía*' is a community-wide social event, at which villagers celebrate their patron saint. Besides other functions, this event helps to redistribute the goods among most members of the community.

On the other hand, the *chinantecos* thought it was impossible to tame the powerful river and took for granted that the works would not reach completion. In that context the society did not have strategies for developing self-generated and self-directed collective responses which would have enabled it to oppose efficiently the situation that was radically altering its existence.

Along the lines of the already-established *cacique*-like structure, the factional leaders strengthened their mediatory capacity and hoarded political capital, gaining a privileged position within the governmental institutions that were present in the project. Thus the lines of action of the affected people were conditioned by promises from the mediators to find and provide their followers with the best options. Those factions organised themselves around the political party in office (Partido Revolucionario Institucional, PRI), its peasant organisation (Confederacion Nacional Campesina, CNC) and also around a political party and another peasants' organisation of moderate opposition (Partido Autentico de la Revolucion Mexicana, PARM and Confederacion Campesina Independiente, CCI), which actually function as magnets for those unhappy with the group in office.

During the process, which can be divided into two stages (1972-75 and 1986-89), various changes in factional affiliations took place, depending on the convoking capacity of the different mediators. In the second stage of the project a new faction emerged and joined the local political orchestra, whose mediators represented a left-wing, peasant organisation, the Union General Obrero-Campesino-Popular (UGOCP) connected to the oppositionist Partido Revolucionario de los Trabajadores (PRT).

The main goal in dispute was municipal government control, through which those factions pretended to negotiate their demands with the state. An indication of the extent of local conflict is the fact that in only one year there were three violent changes of municipal authorities. Nevertheless, the key decisions were made by the state institutions without the participation of the local political players. The scope of demands did not differ from one faction to the next. What every mediatory leader aimed at was the retention of privileges for his clientele. In this way the disputing factions promoted the animosity and the division among the affected people who were losing the capacity to unify for common goals.

Finally, the building of the dam was formally accepted by the *chinantecos* as an act 'for the benefit of the nation', which was actually the result of manipulatory moves by the mediators who claimed to represent a population that had not been consulted. Following this forced consent, the demands were limited to the securing of better relocation areas (more land and of a similar quality to that expro-priated) and more services for the new villages and for the town of Ojitlan, which would lose most of its dependent communities.

In the construction of the Cerro de Oro Dam, therefore, evidence suggests that each of the factions, which were dependent on a politi-cal party and a peasants' organisation, sought to gather around them a heterogeneous group of social actors: *ejidatarios* of several commu-nities, different *caciques*, divergent political and economical regional groups, government officials and technocrats, who embodied and represented their own and others' opportunistic interests related to the works.

These factions accused each other of wanting to have the best share. Every mediating leader was pointed at by the others as being corrupt and conniving with the government at the expense of those whom they represented. As a result of this strategy, internal divisions grew, affecting the communities not only altogether, but individu-ally, creating internal divisive alliances along kin lines, and even bringing about antagonisms within wider kin groups.

As an answer to this context of conflict and anxiety for thousands of Indians, in 1972 a messianic movement started to take shape, based on the hope of impeding the building of the dam and, at the same time, preserving historical territory and a complex of sym-bolic constructions related to the environment which sustained col-lective existence.

In 1973, starting with a number of different sacred apparitions and messages sent by them to their children in disgrace, a cult with millenarian and messianic dimensions was taking shape. In the beginning, this movement managed to overcome the factionalism that had been established and to unite, for once, a great part of those affected around expectations of the conflict's resolution.

Besides having been created from the group's own symbolic codes, it was the only response organised within the traditional struc-tures of power and by those affected, in an attempt to confront the external decisions without the mediators' manipulated and manipu-lating intervention. The contents and organisation of this socio-reli-gious movement were analysed by Barabas (1977). In this chapter, the authors would like to underline the fact that its emergence was based on the revitalisation of the supernatural power of the Elders, who were granted a permit by their deities to defend their territory and people from intruders, through the manipulation of the *nahuales* called 'Men of the Mountain' and 'Watchers of the Boundaries'. These sacred entities which regulate the environment's usage and look after the boundaries of the ethnic territory, were given the responsibility of 'eating' the Papaloapan Commission technicians by trapping them in Cerro de Oro sacred mountain, and of protecting the *chinantec* space from further governmental intrusions. They were also instructed to kill the Mexican President, whom they considered the one most responsible for the works.

The cult was developed from the apparition and the messages of a newly born sacred character, the 'Engineer the Great God' (*Ingeniero El Gran Dios*), which can be understood, at a symbolic level, as being above the hydraulic works' engineers. Other apparitions and reincarnations – Jesus Christ and the Virgin of Guagaloup – opposed through their messages the dam building and the process of relocation, bringing to the present maxims and events protagonised by national heroes such as Hidalgo and Benito Juarez.

The salvationist expectation, sustained by pilgrimages to a sacred hill revealed by the 'Engineer the Great God', in which miraculous cures were carried out, began to fade after 1974. This movement shows the dynamics of the group's religious creation, which incorporates the new contextual reality into its mythical discourse by inverting the positions of power between the government and the indigenous population.

Beyond its symbolic and cultural richness, however, the messianic response we have described did not help in keeping mediation and factionalism away. Rather it was a mediation of the sacred, in which celestial characters acted as mediators and representatives of the *chinantecos* in their transactions with the regional and national societies. Because this mediation failed, the messianic community became a new faction, as questionable as the other factions in the local power networks.

Afraid that those miraculous apparitions might unify those people affected by the project, the CP (Comisión del Papaloapan) began the first relocations in 1974 (Uxpanapa and Los Naranjos), carried out by the CCI and the CNC, even though the work had only just begun. Except for an unarticulated and quite unsuccessful protest by a group from Uxpanapa (1981), aimed at obtaining monetary indemnification and the delivery of promised services, the leadership system's rupture put the relocated populations of both zones into a situation of political inactivity. Once they were removed from the conflict's scene, they were abandoned by the political organisations that were playing the role of mediators.

It was not until 1986 that new pressure groups were created among those living in Ojitlán, who were to be relocated to different municipalities of the state of Veracruz. At that time, the most belligerent indigenous affected faction won the promise of being relocated near the dam. The mobilisations for land and services carried out by those affected by these third and fourth resettlements were equally structured around the mediation system devised by the CCI, CNC and UGOCP, which, segmented into factional groups, had changed their configurations, but did not alter their main lines of political dynamics of representation. The few *chinanteco* leaders that seemed to be getting supporters, that might have threatened the continuity of factionalism, were either bought off by peasants' organisations, political parties and governmental institutions or disappeared from the local scene in very unclear ways. Some of them were killed; others were accused of instigating the indigenous revolt and were imprisoned.

However, the non-fulfilment of promises made by those responsible for the relocations kept the mobilisation of thousands of people going until 1989, bringing about the occupation by protest groups of both all the buildings of the dam, stopping the works for four months (1986), and Ojitlan Municipal Palace (1988), as well as countless meetings, marches and vigils in front of governmental institutions and *caciques'* homes.

There were two major obstacles to the mobilisation of indigenous affected people at this stage. On one hand, there were persistent conflicts among the factions of those affected, which were fighting individually for the best options of land and infrastructure services, preventing the unity towards a common goal. On the other, there were governmental attempts to avoid the leftist UGOCP's activities in organising relocatees, since the other peasant organisations articulated to the government were overrun. This measure for the national security left the *chinantecos* with no representation and, in 1989, the Miguel de la Madrid Dam, started in 1972, was officially opened. The resettlement was completed even though the new villages were still under construction.

Consequences of Resettlement

The consequences of the above-described mobilisations, both for the affected people and for the project itself, were negative. The socioreligious movement, even when it revitalised their deepest cultural symbols and temporarily re-legitimated the hegemony of the Elders, was unable to prevent the dam construction from going ahead and resulted in the discrediting of the gerontocracy as a group with any significant political power, questioning even the efficacy of their very own culture. From that moment onwards, the Elders went on being consulted as sorcerers and medicine men but were marginalised from the political scene. Secular mobilisations did not therefore give rise to a new system of indigenous leadership and nor were the Elders supplanted by another *chinanteco* generational group. Instead, they were encapsulated by the mediation of national peasant organisations that represented those affected as part of a co-options game.

None among the four relocated groups managed to have its basic demands fulfilled. In Uxpanapa, where the situation is similar to that of the other relocations, for example, the indemnification lands were of a most inferior quality to those lost, and they were only regularised several years after the relocation. In addition, the official loan system given by the government institutions was cancelled because the relocated people could not afford to pay off loans formerly granted.

In the resettlement sites, the production projects failed and those relocated either went back to growing maize for their own consumption, but with a lower yield, or decided to migrate.[5] Infrastructure works and services for the new towns were carried out after the resettlements, and in such a temporary way that some of them (irrigation and drinking water, etc.) stopped working shortly after the resettlement or became inadequate and useless (houses), while others were never installed (electricity, latrines).

Twenty years after the beginning of resettlement in Uxpanapa and Los Naranjos and six years after the resettlement of several Veracruz populations, the leadership system follows the same factional and mediative lines, which obstruct the collective organisation. Those resettled around the dam, since they remain within the setting of the conflict – because this area included the most disputed land by all the affected communities – continue being represented by the afore-mentioned trade unions and political groups, joined by independent indigenous organisations such as the Comite Regional Chinanteco, Mazateco, Cuicateco – Frente Independiente de Pueblos Indios, CORECHIMAC-FIPI, and non-governmental organisations, which negotiate, with state institutions, unfulfilled services and the granting of credits for the faction they represent.

The intrafamilial and intergenerational conflict around the possession of land is a dramatic example of social disarticulation revealing the disintegration of a community following dam construction, population displacement and resettlement. The conflict was a result of the erroneous distinction established at the beginning between *derechosos*. The *derechosos* were *ejidatarios* with legal possession of lands

5. People migrate preferably to the oil industrial cities of Veracruz and Tabasco, and to Mexico City, all hundreds of miles from the resettlement towns. Such movements may prove permanent.

and thus with the right to territorial indemnification. The *avecindados* were people without *ejido* and therefore with no right to territorial indemnification and services. This explains why belonging to the category of *derechosos* was one of the main goals of *chinantecos* without land to improve their living conditions.

In the dam area, from 1989 onwards, the large number of the *avecindados*, most of them young people supported by different mediating organisations, have tried to work on the strip of federal land exposed when the water level of the reservoir is at its minimum – and to get the legal permit to do so – but have been obstructed, sometimes in a violent way, by their older relatives and elders, who do not let them make use of the lands.

This conflict has destroyed traditional patrilocal residence patterns and the production and consumption styles of domestic groups, and has forced young people of both sexes to migrate from their familial and communal spheres, bringing about their uprooting and the loss of cultural and ethnic ties.

This style of mediated mobilisation, which at a group level has meant the breaking of parental ties and the strengthening of illegitimate leaderships, has also been damaging for the project. Firstly, because the halting of construction works (1988-1989) implied a huge economic loss, and secondly, because the amount of money spent in badly planned resettlement works – which had to be repeated several times because the resettled returned to their original homes – was much higher than that considered in the original budget forecast.

On the other hand, as a result of its inability to create the grounds for a permanent residence for – and the economic development of – the resettled, the state has created 26,000 new poor. It is also possible that the structuring of a collective and self-managed movement of those affected would have been less damaging for the state than the divisions and ever-growing costs which arose as a result of factionalism and mediation.

The *Nahuas* and San Juan Tetelcingo Dam

The *nahua* population in Guerrero state belongs to the like-named ethnolinguistic group which nationwide has more than a million members. Nevertheless, as with most Mexican groups, as a result of the process of colonial fragmentation the mechanisms of collective identification of this population have broken down.

It is likely that the *nahuas* from Guerrero did not know that there were also *nahua*-speaking peoples in other states. Their identity consciousness tended to be centred on their community of origin and residence. It has thus been called a 'residential identity' (Bartolomé, M. 1992). However, as we shall see, the mobilisation against the building of San Juan Tetelcingo Dam broke the local barriers and revitalised the potential identity of *nahuas*.

Within Guerrero state, the *nahua* people have an important historic habitat, at the basin of Balsas river, where they carry out a form of agriculture that makes use both of the humid alluvial lands and of rainfall farming lands *(tierras de temporal)*. As a complement to this agrarian economy, they have a well-developed, nationally and internationally oriented handicrafts production. Their paintings on amate paper, made according to a pre-Hispanic technique, are particularly well known. Those domestic groups which have managed to combine agriculture and the selling of crafts have become relatively prosperous (Ramirez et al.1992).

On the area of the Balsas basin, there are more than sixty thousand people in thirty-seven indigenous communities. These peoples are related by linguistic, kin and cultural ties, expressed by means of a general participation in the rituals for the patronal feasts in each locality. On the other hand, they are also tied by handicrafts production, and many of their members serve as nation-wide traders for this industry. As a result of these socio-economic dynamics, some natives have taken permanent or definitive residence in national state capitals or in the United States.[6] Thus, even when they are inter-related and have some external trade connections through a commercial network based upon the production of autonomous domestic units, we are dealing with a group of basically independent communities.

The basin of the Balsas river was first considered for its hydroelectric potential as early as in the 1940s, during the developmental trend years, but it was in the 1960s, with the construction of El Caracol Dam – officially called *Ingeniero Ramirez Ulloa* – that the idea began to take shape. El Caracol and two other smaller dams, built in the 1950s, generate around 2,000 megawatts, not enough for a country with an estimated energetic deficit of 8,000 megawatts. That is why the necessity of building a new hydro-electric plant, on the river near the locality of San Juan Tetelcingo, from which it takes its name, arose. The estimated output of this dam is a relatively modest 300-600 megawatts, but it is planned to supplement the output of El

6. Peasants give part of their production to the full-time artisans who in turn invest in agriculture with capital that is obtained through the selling of the crafts. Since the *amate* demand became international, some members of the kin groups live temporarily in the United States (Ramirez et al. 1992).

Caracol, whose working life is seriously at risk because of the amount of sediment collected by the dam.

Following the sadly traditional institutional practice of not informing those potentially affected by this kind of project, and repeating the strategy used eighteen years earlier at Cerro de Oro Dam, no one considered it necessary to let the population know about the San Juan Tetelcingo Project. But by August 1990, the local people started to notice that workers from the Federal Commission for Electricity were around, clearing trees in an area designated for the future reservoir.

Other signs that development was about the take place included the refusal by the agrarian authorities to issue property titles on the lands in the area reserved for the dam and the building of a large bridge on the highway from Mexico City to Acapulco, which was constructed with the necessary height for escaping from the water level. Finally, a journalistic leak (19 August 1990), enabled the population to receive news about its dramatic immediate future (Good, in Scott 1992).

The San Juan Tetelcingo population reacted very quickly and showed an extraordinary capacity for organisation when they became aware of the situation of the affected people at the neighbouring dam of El Caracol, who were, and are still, demanding that the compromises agreed upon be fulfilled.

These communities resorted not only to their local networks but also to those formed, nationally and internationally, by their migrants. As a result, barely two months after the news was published, a meeting between the authorities and agrarian representatives for fourteen of the potentially affected towns, with no outsiders, took place in the locality of Xalitla. Three weeks later, the Council of the Nahua Peoples from the Alto Balsas (CPNAB), which brought together forty thousand inhabitants from the twenty-two communities that were eventually going to be displaced, was created in San Agustin Oapan.

One of the first actions of CPNAB was to ask the director of the Instituto Nacional Indigenista (National Institute for Indian Policy), and the governor of the state to stop the works. By February 1991, the CPNAB was already campaigning across the nation, having published a bilingual appeal in an influential newspaper and carried out a hunger strike in Mexico City's central square. In the following months, the CPNAB consolidated its organisational structure by means of five secretaries and a group of commissioners who perform their task in the extra-communitarian sphere. They even managed to send representatives to the World Bank in Washington, asking them to reject loan applications for the works. They also carried out propaganda campaigns at local, national and international levels asking for public support. In 1991 their representatives went to the International Congress of Americanists in New Orleans, to the World Conference of Non-Governmental Organisations in Paris, and in 1992 to the NGO's forum held in Rio de Janeiro paralleling the meeting on Environment and Development – the Earth Conference (Negrete 1993). Most of the national press, and even foreign media, were aware of the existence of the CPNAB and published their demands. As a result of their propaganda work, they also gained the support of many organisations and groups of intellectuals.

At the same time, at a regional level, the movement expanded, by the addition of thirteen small localities (*rancherias*) that would also be affected. Local protests included mobilisations, marches to Mexico City and other strategies. In spite of having obtained, in February 1991, the promise that the works were going to be 'indefinitely suspended', the activities of the movement did not cease, because they considered that that promise did not offer any assurances of firm action.

In October 1992, the movement managed to secure an audience with the President of Mexico, who gave his word that the works were not going to be carried out as long as he remained in office. Nevertheless, his promise was not a guarantee for the future, and the movement has not stopped. Besides continuing with their promotional activities, they have become governmental speakers for the development of infrastructure works in the local sphere. Furthermore, during their second anniversary celebrations in 1992, the CNPAB set itself as a goal the promotion of their formal juridical constitution, so that they can have access to governmental resources.

It is useful to point out that since February 1991 members of CPNAB have been in touch with a non-governmental environmental organisation, Group for Environmental Studies A.C. (GEA), which strongly backed their actions against the building of the dam, and helped with the staging of forums and the production of publications. In such a way they worked together on an alternative project for the development of the area, aimed at maximising the sustainable use of natural resources and the betterment of the living conditions of the local population, including the use of alternative (aeolian, solar, microturbines, etc.) energy sources.

One of the points made was that all the planning and execution process of specific aspects of the programme should be discussed with the affected communities and carried out with their participation. Such recommendations have not yet been implemented, but it has been an active part of the negotiations between the movement – still considered a legitimate speaker for the affected people – and regional and federal authorities. The cessation of construction work has not meant the disintegration of CPNAB, which nowadays is a very organised movement that goes on record with its opinions on national issues, such as its recent manifestations of solidarity with the cause of the Zapatista Army of National Liberation.

Consequences of the Protest

So far, given the characteristics of the national political reality within which action against displacement and resettlement have taken place, the movement's consequences for the peoples of Alto Balsas have been more significant than initially expected. This is not, of course, the same Mexico that in the 1970s felt that authoritarian behaviour towards the *chinantecos* was permissible, but the logic of the system is the same, and that could have brought about a co-option of the movement. If it did not happen, it was as a result of the special political rationality of the *nahuas*.

From the beginning, the integration of the interest group, whose members were the potentially affected, resorted to ethnic solidarity and political, parental and kin networks of the region, which excluded external agents and state-oriented mediators. If they did not need to appeal to those agents, it was basically as a result of having their own agents – the traders and temporary and permanent migrants – whose former experience with craftsmen and producer co-operatives and associations in dealing with institutions and university life gave them good grounds for dealing adequately with the governmental bureaucracy.

The configuration of the interest group was, therefore, comprehensive with regard to both the reality of those potentially affected and ethnic solidarity. In such a way, after a short time, the interest group became a pressure group, i.e., an association for the defence of shared interests, by means of an organisation based upon objective and subjective experiences, aimed at exerting influence on the government's policy (Ehrmann 1975). Progressively, the pressure group took shape, relying on a self-generated organisational logic and anchored within its own culture, which did not need to appeal to other organisations to channel their demands.

This process of institutionalisation of the group was also directly carried out by the *nahuas*, who deliberately excluded even their municipal authorities because they were generally considered to have one kind of commitment or another to political parties. In such a fashion, the movement acquired a formal organisation without losing autonomy and representation regarding their main causes of its creation.

The CPNAB did indeed become a new social movement (Dalton and Kuechler 1992; Escobar and Alvarez 1992) because its members redefined their previous experiences and adopted a non-mediated and participatory style of political action, which implied a defined and all-comprising politicisation of daily life. Having this as a starting point, the mobilisation towards public goals represented a transformation of the local political traditions, restructured from a new perspective which included the, until then, tendentiously exclusive communal loyalties. They were inserted into a proposal based upon the appeal to global ethnic identity, orchestrated for political struggles.

However, the understanding of these facts does not seek to infer that ethnic interest groups are somehow identical. Ethnicity cannot be exclusively reduced to a tool to be used in the competition for resources, even when, doubtless, it can be given such a use. The *nahuas* from the Alto Balsas were members of an ethnic group before the San Juan Tetelcingo project, and are going to be so in the future. This assertion is backed by the fact that their experience of political and identity action has turned them into an ethno-political movement, which – at the beginning – was oriented towards defending regional interests, but with every passing day is more interrelated with other indigenous movements in the country, and whose manifestations of solidarity surmount the search for immediate interests. In such a way, the potentially affected did not only acquire a political experience valid for their regional sphere, but turned this experience into a new national leading role.

The consequences of the movement for the infrastructure works could not have been more negative, since the work had to be stopped and perhaps will never resume. This was brought about not only by the movement, but also by the authorities in charge of the works, who, following an authoritarian and verticalist tradition, pretended to perform them without even carrying out a clear information campaign among the affected population. This fact worsened a confrontation which, by any means, was unavoidable.

However, from another perspective, the results were advantageous not only to the *nahuas*, but to the state as well. The repercussions of the conflict socialised, among the civilian population, including specialists in this and related fields (engineers, ecologists, etc.), not only the issue of the dam, but also that of the national energy policy. As a result, a debate took place, technically questioning the usefulness of the dam, which took the discussion outside the tight scope of the institution in charge of the works and enabled the flow of different opinions on the subject.

Reflections

In the two cases shown, participation in the movements that appeared as a response to the dams should not be interpreted as a 'birth' of both ethnic communities into political life, but as a reiteration or restructuring of previous experiences. For the *chinantecos*, it meant the reiteration and 'informal institutionalisation' of an inefficient model of political behaviour, based upon external mediation, whose action lines were reinforced by the increase of the needs of articulation with the exterior. However, for the *nahuas*, it meant an opening to the recovery of a notion of political collectivity, having as a starting point the actualisation and dynamism of ethnic identity.

Ethnicity did not play the same role in both cases, because it never represents an element for a foreseeable behaviour, but intervenes according to specific situations: the convoking capacity of ethnicity depends upon its possibility to generate loyalties of a stronger power of definition than the belonging to other kinds of social groups (communities, classes, parties, etc.).

In contrast to what has happened among peasant or urban marginal groups affected by the dams, indigenous mobilisations do not presuppose a group political socialisation of its protagonists through which they would become a collective, but the reformulation of existing traditions so that they gain in efficiency within the new system of interethnic articulation that takes place in each case. This reformulation does not necessarily imply a greater rationality (in Weber's sense of 'efficacy of purposes') of the joint political action, because, as the *chinanteco* case shows, the tendencies leading to community disintegration can be increased by the impossibility of generating a truly collective action.

As the political action of the *nahuas* and the messianic response of the *chinantecos* have shown, ethnicity can play a leading role in the structuring of protest movements against displacements. This has been reaffirmed by the experiences of other movements, such as that of the *mapuches* from Pilcaniyeu, in the Argentinian Patagonia, who were displaced by the building of the Cerro del Aguila Dam and appealed to their ethnicity in order to reach a cohesion that other groups affected by the same dam did not manage to achieve (Radovich and Balzalote 1992:308). In a similar way, in the mobilisations of the *kunas* and *emberas* in Panama against the Bayano Dam, ethnicity has had a key position in collective dynamism, as Wali's work (1991) has extensively documented.

The *chinantecos* did not manage to appeal to ethnicity as a consolidating force for collective action because they were fragmented by a multitude of excluding loyalties as a result of factionalism and mediation. Likewise, the 'contemporary state' of a group's ethnicity will significantly influence the structuring of its social mobilisations. It could perhaps be proposed that, if it is true that economic demands and territorial defence play a *determining* role in the indigenous political response, cultural and identity factors represent a *dominant* factor in the configuration of this kind of social movement.

Another significant aspect of indigenous mobilisation is the fact that they explicitly or implicitly wield an opposing argument, which could be conceptualised in terms of a 'criticism of a civilising style'. By this we mean a critical perspective that alludes to the confrontation of two cultural styles perceived as antagonistic, as two opposite ways of satisfying the necessities of human collectivities that regard social reproduction from different ideological perspectives. It is not only a 'criticism of modernisation', carried out by nostalgic sectors of a society exposed to an accelerated transformation (Brand 1992: 53), but with a radical questioning of the relation of man and nature, especially with regard to the capacity of producing massive transformations. Both the *chinantecos* and the *nahuas* perceived the works as a dramatic transgression of the natural order. In what concerns the *chinantecos*, this perception is implicit in their socio-religious mobilisation, and, for the *nahuas*, it is explicitly manifested in their demands to national authorities.

A similar question appears as one of the arguments of the movement of those affected by dams in Brazil (CRAB) and blossoms in the processes of opposition to these large works. On the other hand, this very criticism of a civilising style has determined the support for movements against dams by NGOs with an environmentalist orientation, which helps to put them within the framework of the new social movements.

These processes presuppose a style of political action with more participation as compared to traditional strategies of delegation of representation (Dalton and Kuechler 1992). The creativity of these new movements lies precisely in the fact that they have not set limits for themselves in the defence of their immediate interests, even when this might be the detonating cause, and also because they propose a global questioning of the societal project exercised by hegemonic sectors.

10

State Power as a Medium of Impoverishment

THE CASE OF THE PANTABANGAN DAM RESETTLEMENT IN THE PHILIPPINES

Susan D. Tamondong-Helin

Introduction

Over the years many countries have adopted the dominant paradigm for development, that of industrialisation leading towards economic progress. As discussed elsewhere in this volume, since 1984 an estimated ninety million people in the world have been displaced from their homes and traditional lands as a result of major infrastructural development projects. This number is still expected to rise as the world continues to industrialise. Dam construction as an example, for purposes of generating electricity, irrigation and water supply, has become a common strategy for modernisation. In the pursuit of better living conditions, governments continue to construct dams for their people.[1] However, does the quality of life improve for the displaced population?

Involuntary resettlement is a consequence of dam construction and of other infrastructural projects. On average, three hundred large dams are constructed every year, causing the displacement of

1. Dam construction, like many large-scale development programmes aimed to accelerate economic growth, are usually funded by international banks providing loans at commercial interest rates.

more than four million people. Dams are perceived as status symbols of industrial prowess in many developing countries even if, like in Africa, they have rarely produced development that is sustainable. This was the case in the Philippines during the construction of Pantabangan Dam in 1973, when the population of 1,300 people was resettled from a valley to a mountain top. Pantabangan, one of the oldest and most historic towns of the country, was totally inundated due to the dam project. Pantabangan Dam was the biggest of its kind in South-east Asia in the 1970s, as it was the dream of the dictator President Marcos to make his country a 'showcase' industrialised state. At the time of Martial Law, the dam was completed seventeen months ahead of schedule.

In this chapter, I would like to illustrate the case of Pantabangan resettlement, wherein state power can be seen as an efficient way for a government, such as the Philippines, to deliver goods, such as a dam, for its constituents; but it can also be a devastating medium of impoverishment in the affected community, as experienced by the people of Pantabangan town.

The Setting

Located in the highlands of Nueva Ecija Province in central Luzon, 140 kilometres north of Manila where the Sierra Madre and Caraballo mountains merge and where the famous treasures of Yamashita were believed to have been found after the Second World War,[2] lies the new town of Pantabangan. When the old town with the same name was inundated twenty years ago, due to the construction of Pantabangan Dam, the people fought to retain its name and political identity. Like a ritual, from the high elevation where the new town lies, older relocatees still nostalgically watch the sun go down in the direction of the old town now under water. Their attachment to the lost land where their main source of livelihood came from can still be observed even after twenty years. The old Pantabangan town was a self-sufficient farming community where kinship ties played the strongest influence in the political and cultural life of its people. Pantabangan town has undergone development from an isolated valley into a mountain community, devoid of the concepts of modern town planning that were earlier introduced to entice the residents to move prior to submergence – beautiful concepts that were promised but were never put into practice after resettlement.

2. People's testimonies.

This study focuses on the town proper, consisting of east and west Poblacion (town centre), excluding the nearby villages that were affected by resettlement.

The Project

In 1969, the Philippine President Marcos signed into law R.A. 5499 authorising the construction of the multi-purpose Pantabangan Dam. The International Bank for Reconstruction and Development (IBRD) loaned U.S.$34 milllion to cover part of the total cost of the Upper Pampanga River Project, where the dam was the main feature, amounting to 242 million pesos.[3] Consisting of two zoned earth-fill dams, the Pantabangan Dam is 1.61 kilometres long, 107 metres high from the river bed and 480 and 12 metres wide at the base and crest respectively. The reservoir has a storage capacity of 3,000 million cubic metres and was envisioned to provide year-round irrigation for rice and diversified crops, domestic and industrial water supply, generation of hydro-electric power, mitigation of flood damage, recreation and fish conservation. The economic benefits to be generated by the project have been estimated to amount to as much as 121,260 billion pesos annually, when completed, and sixteen communities were expected to directly benefit from it. However, there has not been any known evaluation to assess whether this projected benefit was ever realised. After twenty years, even the National Irrigation Authority (NIA), which was the main implementing agency, had difficulty paying its field employees from the project-derived income, i.e., fees from farmers' irrigation requirements.

The creation of the reservoir required submerging the town of Pantabangan and seven outlying villages.[4] These areas represented 7,000 hectares of land, 4,000 of which were classified as residential areas, and required the relocation of 13,000 people. The relocation of families started in May 1973 with the provision of NIA trucks to haul their personal belongings and to transport the people to temporary bunk houses. Many families stayed there for more than a year while awaiting completion of their replacement core houses in the resettlement sites. The early closure of the dam and the water impoundment required an accelerated transfer of one thousand families, which took place towards the end of 1973. More than 60 per

---

3. At 1995 rates, one U.S.$ exchanged for approximately 25 Philippine pesos.
4. Villagers here refer to the *barrios* or what are now commonly referred to as *barangays*, which are the smallest political units in Philippine society.

cent of the original families to be transferred had to be relocated on a crash programme basis, which meant that the temporary bunk houses were full to capacity because most of the core residential structures were not ready for occupation.

The Resettlement Programme

Three sites were initially identified as resettlement areas: a 1,500 hectare area in SitioTanauan[5] which was later extended to 3,000 hectares including the village of Delacay, twenty kilometres east within the present territorial limits of Pantabangan town; an area of about 3,000 hectares called Lublub within the boundaries of Maria Aurora, Quezon Province and Dupax, Nueva Vizcaya; and a 1,000 hectare area in Palayan City, 18 kilometres from Rizal town at Bongabon Stock Farm, which was also called Marcos Village.[6] (See Map 10.1). All these sites are in generally hilly areas and are thus very different from the old submerged settlements located in a valley.

The relocation sites were not fully prepared, and in some areas clearing and levelling of lots were done simultaneously with resettlement. Some were designated residential lots vulnerable to heavy erosion. A number of families abandoned their lots because of poor land conditions and the lack of materials for housing construction, sold their rights of occupancy, out-migrated or lived with relatives in better locations. Resources, including land for development, were particularly limited in the main resettlement area of Tanauan, and people generally complained of the lack of farm lots close by.

The majority of the residents belonging to one *barrio* wanted to be resettled within the jurisdiction of their own municipality. The few who did not want to stay out-migrated to the cities for jobs or to other provinces with relatives. Retention of the original town layout was not possible due to the rough topography. There were not enough level areas to accommodate the residents of the old Pantabangan and its nearby *barrios* and *sitios.* The relocation of families according to their territorial, i.e., *baranggay,* grouping resulted in community layouts which were neither similar to the layout of the original communities, nor reflective of neighborhood and/or ethnic groupings that existed in the old Pantabangan.

Because no proper planning was carried out beforehand, the six major components of the resettlement programme were implemeted randomly. The components were as follows:

5. *Sitios* are units within a *barranggay.*
6. This place was an existing resettlement site.

Map 10.1 Upper Pampanga River Project, Luzon Island
(The Philippnes)

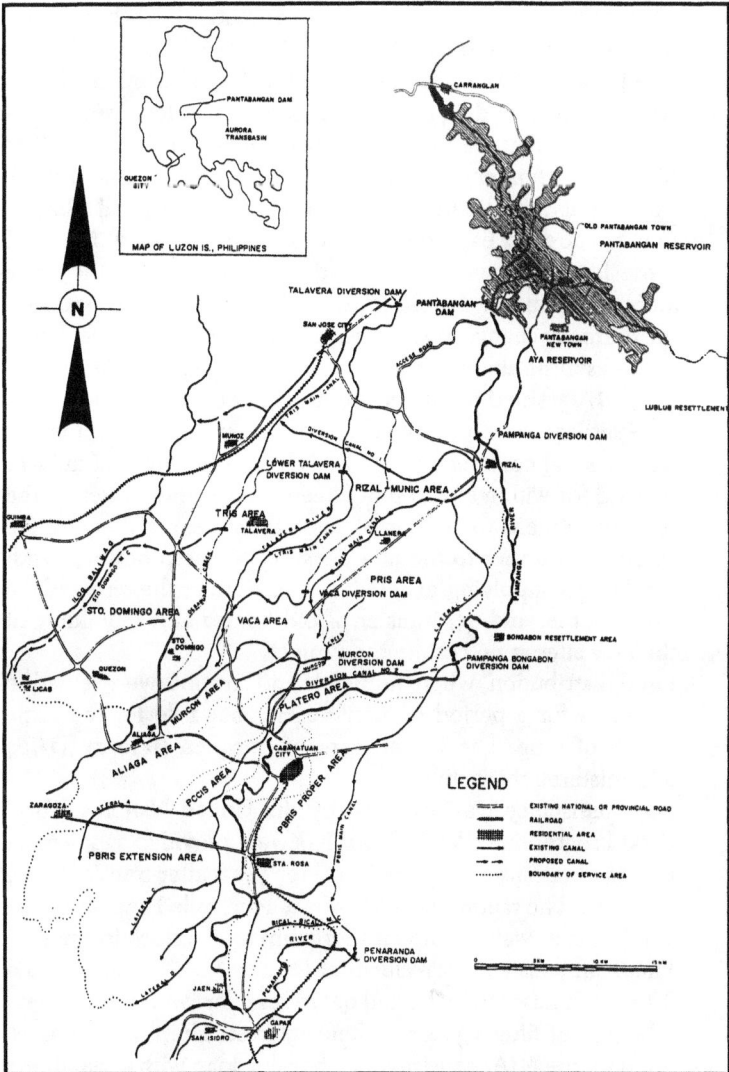

Source: National Irrigation Authority, Upper Pampanga
River Project.

1. Immediate payment of compensation for the loss of properties according to on-the-spot assessments done arbitrarily by NIA engineers. The Resettlement and Reservoir Division paid compensation for private properties submerged, such as land, houses, plants and trees. Payments were based on the Schedule of Appraised Values established by the Provincial Appraisal Committee, according to current market rates. However, people complained that their properties were under-valued, and other plants not compensated. To compensate for the loss of work opportunity, an allotment of farm lot of about two and a half to four hectares to each resettler family was provided. Many of these families owned or cultivated approximately the same amount of land in the old town. To help the settlers cope with the dramatic change in their mode of agriculture and livelihood, several skills-training programmes were implemented.

2. The NIA assisted resettlers in building houses in the new sites. The settlers were permitted to choose one of three housing schemes: (a) construction by the NIA of core housing units to be paid for within a period of fifteen years without interest, the first installment to be started after three years following the resettlers' transfer to the new sites; (b) self-help housing, with the Project supplying materials payable under the terms of the first scheme; and, (c) transfer of old houses and rebuilding at the new sites at no cost by the Project.

3. Land distribution, where homelots and farmlots were leased to resettlers for a period of forty years renewable for the same length of time. The Department of Agrarian Reform (DAR) administered this activity.

4. Food assistance was provided by the United Nation's World Food Programme (WFP). Resettlers were provided supplementary food rations during the first three years after transfer to the new sites. The rations included wheat flour, rolled oats and corn-soya milk, as well as corn and sorghum for livestock feeding.

5. Financial assistance. Presidential Decree No. 35 appropriated 20 million pesos to be loaned out to resettlers with a repayment schedule of fifteen years without interest. The fund, administered by the NIA, consisted of a housing loan with a maximum amount of 6,000 pesos per resettler family, a subsistence loan of 1,000 pesos and a project loan amounting 2,500 pesos.[7]

6. Cooperatives development. The NIA encouraged the organisation of the Pantabangan Pre-cooperative Consumers Associ-

7. At the present rate the minimum wage is approximately 40 pesos per day.

ation. A number of them were formed; however, none lasted long due to problems with leadership.

By virtue of a series of presidential proclamations, decrees and memoranda of agreement, the resettlement and relocation of residents displaced by the construction of Pantabangan Dam became a joint undertaking of NIA and DAR, as well as the involvement of twenty other government agencies. Overall coordination was carried out by the lead agency, the NIA. However, despite the enormous in-pouring of assistance from various agencies in the initial years, the resettlement programme encountered a number of major difficulties and constraints, many of which can be attributed to firstly the lack of proper planning and secondly the absence of appropriate persons handling its implementation. These two major reasons are manifestations of the state's lack of political will to resettle the people properly. Resettlement became a construction project managed by engineers unequipped to handle the intricacies of social problems associated with displacement.

Despite some degree of initial resistance[8] from the people, resettlement was carried out within reasonable grounds, as everyone was afraid and was convinced that the NIA was only following orders from above. The political climate during this period was tense due to the declaration of Martial Law in the Philippines in the early 1970s. In fact, Martial Law became an instrument in the resettlement operation to silence the people, diffuse resistance and facilitate the smooth and speedy transfer of people to the resettlement sites. Martial Law became an effective force that sped up the dam construction in Pantabangan.

Issues after Resettlement

As work on the Pantabangan Dam began in 1971, it is unlikely that the government realised that the-hoped for economic benefits would have to be obtained at the expense of social and economic dislocation of significant dimensions. However, as early as three years after resettlement, despite the millions of pesos having been invested in the development of the resettlement areas, no one seemed satisfied about the conditions prevailing at Pantabangan: not the national agencies

8. Local leaders and students staged two demonstrations in Malacanang Palace to protest against the construction of the dam in the early 1970s. However, their Mayor was co-opted by the government and people could not gather sufficient support for an effective campaign.

involved, led by the NIA and the DAR, the municipal government of the newly created town, not most especially, the resettlers themselves. Some of the critical planning issues that were never resolved originated from the political and inter-agency decision-making which took place even before resettlement, without proper consultation from the people. Due to the early completion of the dam, relocation occurred prematurely to geographic areas that were politically expedient. No importance was given to the search for suitable land with greater development opportunities. Thus, the resettlement site became an area of convenience for those carrying out the task and an area of perpetual inconvenience for those who had to live in it.

As previously described, the new townsite of Pantabangan is located on a hilly terrain with very few level areas for building infrastructure. In the process of levelling, the area was scraped, leaving certain areas with little or no topsoil. As a result, even backyard garden planting became a challenge. The old town was a farming community, and the majority of the people were traditional farmers who could not continue to practice their traditional modes of livelihood in this new, unsuitable environment.

Less than half of the total agricultural land set aside for the displaced population in Tanauan, the largest resettlement area, was arable. Many farmers had nothing to farm on; for those who were allocated arable land, the location was distant and hilly, and the majority of them did not even bother to cultivate it. Many who used to be lowland farmers were required to be upland farmers, and at great distances. In order to survive, some resettlers cultivated plants and livelihood crops in whatever public areas they could find available, such as the *kaingin*.[9] Other farmers planted onions along the lakeside when the water level was low, risking their farms being swept away when the water level rose, especially during unexpected heavy rains.

Becuase of the difficulties of the new farming situation, many resettlers who had left their farmlot allocations idle sought temporary contractual labour from the NIA. In their absence, farmer migrants from other provinces with capital bought the 'right of occupancy' to vacated farmlots and developed them. Other resettlers gave their farm lots to relatives.

The wage economy of the new townsite became heavily dependent on temporary employment with the NIA. But in 1991, the NIA

---

9. *Kaingin* are areas of land cleared by slashing and burning the bushes and trees in order to clear space for the planting of upland rice with intercropping vegetables and fruit trees.

laid off most of its contractual labourers due to lack of funds and as a result of the project's gradual closure. Since almost 90 per cent of the town's original population were NIA employed, the mass lay-off created an economic collapse for the affected families, and the jobless workforce, who were originally farmers, no longer had farms to return to.

With the sudden rise in the level of unemployment in the early 1990s, the illegal cutting of trees in the command area for charcoal-making and other commercial purposes was dramatically aggravated. Slashing and burning of forests for upland rice farming also increased. The municipal government, mindful perhaps of the economic situation, could not enforce much control and practiced tolerance.

Interagency coordination was an important issue that came about as a result of resettlement. The presence of so many agencies in the initial years, each having its own exclusive sphere of activity, made the resettlement programme difficult to manage. Coordination among the different programmes was a problem – a common scenario in emergency situations when various groups compete for the provision of various services, such as in refugee camps. The various projects have different life spans, as in the case of training programmes, and when turning a certain activity over from one agency to another, for example from the NIA to the DAR, one major problem is the manner in which the agency could effectively assume the functions considering the differences in financial, manpower and organisational resources. The NIA, being the lead agency, needed the cooperation of the DAR and others, but because the other organisations did not have as many resources, nor were they as efficient, the NIA became the patriarchal agency figure not only to other agencies but also to the people and to the newly created municipality. This has remained for many years up, until recently, when the municipal government increasingly became more independent and the NIA has progressively decreased and scaled-down its operation.

Assistance from the WFP, which lasted for three years from the mid 1970s, was welcomed by the resettled population, but it also created some degree of dependency and counter-motivated the beneficiaries to look for other food sources. It was only when the rations were over that people learned to be more resourceful and started backyard gardening.

Skills-training programmes were introduced to help people cope in their new setting. Such programmes included sewing, animal-raising, small-scale business, pottery, leadership training, fruit-tree cultivation, auto-repair, welding and cooperatives management. However, many of the training programmes were not planned appropriately, and there were no outlets for their skills once trained. Some of the skills were impractical, such as pig-raising, a water-consuming activity which was inappropriate because water supply was a problem even for people themselves. People ended up butchering the piglets for consumption, since maintenance and the affordability of feeds were problems. Another unsuccessful training programme was clay-pot making. Trainees were mostly farmers who possessed rough hands for farm work, while pottery required smoother hands. For those trainees who had learned new skills, despite the provision of project loans, few managed to open small businesses. Many of those who managed to secure loans were obliged to spend their money on weddings, baptismal parties and gambling. The resettlers had little experience in managing large amounts of cash since they were used to living in a subsistence economy and had never previously been required to hold large amounts of money. In the new town, however, they became mostly wage earners and had to learn how to manage the expenditures of daily living: this sudden transformation was a source of stress to many of the resettled families.

Transitions

Between 1969, when R.A. 5499 was passed authorising Pantabangan's submergence, and the present time, many processes have affected the lives of the originally displaced people. The initial years up until about 1973 can be classified under Scudder and Colson's first stage of a settlement process, that which is ideally characterised by planning, initial infrastructural development and recruitment. In Pantabangan's case, however, no proper resettlement planning was carried out. Interestingly enough, it was in this stage where initial resistance from the people, despite Martial Law, occurred after student leaders organised a demonstration in front of the President's Malacanang Palace. People were outraged when they heard of the congressional legislation that was passed behind their backs. A protest rally was also held at the construction site during this period, where people barricaded the passage of trucks and other construction vehicles. Unfortunately, the resistance was futile, as by that time there was little they could do to stop the project.

The second stage in the life of Pantabangan oustees[10] occurred between 1974 and 1978, when relocation was in full swing. Many

---

10. Oustees is a term commonly used in India to refer to people internally displaced as a result of government action and development projects.

people were accommodated in bunk-houses, and everyone was receiving rations from WFP. This was the initial adjustment period, where multi-dimensional stress was most eminent. Many people remembered this period as the most difficult one. However, they also considered it as a great learning process where they learned how to cope with hardships and utilise creative survival strategies.

The years between 1979 and 1983 were somewhat happier and could be considered the 'boom years' when people moved out of temporary accommodation and settled instead into the core houses. At this time many families had a wage earner employed by the NIA and were receiving a fixed income enabling a majority to send their children to school, and students were able to pursue higher education outside the town. People were able to buy new house appliances and open up small businesses. This period is remembered as one of progress, despite the difficulties resettlers faced in their new environment.

Economic sufficiency in Pantabangan was extended through 1984 to 1988, although the Watershed Project, utilising most of the labour force and therefore providing most employment, was winding down. The town crisis began in 1989, when the Project was officially completed and consequently, many of the casual and temporary labourersers from the town were laid off. As a result of unemployment, alcoholism increased with people's frustrations in their efforts to find alternative sources of income. Deforestation also accelerated, as people found illegal tree-cutting a convenient way to make money.

The mass job lay off occurred in 1991, when the NIA declared its funding insufficient to support the labour force of the completed Watershed Project. This period was characterised by the town's depressed state; it was a time in which people experienced their lowest morale, and municipal leaders had no idea how to improve the situation. Everyone was hoping for government aid but it never came. The people felt that the government had decided to ignore the problem and abandon the residents to a poverty which was not of their making. During this time, electricity and water-supply maintenance, which for many years were subsidised by the NIA, was handed over to the town, who could not afford to operate the services. Consequently, very few households had electricity and running water.

The municipal government finally managed to obtain financial assistance from the provincial government in 1993 to ease the economic situation. However, as another phase of community life emerges out of the lives of the Pantabangan oustees, many of the old issues remain the same.

Present Situation

After twenty years, the vast ricefields and green farmlots of the old town no longer exist, and the mountains are almost bald from heavy deforestation. The new town is undergoing a new phase as the municipal government develops more autonomy from the NIA, but the picture is bleak. None of the loans provided in the initial years have been repaid. There are not even any records of such transactions anymore, as filing and record keeping was not systematically done by the field office. None of the allocated farmlots has become productive, not even the demonstration farm that was started by agriculturists and researchers from the University of the Philippines. None of the cooperatives formed are effectively functioning, except for one onion cooperative recently founded and headed by a woman.

The fish cages[11] cooperative, which was reasonably successful in the past and was previously administered by the former parish priest of Pantabangan, is in the process of re-organisation and offers promise. Many of these cooperatives are set up to have access to credit from the Land Bank, which provides loans only to organised groups and charges interest at a market rate.

Most of the people who now remain in the new Pantabangan town are elderly and were the original household heads in the old town. The younger productive members of the community are working and living in other vicinities and nearby cities that could offer them better opportunities. However, they return to the town on short visits to their relatives. There are also those who had gone abroad as domestic helpers and labourers, and who in turn remit money to their families in the town. Families who have relatives abroad normally have better houses and appliances and are able to invest in small businesses such as the operation of tricycles and jeepneys.[12] In-migration is minimal, except for those nomadic merchants who started to set up small businesses along the roads, such as the 'sari-sari' stores. Inter-provincial marriages have also brought new families to the town.

The literacy rate has increased with the education of more people and the building of a new high school in the town centre, but unfortunately the job market is almost non-existent locally, pushing away the educated young people to seek opportunities elsewhere.

11. Fish cages were set up on the lake to culture tilapia fish and were maintained by a group of resettlers who formed themselves into a fishing co-operative, with limited membership.
12. *Jeepneys* are the most popular mode of transport in the Philippines, especially in rural areas, due to their capacity to take an enormous number of passengers in long parallel seats.

One of the few visible positive aspects of the new community after twenty years is the presence of fruit trees in the backyards and along the streets. Fruit tree planting was part of the training programme initiated during the early years of resettlement, and people were given free seedlings with incentives to plant them. However, no training programme on fruit preservation and marketing was introduced.

Electricity, which was provided free of charge during the initial years, is now an expensive and rare commodity in the new town for which only few people can afford to pay. Ironically, the National Power Corporation (NPC) plant supplying electricity in Central Luzon, is within sight from the new town. Water supply remains a major problem, with water pumps functioning only in lower geographic areas and drinking water running in the faucets only twice a week, and then for a few hours only. Many people have pumps that cannot generate water, and so they have to fetch water from the lake or hire tricycles to transport water from the wells. The prices that people pay range from five to ten pesos per gallon of water brought directly into the home. Normally, water is free in public pumps and faucets in other parts of the country.

Infrastructure is limited to one basic health clinic, one Catholic Church under repair, a Protestant Church under construction, a typhoon-damaged public market, two public school buildings in addition to one private school, a public park with a basketball court and a well-built municipal hall perched on top of a hill overlooking the town centre. There remains a plan to erect a market building, but it has not yet materialised. A town museum, which was the oldest house (1863) in the old town and was an important reference to the the town's history, was moved to the new townsite in 1973 but unfortunately mysteriously burned down in 1980. Most of the residential houses at present are made of concrete materials from the core housing constructed by the NIA. Streets have been paved and asphalted recently, although repairs are needed. Regardless of the increase in tricycles and private *jeepneys*, public transportation is still a problem. There is an absence of regular transport between Pantabangan and the outside world.

Despite all the changes in the economic and daily life of the people, patronage politics remain strong and unchanged. When a person runs for public office in the municipal government of Pantabangan for example, victory depends upon his or her number of relatives. Relatives who are eligible to vote patronise their candidates from the same clan, not according to the candidate's political platform. However, since the old town's original population composition remained reasonably intact after the move, most of the people are related to one another. This results in friendly competition among clan-mates during election. Politicians have to woo their relatives in order to gain votes, making the election season a chance for poor voters to take advantage of favours and promises from competing kin.

Taking these political alliances into consideration is an important part of a resettlement activity, as when political leaders agree on certain issues, their constituents will follow. The efficiency of resettlement operation therefore becomes politically driven.

Conclusion

In the face of conflicting interests between the people and the state, those of the latter's invariably predominate. Since it is the state that causes the disruption of people's lives during their displacement, it has a moral obligation to restore what was disrupted during their resettlement. Proper resettlement of individuals and communities should be borne by the state in any project causing displacement for the sake of national interest.

The experience in Pantabangan resettlement is just one of the many similar circumstances faced by oustees in other parts of the world. Since state power was used to dramatically change the life situation of 1,300 people in Pantabangan, the state should also take responsibility for ensuring the restoration of community life and progress of the displaced even after twenty years.

Power, according to Max Weber, is manifested when an actor within a relationship is in the position to carry out their own will despite resistance. He adds that since the concept of power can include a multitude of situations resulting from innumerable combinations of the personal qualities of actors and circumstances, concepts of imperative control, authority and discipline must also be introduced. What happened in Pantabangan was a manifestation of the use of state power over the community, using the NIA as a medium to carry out the objectives of the state.

It has been argued that all networks and hierarchies of power, and often the very basis for legitimising authority from the local level and beyond, are modified and reconstituted via negotiation. However, in a dictatorial political situation, as in the case of Pantabangan under Martial Law, there was no negotiation. Without fair negotiation, there could be no sustainable progress. This was clearly demonstrated in Pantabangan. In the absence of a reasonable partnership between the NIA and the displaced population, there was no motivation to strive. Dependency on the government resulted and was very much in the forefront of people's lives.

With the increasing demand for dams and similar infrastructure causing displacement, it is important for the state to reflect on the past experiences of communities such as that presented here, to avoid repeating the same mistakes. Many lessons can be learned from the Pantabangan experience, but two major points deserve emphasis:

Firstly, that proper planning involving the project-affected people in *all* stages should be made before any plans for resettlement can be conceptualised, let alone finalised, to ensure appropriate approaches. People's participation must be taken seriously. The Pantabangan case is not unique in terms of the absence of democratic consultation from oustees; many other countries practice it, dictatorial or not. However, state power, be it through Martial rule or another dictatorial system of government, should not be used to push through a project that could potentially marginalise a whole community for an indefinite period of time. Any existing government system whose ultimate goal is to help the people must adhere to its development objectives rather than political motives.

The *second* lesson points at government responsibility. The state's moral obligation should not end with the project's completion when a displaced population results from it. As Cernea (in this volume) and others have emphasised, resettlement operations should be viewed as development projects. Institutional monitoring from the national hierarchy all the way down to the field level has to be effectively carried out by appropriate personnel. The proper implementation of resettlement activities are major roles that any socially responsible government must undertake in order to ensure development sustainability that will benefit not only the country itself but the global community.

PART FOUR

TACKLING THE CHALLENGES OF IMPOVERISHMENT

11

Land-Based Strategies in Dam-Related Resettlement Programmes in Africa

Véronique Lassailly-Jacob

'The tree that's been transplanted will never make as pleasant a shade as the tree that grows where it has always stood.'

(Baule proverb)

Introduction

During recent decades, increasing investments in development infrastructure and growing population densities have been the main factors underlying the relocation of populations on a large scale.[1] Since the 1960s, the construction of large hydro-electric dams and the formation of artificial lakes in Africa have been the most frequent causes of the forced displacement of communities. The data presented in this chapter are drawn from a few major dam-related resettlement operations that took place in Africa during the 1960s and 1970s (Volta, Kossou, Kainji, Kariba, Aswan)[2] as well as a few

1. My grateful thanks go to Michael Cernea and Noal Mellot for their valuable comments and suggestions for rewriting this chapter, which is based on data collected by the author during fieldwork in the Ivory Coast (the Kossou project), Ghana (the Volta project) and Egypt (the Aswan High Dam project).
2. Built across the Volta River in 1964, the Akosombo Dam in Ghana disrupted the lives of 80,000 people from various ethnic groups. Built in Egypt in 1969, the Aswan High Dam flooded the homeland of more than 100,000 Nubians who were resettled, half in Kom-Ombo (New Nubia), Egypt, and half in Khashm El Girba

medium-scale schemes that have been carried out since then (Manantali, Kpong, Nangbeto, Kiambere).[3] (See Map 11.1.) All these dams disrupted communities' lives, dramatically forcing people to move. Mostly subsistence farmers, herders, nomadic pastoralists and fishermen were affected. However, the towns of Bussa and Yelwa in Nigeria, as well as Wadi Halfa in Sudan and part of Kete Krachi in Ghana, had to be moved and rebuilt.[4]

To compensate uprooted rural people, whose primary occupation is farming, governments have usually resettled them in planned agricultural areas. It has recently been assumed that cash compensation by itself was inadequate to allow resettlers to replace their resource base that is the land. In the Kiambere case for example, resettlers were paid for the loss of their land. This compensation did not suffice to buy equivalent land elsewhere; besides, families were not powerful enough to struggle individually for land purchases. As a result, they spent the money on bridewealth, old debts, household items or home improvements, and 'marginalisation' soon followed (Mburugu 1994). This chapter deals with resettlement programmes that apply a so-called 'land-for-land' strategy, which replaces lost land with new land of equal potential. In these government-sponsored resettlement schemes, new 'settlers' have received, in compensation, land and assistance to help them regain self-sufficiency or even raise their standards of living.

Despite governments' commendable efforts and substantial international aid, the goal of developing new, viable production systems to sustain relocated communities has seldom been achieved. Three observations can be made from the start. First, there is an often massive exodus of settlers from the new settlements. Second, it may take several years before the original level of subsistence is reached. Third, when newcomers do, once again, become self-sustaining, they usually do so thanks to activities other than the farming programmes planned for them. What are the reasons for these disappointing results? Can we draw lessons from these previous resettlement operations? By examining the production-based components of resettle-

---

(New Halfa), Sudan. The Kossou Dam, built in 1970 on the Bandama River in the Ivory Coast, forced 75,000 people to move. The Kariba Dam, built in 1958 on the Zambezi River between Zambia and Zimbabwe, affected the lives of about 50,000 people, as did the Kainji Dam, built in 1968 on the Niger River in Nigeria.

3. More recently, dams constructed in Ghana (Kpong), Mali (Manantali), Togo (Nangbeto) and Kenya (Kiambere) have displaced a few thousand people each.

4. We do not have much information about these urban resettlers. The literature on dam-related resettlement operations mainly focuses on rural rather than urban relocatees. Urban resettlement plans and urban resettlers have not been studied enough.

ment programmes, I shall point out why most resettled communities encounter difficulty reattaining self-sufficiency through the allocated land and new farming programmes.

Map 11.1 Main Dams Which Have Led to Important Transfers of Populations

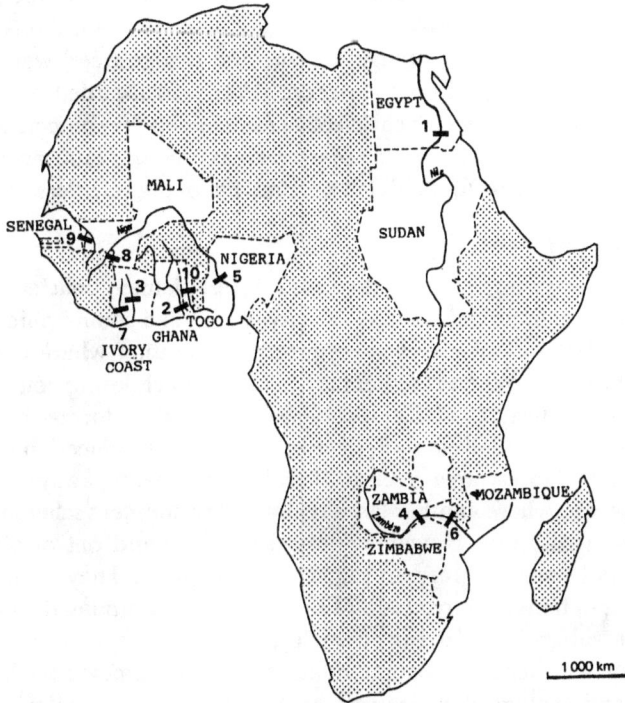

Name of Reservoir	Country	Date of Inundation	Population Displacement
1 - Assouan (Nile)	Egypt-Sudan	1969	108,000
2 - Akosombo (Volta)	Ghana	1964	80,000
3 - Kossou (Bandama)	Ivory Coast	1970	75,000
4 - Kariba (Zambeze)	Zambia-Zimbabwe	1958	57,000
5 - Kainji (Niger)	Nigeria	1968	44,000
6 - Cabora-Bassa (Zambeze)	Mozambique	1974	25,000
7 - Buyo (Sessandra)	Ivory Coast	1980	16,000
8 - Selingue (Sankarani)	Mali	1980	15,000
9 - Manantali (Bafing)	Mali-Senegal	1982	12,700
10 - Nangbeto (Mono)	Togo	1987	10,000

Source: Véronique Lassailly-Jacob

Land-Based Resettlement Programmes

Land Compensation Policies

Whenever public authorities decide to compensate victims for lost goods, they seldom take the land – the most precious belonging of the evicted – into account. Only arable land developed through an irrigation network is compensated for (as in Old Nubia). In the Kossou and Akosombo projects, flooded arable lands, food crops and fruit trees (palm, cola, orange, banana and mango trees) were not considered worthy of compensation, which was awarded only for coffee and cocoa trees. Such selective assessments for compensation purposes reveal the 'vision' planners have of the land and the resources, a 'vision' quite different from that of the resettlers.

Resettlement Policies

Planners have implemented two sorts of resettlement policies, each with a different impact on the viability of resettled communities.

The first sort of policy takes into consideration where people want to move. When resettlers are involved in choosing new locations, they always prefer to resettle as close to their former habitat as possible. In the Kossou Project, evacuees were induced to move toward the forest area over six hundred kilometres away, in the south-west, where another large regional development scheme was being carried out. However, only three thousand out of eighty thousand people agreed to migrate to this place. They preferred settling in familiar surroundings on the lakeshore among their own ethnic subgroup. Moving to such a close relocation site is less painful. Furthermore, people adjust better to the new social, cultural and ecological environment when it is closer to the previous habitat. But two problems can arise. First of all, upland soils may have less agricultural potential than the rich alluvial soils of the inundated floodplains, as Scudder pointed out in one case: 'Because the majority of the Tonga were moved inland from their former homes along the Zambezi, most relocatees found themselves in areas with less fertile soils which could only support bush-fallow systems of cultivation' (1980:391). Secondly, there may be land problems because resettlement sites are located on vacant land owned by other people. If relocatees and their hosts come from the same ethnic group, relations may be cordial, at least at the start (as in the Kossou Project). If they do not belong to the same ethnic group, relations may be strained straightaway (as in the Volta Project). In any case, tensions mount as time passes. Resettling people on unflooded ancestral lands or government reserved lands (such as forest reserves) is the most fitting solution when feasible, as in the Kpong and Manantali projects.

The second sort of policy forces people to settle in a new area, far from their former habitat. The Nubian Sudanese had to move more than one thousand kilometres to settle in the Khasm El Girba area. Similarly, six thousand Gwembe evacuated from Kariba were required to move one hundred kilometres downstream to the Lusitu region. In Egypt, the people of Lower Nubia were given the choice of either resettling individually on a site of their choice or being resettled collectively a few hundred kilometres northwards in the Kom-Ombo area. As the Nubians wanted to avoid the dispersion of their community, the second option prevailed despite the distance. Far-distant resettlement means moving to an unfamiliar environment and entails increased hardship. The further people are moved, the greater the resistance and trauma even though resettlers may receive relatively large tracts of arable land at the new sites (fifteen-acre plots in the New Halfa Project). In New Nubia, Egypt, and New Halfa, Sudan, many Nubian families left the resettlement area to go back to their homeland and settle on the lakeshore. Furthermore, tensions with hosts in resettlement areas are exacerbated, partly because of different ethnic origins. Talking about the relationship between Gwembe resettlers and their Goba hosts in the Lusitu area (Kariba case), Scudder (1993) mentioned that conflicts over boundaries and sorcery accusations have increased over the years, and land initially lent to the newcomers was taken back.

Land Acquisition, Preparation and Distribution

In Africa, two systems of imbricated land tenure operate on the same territory: national law and customary laws. There is no piece of land, even vacant land, without a customary owner, i.e., an ethnic group, a clan, a lineage or a family. Informal customary rights to the land still prevail in many rural areas. Furthermore, lands in many rural savanna areas have no market value and no registered deeds. Finally, while States are equipped with the legal means to take away land needed for the public good and to compensate the expropriated, they lack legislation for carrying out legally workable resettlement operations, which involve purchasing replacement land for the evicted communities and compensating the hosts. Given this legal vacuum, acquiring, distributing and developing new land is an almost insurmountable task for planners.

Two major policies have been pursued in acquiring land for resettlement schemes: the first calls for governmental intervention. In

New Halfa, Sudan, the government acquired fifty thousand *feddans* (1 *feddan* = 1.04 acres; 0.42 hectares), i.e., 2,000 sq. kms, and provided resettlers and their hosts with large holdings in tenancy. In New Nubia, Egypt, 200 sq. kms were reclaimed from the desert. However, even when authorities do acquire enough arable land for relocatees, the allocated land may not be ready to farm by the time of resettlement. Too often, planning starts too late and leads to a 'crash' programme. In New Nubia, at the time of relocation, less than 10 per cent of the new land had been reclaimed. As a result, settlers received only one *feddan* and depended on food relief for several years after 1965. Not until 1980 did each eligible person acquire his full allotment of land. In Ghana, the agency in charge of acquiring land for the relocatees encountered customary landowners' refusal. Four years after resettlement, only sixteen out of fifty-two settlements had received cleared land. A few years later, relocatees were back on relief from the World Food Programme, and some new settlements had become ghost towns. At that time, Ghana's government 'enacted a law amending the Volta River Development Act in 1961 to provide for the acquisition and payment of compensation for all flooded land as well as land required for resettlement purposes' (Adu-Aryee 1993:140). Despite this new law, many original landowners continued denying relocatees access to their three-acre plots. Many of the them had not been compensated for expropriated land because they had no written evidence to support their claims.

A second land acquisition policy is based on friendly agreements. At Kossou, for example, the resettlement agency acquired tracts of arable land in the savanna area for the forty new settlements, under friendly agreements with host populations who belonged to the same ethnic group. One or two tracts of 150 ha. each (according to the size of the settlement) were cleared for each settlement with heavy machinery. Each tract was then divided into 5 ha. for thirty households. There were about two hundred households in each village. The resettlement agency assumed that the host population would agree to share land with the other newcomers out of generosity for brothers and sisters in need. Having no land rights, these newcomers became indebted to their hosts, and their survival still depends on maintaining friendly relations with them.

Too often, friendly agreements are worked out with very little compensation. In the Kossou Project, the uncompensated hosts often refused to allocate farmland to newcomers. Or, in order to prevent relocatees from cultivating already-rented land, they placed fetishes there and held never-ending *palavers*. Regarding the New Halfa Project, Salem-Murdoch (1989) has pointed out that 'a result of the government's differential treatment of relocated Nubians and host Arabs was the intensification of ethnic tensions between the two groups'.

Land may be distributed to resettlers in one of three ways. First of all, anyone who owned now-flooded land may receive new land as a function of the size of his previous farm. In New Nubia, the size of the holding was based on what each head of household owned in Old Nubia. Those who had less than three *feddan* or those who had no land received two *feddan*. The largest landowners were given five *feddan*. However, most landholders received only two *feddan*, because the size of their previous holdings had usually been small.

Secondly, every head of household may receive the same acreage. In New Halfa, each head of household received a fifteen-acre farm. Initially, land as well as the other resources (seeds, fertilisers, etc.) were equally distributed by the resettlement agency among relocatees; but over the years, these resources have become concentrated in the hands of a few. Differences in living standards among tenants have increased between those who, capable of profiting from new opportunities, now form an elite supervising huge domains, and the others who, excluded, only dispose of the labour their families can provide. This is one of the Project's major consequences (Salem-Murdock 1989). In the Volta Project, each household was entitled to a three-acre farm. Since this was too small, the fields could not lie fallow, and the soil was impoverished. In the Manantali Project, 0.8 ha. of farmland was cleared for each individual over eight years old.

Thirdly, only a selected number of resettlers may be given arable land. This happened in the Kossou Project, where 'volunteers' received 5-ha. farms in the savanna area. In all three cases, relocatees receive only land for fields. No land is set aside for other activities, as we shall see.

Farming Programmes

Before construction of these dams, production systems were quite diversified. Riverine dwellers, particularly in savanna and desert areas, practised an intensive cropping system on the floodplains, sometimes based on irrigation and often associated with recessional cultivation during the dry season as floodwaters receded. This was true of Gwembe Tonga in the Kariba Project, Nubians in the Aswan project and Gungawa in the Kainji Project. These intensive farming systems could support high population densities. In more humid areas (for example, among the Baule in the Kossou Project), an extensive subsistence farming system based on shifting cultivation and slash-and-burn techniques was practised.

On the new sites, farmplots are usually allocated on an individual basis to each head of household. Planners tend to resort to one of two agricultural policies. The first is a policy of replacement, where the goal is to re-establish existing production systems and reattain the previous standard of living. Accordingly, relocatees receive little support. They are supposed to use their former farming practices or to adjust spontaneously to the new environment. This occurred in the Manantali and Kariba Projects. However, because planners did not clearly understand previous agricultural practices or did not carefully study the new site's human-carrying capacity, the allocated land was insufficient; and erosion resulted. The Gwembe Tonga had to re-establish their former agricultural system in the Lusitu area, where resettlement increased population densities fourfold! Twenty years later, desertification has, not surprisingly, turned this area into a dust bowl (Scudder 1980). Although the cultivated land requires periodically lying fallow, the exiguous land allocation keeps farmers from carrying out an extensive farming system. In Manantali, several resettlement villages have not received enough land to practise bush fallow cultivation, herding, hunting and foraging. As a result, resettlers are impoverished, and shorter land rotation cycles may damage vegetation and erode the soil (Horowitz et al. 1993). It can be seen therefore that the lack of a comprehensive understanding of native production systems leads to a development that cannot be sustained in the long run.

The second agricultural policy, which is more frequently adopted, calls for intensive farming techniques. Since there is not enough suitable land for traditional systems of shifting cultivation, permanent fields are cleared and cultivated under intensive, integrated farming programmes. 'Intensive' means using modern farm equipment and making major investments. 'Integrated' means providing farmers with both the food and income they need. This system, which is strictly supervised and amply financed, is supposed to be highly productive and profitable. In New Nubia, the reclaimed land was irrigated with free-flowing water thanks to heavy investments for developing a perennial, intensive agriculture. Each new village's arable land was divided into sections for different crops. One section was reserved for sugarcane, a compulsory, government-sponsored, cash crop that Nubians had not grown before. Many families had at least two plots, one for sugarcane and one for whatever other crops they decided to grow. In New Halfa, Sudan, Nubians and settled nomads had to rotate cotton, groundnuts and wheat on their tenancies. In the Kossou Project, a rain-fed mechanised farming scheme for producing annual crops was associated with raising livestock. A selected number of relocatees participated therein.

Overall results were disappointing. Maintenance of sophisticated farm machines was a major problem; yields were far below predictions, and the failure of most programmes has left many resettlers worse off. Over ten years into the Kossou Project, the mechanised farming system had failed; most tracts were deserted, and many able-bodied adults had been migrating out of the resettlement area while others stayed on as farmers without land. Many relocatees had taken to fishing in the lake and farming the unflooded ancestral lands, and thus made a better living than under the agency programmes. Adu-Aryee, an anthropologist and former Deputy Director of the Volta River Authority, has made a similar point: 'Ironically, it is worthy of note that it is more the unprogrammed and spontaneous economic activities, such as fishing and drawdown farming in the case of Akosombo, and irrigated rice farming and fishing in the headpond in the case of Kpong, than the planned and organised farming programmes that have attracted and supported the settlers' (1993:148). In some parts of New Nubia, agriculture has been diverted from its planned-for purposes. Raising livestock has generated more income than growing cash crops. Hence, allocated farmland is being used mainly for feeding livestock; during the sugarcane harvest season, Nubian women go to the fields in order to collect the high green stems and leaves to feed their animals, as well as the stems' dry envelopes to be used as fuel.

Land Tenure

In the African countryside, land is an owned, developed space marked with local community's identity. Butcher wrote in his operational manual for resettlement, 'more than houses, land ... is the peoples' most valuable property. Not only does it enable them to grow food for subsistence and cash crops with which to obtain money to buy the essentials of presentday life, it is often considered to be sacred. Land is the property of the ancestors, the living and the unborn children. Often key parts of the local religious beliefs and customs are closely associated with the land' (1971:24-25).

Land is the ground upon which social, cultural and religious beliefs are grown. 'Units of social organisation such as the family, lineage, clan, tribe or ethnic group are also territorial units. Such territorial units are viewed as permanent elements in the lives of individual families and communities' (Mburugu 1994:49). This is the land that, once flooded, is to be replaced.

Very often, the new communities do not obtain full title to the arable land allocated to them, at least not in the case of major development projects. Settlers are usually tenants on the developed land.

This was true of the relocatees involved in the mechanised farming scheme in the Kossou project. They were forced to adopt an inflexible, controlled modern farming system. They were allowed to farm provided that they respected agency guidelines. Consequently, they thought they were working for the Agency, not for themselves. The fields were called *blofue fie* (fields belonging to white people). As a safety net, farmers preferred growing traditional crops 'on the side' to the detriment of the time spent on the new farming system, which was considered to be tiresome, compulsory and barely profitable. In New Halfa, Nubians received fifteen *feddan* tenancies for growing, in rotation, cotton, groundnuts and wheat. In New Nubia, settlers were forced to grow certain crops in the fields appointed. They had no security of tenure on the irrigated lots. Lack of land ownership has discouraged resettlers from fully committing themselves to farming on the plots run by the agency.

In general, land-based resettlement strategies have had disappointing results. Planners see the land only as a productive asset and see resettlers merely as producers who are to be allocated sufficient arable land for farming. Too often, planners use resettlement as an opportunity for introducing modern farming without giving due consideration to the improvement of local production systems, nor even to the new possibilities offered by the project. Relocatees usually do not share in the benefits of the project that has displaced them.

There is a gap between two rationales or two perceptions of the land. The planners' land perception focuses on productivity and profitability, whereas the resettlers' land perception encompasses a wide range of social, cultural and religious elements as well as the productive factor. As long as this gap persists, 'the challenge of "solving" the resettlement dilemma can only grow' (Cernea and Guggenheim 1993:2). Under these conditions, land-based development programmes will never satisfy the resettled population's needs and wants. Impoverishment and marginalisation will ensue.

Land-Based Strategies for Preventing Impoverishment

A 'land-for-land' strategy would entail replacing the lost land of the displaced communities. But, what does 'replacing land' mean? It means giving resettled rural communities full title to an adequate, clearly defined surface area. There are four prerequisites to doing this. First, an adequate surface area means not only providing relocatees with enough productive farmland but also providing communities with common land. Besides growing crops, land also provides other basic resources for meeting daily needs of energy, shelter, medicine, food and income. Gathering wild resources is still a major way of obtaining food in most rural African societies. 'Bush foods' add seasonal diversity to the diet and provide sustenance during shortages. Furthermore, 'bush' resources also provide the most vulnerable with a source of income. Resettlers are too often – mistakenly – viewed as full-time farmers whose only source of income is agriculture. Planners tend to forget that resettlers are also gatherers, hunters and herders and that they need extra land to practise these activities which are part of their traditional production systems. Planners fail to attach importance to 'bush' land or common land. They too often rely on the host population's traditions of hospitality and solidarity for granting newcomers access to these resources. While such generosity often does occur at the time of resettlement, it does not last long, at least not in areas with high population densities. Under these conditions, previously available natural resources suddenly become scarce and precious, and customary rights of access to the land are tightened. Previously treated as unfortunate brothers and sisters, relocatees are soon seen as competitors and intruders. Relations are strained, and conflicts break out due to competition over common resources. Planners should not rely on the hosts' hospitality. They should acquire a large enough, clearly delimited area for the resettled community and not just plots of arable land. If the importance of common land and of its resources is underestimated and if extra uncultivated land is not allocated, resettled communities will grow poorer.

Second, an adequate surface area also means enough productive farmland. The size of allocated farmland should be determined as a function of the soil potential and of the production system to be introduced. The size of the adequate surface area should be determined according to one of three situations. First, when intensive farming programmes are introduced, resettlers should be granted extra arable land for traditional farming. Intensive farming programmes have never totally replaced traditional farming systems. Some staple, or other crops, (for example vegetables or condiments grown by women) are usually not taken into account under intensive farming programmes. As a result, resettlers, especially women, need to keep traditional farms at the periphery of the modern farming scheme. Furthermore, when planners decide to acquire land for re-establishing the previous farming system with its technology, they must carefully study all the components of these systems. Forgetting to take into account the fallow land in a shifting cultivation system will result in declining soil fertility, poor yields and land degradation (Scudder

1993). Finally, in all cases, planners must take into account the need for 'reserve land' that can be used to meet the growing population's future demand for arable land. An exiguous and inadequate land base leads to impoverishment of the soil and of the people.

Third, the resettled community should be given full title to a clearly defined surface area. Full title means security of tenure, a capital point. Newcomers without clearly defined property rights soon become indebted to their hosts and may be evicted from the land they occupy. The government itself and not the agency in charge of resettlement should negotiate for the land acquired on behalf of relocatees. As pointed out, the state, to do this, must provide the necessary legal framework. The original owners, even though their title to the land may not be registered, should be identified and fairly compensated. Whenever possible, the host population should be integrated in the development programme. Overlooked hosts become jealous of government efforts on behalf of relocatees. Envying the improved housing, water supply and new schools or clinics provided to relocatees, they may turn against them and threaten the project's sustainability. Only a strong institutionalised intervention which starts well before resettlement, can solve the problems that arise in land cases under customary law. A well-delimited territory including cultivated land as well as bush land should be allocated to each new community.

Fourth, at the time of resettlement, planners should not focus exclusively on 'sophisticated' agricultural schemes. Under such schemes, the land prepared at high cost does not belong to the resettlers, who are only tenants. Furthermore, ambitious farming programmes promote unsustainable development, creating enclaves that will remain dependent for a long time. In addition, dependency entails impoverishment. More modest programmes will reap the new opportunities created by the project itself such as developing the new lake's shore through draw-down or small-scale irrigated agriculture, animal husbandry or fisheries, as well as downstream areas. Relocatees should share in the benefits of the project that displaced them. While analysing the enormous physiological, psychological and sociocultural stress that accompanies involuntary relocation, Scudder and Colson (1982) stated that major innovations must not be introduced during the initial stages of resettlement, when stress is especially intense. At the time of resettlement, development programmes should be kept as simple as possible, and new available resources should be exploited. Relocatees should first re-establish themselves and be able to fend for themselves. When feasible, 'Leave the people to farm in the way they know best at first' (Butcher 1971). Thereafter, a development phase may follow that judiciously combines 'development from above' with 'development from below'. Instead of flooding resettlement schemes with government-desired innovations, planners should lay more emphasis on facilitating local initiatives and enhancing local production systems (Scudder 1980). Ambitiously planned resettlement schemes that try to radically transform the relocatees' economy and ways of life are likely to fail with, as a consequence, the impoverishment of resettlers.

Conclusion

According to one of the World Bank's resettlement guidelines, 'all involuntary resettlement should be conceived and executed as a development program' (Cernea 1993a:24). But how can land-based resettlement programmes also become development programmes? Giving relocatees an adequate productive land base is part of the answer. Giving them the opportunity of sharing in the project's benefits by, for example resettling them downstream in newly irrigated areas (Cernea 1990a) is another part. According to Shihata, '... balanced development can only be achieved if the basic human rights are secured for the people adversely affected by development, as well as those who receive direct benefits. This requires creating an environment that allows them to preserve their cultural values while improving their living standards' (1993:53). Creating this kind of environment means giving the resettled community clear and full title to an adequate, well-defined territory which will serve as the basis of its production system and as new grounds for its cultural and social values.

12

Policy Implications
of the Involuntary Ownership of
Resettlement Negotiations

EXAMPLES FROM
ASIA OF RESETTLEMENT PRACTICE

Alan Rew

Introduction

The design and evaluation of resettlement continues to prompt strong reactions and controversy. Many would agree with the comment of David Aberle (1993:191) that 'Relocatees are removed from their homes because they are relatively powerless ... Hence relocation will almost always be a tragedy of greater or lesser proportions.' At the same time, other social scientists have sought to avoid academic fatalism and insouciance and pioneered the successful application of social science concepts to resettlement problems (Cernea 1993b:26-29). This second experience strongly suggests that the worst resettlement outcomes and impoverishment can be avoided or minimised through resettlement planning (Cernea 1994c:47) and that a vision of resettlement policy reform is necessary and practical.

Despite this contrast in resettlement analysis between the recognition of tragedy and the necessity of hope there appears to be widespread agreement in the literature about the scope for *volition* in resettlement planning. The relocatees, it is widely agreed, are *forced* to relocate because of land, infrastructural and other development investments. They are 'oustees' or 'involuntary' migrants, forced out of their homes indiscriminately, all facing, as large, disorganised groups of people, the same quandaries of coping and survival (Cernea and Guggenheim 1993:3).

When analysis turns to the action of state agencies in acquiring land from the existing occupants, it is often first recorded that the actions have been more or less regrettable – the acquisition has disrupted a community or has been ill-considered and led to conflict, and so on. However, there is almost always a second assumption that the agencies could, and should, somehow have acted differently. Often the volition that is implied is referred to elliptically and in terms of the active avoidance of action; for example, aid borrowers are blamed for 'lack of commitment', as if, somehow, they could readily raise the level of their interest and concern if they chose to do so. Periodically, the assumption of volition is explicit; for example, in the statement that 'resettlement works when governments want it to work' (World Bank 1994a:ix).

Social science has made a notable contribution to the amelioration of suffering and distress from the involuntary displacement of local populations. It has done so by concentrating on the threats to cultural identity and economic well-being imposed by enforced disruption and displacement. Cernea points out that these findings have altered the language that World Bank staff use to describe 'their' projects; increasingly, Bank staff discuss 'powerlessness', 'social cohesion', 'traditional authority structures' and so on (1993b:30).

My argument is that while it is essential that resettlement planning is based on ethnographic detail and on a full recognition of the *social* fabric of the resettled population, the state-of-the-art literature pays insufficient attention to the institutional processes of relocation and displacement. The need to understand the organisation of resettlement programmes is, of course, mentioned in that literature. Indeed, there is ample recognition in the secondary commentaries that borrower 'ownership' and government commitment is often lacking. It is difficult, however, to find coherent analyses of the *reasons* for government reluctance or for the occasional successes.

In part, the explanation for this lacuna in the political and institutional analysis of resettlement concerns the combined effects of low disciplinary and donor priorities. The institutional analysis of resettlement operations is not viewed as of equivalent priority to policy dialogue on legal frameworks by the donors nor, by academics, as equivalent to research that adds to our moral understanding of resettlement tragedies, failure or the scope for local resistance. Michael Cernea has drawn our attention to the importance, or potential importance, of a social analysis of institutional procedures (1993b:30-31).

Nonetheless, his comment clearly recognises the prevailing attitude to analysis of this kind – he is forced to describe it as rather 'technical' and 'mundane', although worthy (to varying degrees). Thus on the one hand, moral outrage at displacement and the disruption of social and economic relations induced by project investments leads many social analysts to shun resettlement operations, while those that see the practical and theoretical challenges in resettlement planning are usually led by donor priorities towards the production of guidelines and proposed frameworks for borrower action.

This chapter hopes to address and help fill this gap in the analysis of resettlement. Its specific aim is to contribute to the solution of practical operational problems and to policy. The closely administered life of the relocating population also shows state-household-community relations that create possibilities for the development of anthropological theory. I have recently tried to develop the implications for anthropological theory elsewhere (Rew 1994:284-294). In this present paper I aim to show that a closer understanding of the parallel institutional processes of reluctant resettlement management and household and community disorganisation has substantial implications for donor-borrower dialogue and for institutional strengthening and the sequencing of resettlement programme operations. Of potential key interest to social analysts in both the universities and in the agencies is how to organise and timetable repairs to the *social fabric* of dislocated communities in relation to their *physical rehabilitation* and to the regeneration of *economic production*. If these relationships are more closely analysed, they suggest arrangements for organisational responsibility that could both encourage government commitment and lessen the chances of disorganisation and impoverishment.

The paper first assesses the recent World Bank review of resettlement and development projects initiated between 1986 and 1993 (World Bank 1994a) and the weighting given in the review to considerations of organisational and institutional design. This review (hereafter WBR) is both extensive and comprehensive and provides a key international benchmark for policy, operational standards and future research. Its treatment of institutional processes will thus guide the way that borrowers and development researchers view their importance.

The WBR conclusions and recommendations provide a context for an analysis of my own experience of projects with resettlement components. I have started by analysing what government agencies actually do, *not* what governments and donors *hope* or *aim* for, or what they say is intended to happen. The analysis suggests very strongly that one of the most 'involuntary' aspects of resettlement is that of borrower or executive agency ownership. Few agencies want to accept responsibility for resettlement easily, and even if they are specifically charged with resettlement responsibilities, they are very conscious of the difficulties involved in managing community and political disruption and in dealing with human distress and impoverishment. Indeed, in each of the nine projects with resettlement components in which I have been involved, there were varying but substantial degrees of organisational discomfiture. The detailed problems of displacement and the need for subsequent access to a range of supports and services were often handled in an involuntary, rather than a planned and considered, way. I am fully aware that, with experience of managing resettlement, specialist agencies gain confidence and ease; and that I have generally taken on more difficult cases where normal administration and design has either broken down or was never properly established.

Following this review of my own experience, alternative ways of arranging the structure of resettlement management are listed and the result compared to the main thrust in the WBR. The aim of this comparison is to refine an operational model that, while based on the authoritative findings of the WBR, also takes the constraints and opportunities for institutional performance more fully into account. I believe that the result is a sharper definition of the scope for participatory planning and of the asset-building process that leads to rehabilitation.

The World Bank Review and the Policy Imperative

The WBR stresses that involuntary resettlement consists of two closely related yet distinct processes that are among the most difficult to achieve in development work. These are the orderly relocation of people from their homes and lands and the subsequent rebuilding of their livelihoods. The key message is that well-planned resettlement can prevent impoverishment as it rebuilds sustainable livelihoods, and that it can even reduce poverty.

The WBR is also concerned to show how the World Bank's own portfolio of projects bears on worldwide resettlement patterns and solutions. The scale of development-induced population displacement has grown rapidly in developing countries in the recent decade, especially in the countries of Asia. This phenomenon reflects the accelerated provision of infrastructure and growing population densities. It is estimated that each year some four million people are displaced by the three hundred or so large dams that are started and six million people are displaced by urban and transportation investments. In 1993 projects in the Bank's portfolio accounted for only some 3 per cent of reservoir-related displacement and perhaps 2 per cent of urban- and transport-related displacement, implying the resettlement of two million people over an eight-year period, mostly in South and East Asia. The Bank is thus significantly involved in resettlement as part of its own project planning but has a circumscribed role through direct project financing.

The Review takes the opportunity, therefore, to move beyond specific project entanglements and to show that there is a need for national or sectoral *resettlement strategy* and for *policy frameworks*. In part, this conclusion stems from the finding that projects that followed the Bank's own policy guidelines performed better in resettlement terms than those that bypassed the requirements. The Bank's resettlement policy, first adopted in 1980 and then later amended, was also found to be sound, and countries with national or sector resettlement policies generally performed better in preventing impoverishment than those that lacked them. The WBR not only confirms the soundness of World Bank internal policy but also argues the need to extend the impact of the Bank's resettlement policy beyond its direct financing influence. Part of the emphasis on policy dialogue for resettlement is to help the Bank to secure changes in national legal frameworks. While resettlement is treated as subject only to property and expropriation law, it is argued, an adequate framework for *development-oriented* resettlement will not emerge (World Bank 1994a:3/2). The adoption and publication of World Bank resettlement policy guidelines also encourages other donors to adopt explicit policy norms and thus to further influence the borrower government's environment for decision-making. Furthermore, the enactment of policy frameworks for resettlement is seen as pivotal in encouraging Bank departments to help expand the borrower's institutional capacity in the context of limited direct project financing.

Finally, the search for policy reform conducive to 'resettlement-with-income-restoration' is seen as an end in itself and not as part of project conditionality or a form of focused sectoral leverage. Improved resettlement policies and legislation are required as part of a programme of 'better governance' (World Bank 1994a:3/10), and this also moves the debate on resettlement 'upstream', within the Bank's policy and operational discourses.

It is acknowledged that in some countries there is a policy vacuum. The argument in favour of policy dialogue has been countered by the contention that formal policy commitments will limit operational flexibility. The review is clear, however, that the World Bank should persevere with policy dialogue. It cites resettlement policy and implementation in China – a country with 25 per cent of the World Bank's resettlement project portfolio (1994a:4/7) – as an exemplar to be followed and a justification of the approach. Laws and regulations adopted between 1978 and 1992 protect the living standards of those people displaced. Moreover – and of crucial importance for the issues tackled in this paper – it is concluded that the establishment of general principles by national resettlement law has led to the definition of clear institutional responsibilities and the acceptance of resettlement responsibilities at national, provincial and local levels.

The major risk in resettlement is that infrastructural development and its benefits will be achieved at the cost of loss of livelihoods and incomes and the creation of poverty for the relocated populations. This is an ever-present risk because the people living in the remote or inner-city sites usually chosen for infrastructural development are already vulnerable. The risks to them arise from their social marginality – whether as farmers or indigenous people in remote areas, as urban squatters or because they have livelihoods based on the extensive use of land for pastoralism or hunter-gatherer activity.

The restoration and improvement of pre-move incomes is the ultimate test of the key WBR conclusions, and of consistency between policy norms and resettlement operations. The vehicles for income restoration and improvement are policy dialogue and the production of development plans that set out timetables relating pre-displacement incomes to incomes at agreed 'resettlement-with-development' programme stages (1994a:4/3). Cash compensation for expropriation and disruption will play its part, but land-for-land, the provision of adequate services and the restoration of gainful employment and self-employment are of even more importance in preventing impoverishment. In the case of tribal populations there is a marked need for compensatory benefits other than cash in order to prevent impoverishment.

Although Bank policy defines income restoration as a measurable goal for all resettlement operations, the WBR concludes that very few projects include adequate methods to assess whether or not income restoration is being achieved. On the whole, it concludes, as did an Operations Evaluation Department study before it, that the weight of available evidence points to unsatisfactory income restoration more frequently than to satisfactory restoration. There is particular cause for concern in the case of the Indian and Indonesian portfolios. The key explanatory variable for success in restoring livelihoods is the presence of a national commitment to help resettlers. The lack of commitment is seen in compensation packages that do not allow resettlers to purchase replacement lands, unwillingness to use institutional resources to find alternative land parcels, inadequate financial resources allocated to resettlement, institutions that lack the appropriate legal mandates and skills to assist resettlers and lack of resettler and host participation in the definition of solutions (xi-xii).

It is hard to disagree with the key message or the findings about resettlement programme performance. My own project experience suggests that the risk of impoverishment is ever-present and that actual outcomes are more often disappointing than beneficial. The key explanatory variables in the WBR – lack of borrower commitment, inadequate compensation, inadequate budgets, unhelpful legal mandates, rigid procedures and lack of consultation mechanisms – do not, however, offer fully satisfactory explanations of my own project experience. These factors are present but their interrelationships, weighting and context need more careful thought than the WBR has been able to give them.

I turn then to those case studies and show how, in the middle ground of resettlement management, policy norms are dealt with and how 'borrower ownership' turns out to be a complex of separate factors, some more amenable to reform than others. Inadequate compensation and inadequate budgetary resources – at an aggregate level, that is – did not seem of special importance for disappointing performance. Rather it was the detailed individual determinations of the resettlement plan that prompted questions of equity and survival and often triggered the unravelling of social and community supports. The executive agencies did not so much lack 'commitment' or 'resources' beyond the usual, but did lack management models and direction, legitimacy and an appropriate range of skills, especially those of conflict resolution and participatory planning. It is most important to analyse the middle ground between policy and income restoration schemes since, wrongly specified, institutional strengthening programmes for resettlement could in the short-to-medium term lead to worse, rather than improved, outcomes.

Case Studies in the Organisation of Resettlement Action

I have had the opportunity to study the organisation of resettlement components in a number of projects, sometimes working in an academic research mode, but usually as a consultant involved either in supervision or evaluation. The projects have covered reservoir, irrigation, factory and mine developments and also urban site acquisition. Much of the more detailed work has been in Asia – in the Philippines, Sri Lanka, Malaysia and India – and it is on these examples that I base my main conclusions. But I have also been involved in varying degrees in resettlement in Egypt, Kenya, Zimbabwe, the UK and, more recently through the work of Chinese researchers, in China. These other involvements give me some confidence in my conclusions based on the Asian examples.

The Philippines example involved city-centre site acquisition and the relocation of the residents to serviced lots on the outskirts of the metropolitan area. In Sri Lanka, I evaluated a reservoir development intended for hydro-power purposes but with downstream irrigated land settlement and upstream urban resettlement components. The Malaysian project also focused on hydro-power generation through reservoir development but there was, in addition, a parallel resettlement project compromising agricultural settlement based on tree cropping, reservoir fisheries, township services and rural industrial units. The Indian project has concerned major and extensive industrial development with separate site acquisitions for a factory, a mine, an industrial water supply reservoir and for (eventually) three housing and township complexes with the subsequent upgrading of services in at least three village sites.

All these examples have in common that they are infrastructure development projects with substantial land acquisition and population resettlement components. With the exception of one organisational feature that I will draw attention to later, they had very little else in common. The scale of resettlement varied considerably – from hundreds of people to some thirty thousand people relocated. The character of 'involunary-ness' in the relocation also varied – from forcible demolition of houses and relocation at one extreme, to landowners clamouring to be allowed to sell their land to the industrial development at the other. Compensation modalities also varied. In none of these cases was compensation restricted to 'cash only' – although one executive agency had immediate prior experience of it and was prepared to argue its virtues on social development grounds. There was, however, 'compensation in kind only' and mixed 'cash compensation/replacement land' packages. The four resettlement programmes involved a range of development options: land and employment-based development, an 'employment only' strategy; 'services and land only' options. The populations' responses ranged from demoralised dependency and resentment to organised resistance and active negotiation with the developers. Furthermore, the feasibility of avoiding impoverishment and community demoralisation for the resettlers also varied. In the case of the mine development, the chances were relatively good (Rew 1994:xx). In the case of the industrial water supply component, land-based solutions for the vast majority would prove elusive despite the pressing need to find replacement land since almost all the relocatees came from farming backgrounds, had limited formal educational experience and saw no valid future for them in alternative industrial employment – if, which they doubted, it could be identified.

One factor that each of the projects had in common was the considerable reluctance of key agencies to accept full responsibility for resettlement administration. There is evidence in the literature that our understanding of the risks of impoverishment for the relocatees has been growing. It is not sufficiently appreciated, however, that the risk of planning and management failure for the executive agency is also very significant . Relocation and resettlement are often highly politicised. Local groups lobby government to protest the development, delay it or to seek enhanced compensation packages and other survival options. Rural elites – acting on their own and other's behalf – try to negotiate options for the community and for groups of households and individuals using administrative and political influence and legal sanctions if possible to do so. In some cases, politicians try to mediate – on behalf of groups and/or individuals. This is a high profile and very risky environment within which to try to manage outcomes that are almost bound to disappoint some sections of national or international opinion. The public scrutiny and remedial nature of the tasks also mean that the opportunities to benefit from the usual privileges and rents often associated with public office are few.

In each case, plans were drawn up, whether for physical rehabilitation, for downstream agricultural development or for other means of employment. The failures or difficulties, when they came, were largely in the area of direction and management. Development blueprints and schema – of various levels of sophistication in dealing with the resettlement challenges – that had been arrived at during appraisal provided frameworks of intention but often lacked bite because of the management and implementing staff's lack of clear direction or of the skills needed to resource and adjust the plans.

Many of the difficulties in development management that were faced were generic. Israel (1987), for example, notes the intensity of management that is needed when the organisation's tasks are inherently difficult to specify. The multifaceted, highly emotional and politicised nature of relocation requires particular management skills, intensity and flexibility.

Resettlement management in the case of the projects I report here was seen as a task beset with unusual difficulty. Part of the frequent phenomenon of 'poor government commitment' indeed comes from this *high difficulty and risk* for the implementing agencies. Administrators become especially risk-adverse in such a difficult political and policy climate.

Another typical cause of poor commitment by government bureau arises from a major gap in perspectives and trust. This gap sometimes has an ethnic character and sometimes it involves the contrasted views of resource-poor rural residents and urban professionals. In one of my project cases, there was a major gap in perspectives between the urban resident, ethnic Chinese engineers who were responsible for the project's design and implementation and the resettlers who were indigenous shifting cultivators with a long tradition of riverine and forest dwelling. Considerable anger and resentment was generated, not because of initial ill-will, exploitativeness or incompetence on the part of the engineers, but because these highly qualified professionals made critical mistakes through their inability to put themselves in the shoes of the rural residents. Thus there is always the strong possibility of a deficit in the *legitimacy* of management actions arising from the gap in perspectives and the consequent distrust of implementer's intentions and skills.

Even where there are no obvious ethnic or comparable major differences, conventional local administration can also face major legitimacy deficits because of histories of rent-seeking on the part of field and other administrators. Local-level officials may have reputations of being especially corrupt and under the influence of rural elites, whatever the nature of the reforms from the capital city (see Blair 1978 for a powerful argument about the persistence of local-level class relations in Bangladesh). In one of my cases, the resettlers resisted what some saw as quite a favourable outcome until it became clear that their resistance was less to the solution proposed than to the involvement of the sub-district administrator who was, like his tribe, known to delay paperwork unless he was given a substantial 'present'.

Cutting across routine resettlement decision-making was the strong possibility of explicit or tacit *vetoes by powerful interests*. Otherwise desirable reforms or operational actions were blocked by the need to satisfy a web of interests lying beyond the immediate project stakeholders. In one case the satisfactory relocation of a hamlet of tribal and low-caste people was thwarted because the landowners on whose land they resided, to whom they were indebted and for whom they worked, refused to allow an improvement in the tribals' living standards while they continued 'unimproved'. They were very far away and all attempts failed, leaving a most unsatisfactory compromise that failed to reach the agreed environmental and social development norms and standards that had been agreed. In other cases, the vetoes emanate from indirectly related ministries and departments whose stakes in the project did not seem sufficiently direct to involve them from the outset, but whose reservations in implementation prove difficult to manage. Pragmatic solutions to on-site problems are vetoed because it is feared that although feasible in this one case, they will set precedents that will create difficulties elsewhere.

Perhaps the key variable creating low levels of commitment is *lack of direction*. It could be argued that an agreed legal and policy framework would set the context for project-level management and resolve many of the uncertainties that seem to beset project staff. It could be argued that clear rules agreed at national and sectoral level would frame subsequent decision-making so that project staff and resettlers would have no choice but to agree to the implementation decisions. My experience of the cases quoted above shows that while the national framework was far from ideal, I doubt that its optimisation would have led to easy implementation arrangements. Indeed, I fear that in some cases a more sharply defined national or sectoral policy would strengthen the hands of project staff when forcing through decisions that may not have been always for the best. In other words, 'institutional strengthening' may well be at the cost of 'improved consultation and participation'.

The main uncertainties come as soon as the project implementation comes close to local-level realities and tries to take them on board, and as it tries to devise procedural linkages to ensure that these local specificities and linkages can be administered and accommodated. Indeed, it is the complex and changing multiple relationships between, usually, highly differentiated local populations and differentiated administrative and consultative mechanisms that makes resettlement difficult to manage. The complexity of community to management relations, public sector linkages and flows and the accelerated change of a time-bound development project are difficult for resettlement administrations to model and predict. It is easy for them to lose sight of the many possible responses and trade-offs, and hard for them to know how to coordinate the many and varied administrative demands and procedural linkages that are required.

Each resettlement scheme serves to highlight the great number of social and economic activities and exchanges that exist at local levels. The announcement of the project boundaries threatens to unravel some of these links immediately as people recalculate their choices and options. At the same time, the resettlement management takes on a potentially highly significant role in disaggregating resources in anticipation of individual and community needs and then packaging those resources in terms of eligibilities for service that have to be adjusted to the circumstances of the relocatees and have to be administered in detail. The variety of detailed tasks that usually have to be performed for any one of the resettlement modalities is daunting, especially when set in terms of usually pressing deadlines.

Compensation payments can often continue in dispute for some time after the infrastructure works have been completed. In one case, reservoir flooding had taken place before the inventory of tree crops could be completed, since the surveyors had underestimated the level of disputed surveys and the number of second thoughts on other assets to be taken into account. They simply fell behind schedule in the more distant parts of the reservoir bed; simultaneously, the civil engineering component had made more rapid progress than anticipated, so that a choice had to be made whether or not to flood a season earlier than planned – and so bring forward anticipated benefits. A set of compromise compensation payments were then agreed, which served to add further weight to the claims among the resettler community that there were difficult-to-understand inequities in the compensation payments and that the work of the surveyors was suspect.

At the same time, following compensation determinations, actual payments have to be made and new village areas have to be surveyed and allocated to resettler families in some way and the actual process of relocation and new villages and townships planned and contracted. Often this will involve coordinating the work of a number of bureau – surveys, land titles, finance or treasury offices, public works, transport, district administration – or the equivalent departments and sections within a single resettlement organisation.

The arrangements for coordinating inter-agency actions and the procedures governing the detailed allocations to resettlers do provide the *administrative and management fabric* of the resettlement policy for that country or sector. Even if there is no formal policy on resettlement, an administrative and management fabric will nonetheless provide the glue that will determine the resettlement outcomes and the extent to which impoverishment increases or reduces. In the major countries of South and East Asia, there will already be existing schemes for comprehensive area development, rural and urban rehousing, agricultural intensification, marginal land development and the promotion of small firms and household enterprises. As we know, some land acquisition and population displacement actions simply provide cash compensation and then refer the displaced households to the existing economic development and welfare services. If there is a specific resettlement project or a resettlement policy, it will inevitably need to determine whether to reproduce and repackage elements of the existing schemes and administrations to suit its own purposes and timetables. Alternatively, resettlement programmes can function by coordinating blocked, resettlement programme demands on the existing services. The most distinctive aspect of a resettlement project is the intensity of new demands in a specific geographical setting; it is unlikely that the optimum physical, social development and economic development services provided from scratch for a resettlement scheme will be wholly dissimilar to the existing services provided for the population at large.

Possible Organisational Models for Implementation

My own project involvements suggest that there can be no escape from the need to address the organisational framework for service provision. Furthermore, effective action requires flexibility and a recognition that any organisational framework has both benefits and costs. In Table 12.1 I summarise the range of organisational models used in my case studies and the main implications for the style within which development outcomes can be managed. The extent to which the case study projects used the models listed varied considerably.

The land acquisition for urban-services programme I researched in the Philippines relied wholly on Model A. An initial plan was drafted at municipal level; the police services supervised the clearing of the inner-city sites; the municipality provided the transport for the relocation of families and building materials; the social welfare department coordinated initial assistance to the resettlers; the housing authority administered the consolidation of the physical fabric of the new settlement.

The relocation and resettlement was carried out with minimum administrative cost and without the duplication of services. Nonetheless, there was poor overall coordination, in part because each service failed to interest itself in the details that applied to the others and no one body was especially responsible for coordination requirements, although there were formally designated lead agencies for various stages. There was considerable and unnecessary distress for the resettlers at the beginning and major administrative problems in the later stages of the settlement-scheme when it became clear that the record-keeping system could not provide the information required about the crucial handover periods. Experience has shown that Model A does not cope well with the unusual pressures and timescales of major population displacement. Nonetheless, there are attractive features. Use of Model A does not involve many additional costs, nor does it segregate and marginalise the resettlers or make them dependent on project management. If a way could be found to build in capacity to direct and manage the initial intensive period of relocation and to consult with resettlers over their many and varied initial needs during this period, then a modified Model A would have the benefits of sustainability.

A mining and industrial development I monitored and helped supervise in Rajasthan used Model B. The project was being implemented by a national engineering corporation with some external assistance in specific technical areas, including in resettlement planning. Once the resettlement options were explained and arguments were accepted that cash compensation alone would not solve either the social and economic development problems of the resettlers or the project timetabling needs of the engineering, the corporation proceeded to manage all inputs as part of a multi-faceted engineering scheme with critical paths and appropriate contracting arrangements, all specified and well-managed. The contracting arrangements for relocation and physical rehabilitation were no less well managed than those for road construction.

In the Sri Lankan project, the organisation of resettlement assessment and services moved through a series of stages that resembled the use of Models B, A, E and D in sequence. Confirmation of resettlement requirements was undertaken by international engineering consultants in liaison with, and after initial assessment by, the normal agencies of civil administration. As resettlement proceeded these arrangements proved unsatisfactory and a special resettlement manager was identified and recruited. He then used his influence and networks to call upon a range of contracted services. Eventually, this specialised but essentially 'task force' organisation evolved into a parallel project organisation that administered resettlers' service requirements as a specialised problem.

The virtues of Models B and C are also their vices. Intensive project management and intensive political commitment can both solve the problem of coordinating a multiplicity of tasks against urgent timetables, although they do so in highly contrasted ways. They are not designed to manage the resettler citizen's routine and continuing access to services or the resettler community's re-integration into the surrounding civil society. Thus the Malaysian project was completed ahead of time using Model C, with a major reduction of engineering costs and the stream of hydro-power benefits brought forward as a result. The phase of intensive political support inevitably wound down with the completion of the major works, and the new settlement component was left with integrating information provided, on the hoof and unrecorded, by high-level politicians and policy-makers. The resettlement component was, as a result, very disappointing.

Table 12.1 Organisational Models Used to Implement Resettlement Components

Model	Management Structure and Style
A. Sequencing of defined tasks through separate executive agencies.	A. Containment and routinised management through conventional public administration available to all citizens.
B. Multi-faceted engineering managed by a single engineering entity or firm.	B. Intensive technical planning and limited duration management of the project component.
C. Coordination of all stakeholders through a high-level committee.	C. Intensive, highly pragmatic and non-routinised political management of the interests voiced by varied bureau, firms and community groups.
D. Parallel project management through a separate relocation and rehabilitation agency.	D. semi-permeable routines, designs and long-range management by a specialised authority providing specialised resettlement services and monitoring within the resettlement enclave, but also repackaging elements of services available to all citizens.
E. Specialised sponsorhip plus contracting arrangement for individual services.	E. Centralised regulation and monitoring and the funding and contracting of competetive service delivery from poublic sector, NGO and private-sector suppliers.

The mining resettlement in Rajasthan has worked well, provided the resettlers can maintain links with the mining and processing company and provided the company continues to extend the benefits of company township services to the resettlers (Rew 1994). Model B works well in this context because the company dominates the local economy and employment. It is less appropriate in terms of the aims of the engineering unit when there is a phase of civil engineering design and construction followed by a phase of resettlement administration, as in the case of many hydro-power developments. But the model also works reasonably well in the context of irrigation scheme development where a high proportion of the irrigated lands settlers have been relocated from the non-irrigated lands of the area.

Perhaps the main challenge to resettlement programme adminis-tration comes in the form anticipated in the WBR. High population densities and major and cumulative infrastructure development will increasingly occur in regions with few options for further land-based development if the existing agricultural technologies are employed. In these cases, the normal services of the society must be used to their full *through careful administrative planning* and through the encourage-ment of small firms and household enterprises. This is not as easy task, and not too much must be expected; the challenge to avoid impov-erishment and even to reduce poverty will be especially taxing.

Such a challenge is found in the industrial Indian case study – it has used a combination of Model B and some elements of Model E. That is, it first approached the task of resettlement management through multi-faceted engineering but has had to evolve other man-agement methods involving the contracting out and indirect man-agement of the social development aspects.

It became clear, early on, that its engineering staff were frightened and anxious at the level of overt hostility in the area to be cleared and had discontinued all but token field visits. It had also become clear to the residents and to the authority that there were in fact few devel-opment options available to meet all the resettlers' income needs. The population was much larger than first anticipated – perhaps four-teen villages rather than three; administrative responsibilities were highly confused because of a change of status for a proposed reser-voir from irrigation water supply to industrial water supply; there were few available large agricultural land parcels within reach of the project area; there was a large supply of skilled industrial labour in the area and little scope to employ resettled farmers. There was some scope for reservoir fisheries but, in the general area, fishing is seen as a tribal and low-caste occupation. Those expressions of interest received from the settlers were from higher-caste groups who wanted to organise reservoir fisheries, but would use mainly outside labour to do so. Some better-placed resettlers could, for a period, rely on their traditional occupations as stone-masons and builders and so contribute to the growth in infrastructure in the rapidly growing region. The employment of the great majority was in doubt unless, using their cash compensation, they were to participate in household enterprise, develop small firms or intensify their farming through unfamiliar agricultural technologies.

In these circumstances, a resettlement development programme could only resort to two strategies: the administration of improved access to available, existing opportunities for gainful employment and building self-confidence and self-reliance through the mobilisation of energies and social bases for community development and business enterprise.

In order to implement such a programme, the programme management would need skills in small enterprise development and, for example, awareness of the national Indian experience in implementing household enterprise promotion under the IRDP. An evaluation of this national programme found that it was least successful in giving access to credit for women producers and that training and marketing support were needed before IRDP could effectively support employment ventures by women and the poor (Crow 1992:257).

It is at this point that Model D becomes interesting but also shows it weaknesses. A challenge of the kind just described is certainly not consistent with the styles of Models A, B or C. There will, therefore, be a temptation to use Model D since it allocates responsibility to one public sector entity that will be held accountable for the results and could claim to provide that link in the 'synergy between policies, organisations and resources' that the WBR defines as local institutional capacity. Since this agency will have extensive project management and also regulatory and spending powers, it will inevitably need its own technical staff and a special administrative authority – perhaps as a special department or as a parastatal.

However, bodies of this kind are rarely suited to carry out the empowerment and networking activities which the project case study above suggests are necessary if impoverishment is to be avoided. First, there is the inherent constraint that organisations within the public sector will need, for public scrutiny and familiarity reasons, to be *instrumental* organisations that are commanded from the top and within which instructions are carried out with minimal distortion. The organisation is a piece of state machinery that is available to work for whoever is currently in political control – it must therefore be predictable and accountable. This framework or model may work reasonably well in the invariably complex and changing circumstances of a resettlement programme provided that the key officers are aware that they themselves must be creative and flexible, can command a wide range of specialists to give them advice and can translate the actions of their subordinates into messages that are accepted as politically valid. In this way they can both order compliance from their subordinates and provide liaison and policy advice to their political masters. These are skills that most senior public servants have acquired and perform well.

A public-sector resettlement management unit is far less effective, however, in coordinating relationships with the other agencies or bureau within the set of 'resettlement policy' institutions that must be kept in the picture or involved. Even where the resettlement parastatal is identified as the lead agency and its head given the appropriate senior rank, there will continue to be difficulties in liaison since lateral and subordinate bureau have many ways of resisting and refusing compliance if they wish to do so. Nor are parastatal authorities noted for their skills in linking community groups or the range of corporate and community stakeholders that might be resources for firm and enterprise promotion. Inter-agency and inter-stakeholder relations are complex and marked by negotiation, bargaining and a great deal of strategic behaviours, not by the instrumentalities and command relationships of the public sector organisation. Indeed, for these reasons many of the constituent activities of resettlement development seem better suited to organisations in the NGO or private sectors.

Model E may therefore be the most appropriate organisational vehicle for the increasingly circumscribed development-induced displacements reviewed in WBR. In the case of the Indian industrial project displacement I describe here, the bulk of the displaced farm population may have to find employment outside of low-technology agricultural cultivation. This constraint drastically circumscribes the viability of a development programme that can avoid impoverishment for certain households and a radical change of occupation for many others. The implementing agency took the project so far using a Model B approach. It recognised, however, that it lacked the experience or in-house skills necessary for it to deal with the severe stress placed on the community, to resolve the conflicts between the community and itself and state government or to deal with the long process of repair to the social fabric of the community that would be required. As a result of this recognition it commissioned a local NGO with social survey, social work, community development and business development skills to work in liaison with its engineering managers but essentially according to a programme devised by the social development specialists themselves. In the same manner, it contracted the fisheries bureau and fisheries consultants to set up a strategy for reservoir fisheries development that would maximise local involvement.

The quality of coordination using this model was extremely good. I had feared that the agreement to contract out the social development work might have led the project managers to a purely formal processing of the recommendations. This was not so; the recommendations were taken extremely seriously, and there was a serious exchange of perspectives that lead to the improved implementation of decisions. Furthermore, it led to a welcome organisational response on the part of the engineers. When the contractor organisations began the work, it was found that a relatively junior and unnoticed engineer proved extremely effective in communicating with the villagers and winning their trust. The result was that the project management unit felt more confident and trustful of the work and cooperated enthusiastically, even though the engineers had been, initially, very anxious about community attitudes. As implementation proceeded, this young engineer, despite his status, played a key role in linking advice on social and physical rehabilitation. Indeed, his lack of rank proved a bonus because it signalled that participation mechanisms need not rely on hierarchy but could recognise creative energy.

Recommendations

This chapter ends with recommendations rather than conclusions since my aim has been, hopefully, more practical than theoretical. The recommendations are also mainly to the World Bank Environment Department, although they were not specifically invited as such. They are made to stimulate further reflection by that department on the organisational implications of resettlement policy. Its very important Review of the resettlement features of the last decade of World Bank projects ensures the Review's place as a benchmark document. The key message that impoverishment through displacement can be offset by coherent development programming is welcome, since it will presumably lead to the synergy of policy, organisations and resources mentioned in the Review and will be especially welcome if that synergy can be directed to counter the poor commitment that is also frequently mentioned.

World Bank staff have made a number of notable contributions to institutional analysis and participatory planning in recent years that can be employed to guide resettlement planning. Of particular importance is an understanding of 'institutional policy sets' when trying to make sense of the interplay between organisational responsiblities, policy and political commitment. Inter-agency relations play a major role in the functioning of complex modern state systems, and we need to understand the way in which sets of these relations and the linkages and bargaining within them determine *policy outcomes* – which may be very different from policy statements about aims and intentions. The detail of the case studies I have outlined in this paper, for example, was subject to the influence of vetoes by cooperating departments and lack of direction because of disagreement about effective action. There was no especial difficulty in getting agreement on principles.

A first recommendation, therefore, that flows from this account of project experience is that the administrative planning of resettlement action, based on a good knowledge of existing and feasible responsibilities, is a prerequisite for effective policy advice. It is crucial to know what can feasibly be implemented as a guide to feasible policy targets. Too often, governments embark on infrastructure development and population displacement schemes without the careful planning of responsibilities that would be seen as essential in schemes for industrial production. My advice to borrower governments and to aid donors is: 'if you cannot write down the main set of administrative responsibilities for all resettlement modalities and how they are to be discharged, do not undertake the project'.

Second, this administrative planning should be presented as *visionary* and should not be seen as mundane or dauntingly technical, as Michael Cernea (1993b:30-31) fears will happen. A detailed ethnographic and management awareness of social, economic and political processes within dislocated societies should lead to a more far-sighted and robust understanding of the set of socio-therapeutic and technical skills needed in development resettlement planning and management. Many of these skills are indeed social development and ethnographic skills, since the critical element in rehabilitation is repair to the social fabric torn by the threat of displacement and then further ripped by distrust of government officials and often distrust of their own leaders. Planes of cleavage can easily develop within the community as resistance and accommodation to external pressures both proceed, sometimes with resettler leaders taking one role and then another. In these circumstances the social exchanges and ties that underpin the economies of many of these communities also break down with disastrous material consequences. Radical distrust and impoverishment are both frequent results. Resettlement management must therefore include skills in conflict resolution within the community at risk of impoverishment, coupled with facilitation skills to encourage residents to voice their needs and to put pressure on decision-makers to provide adequate information, compensation and alternative livelihood supports.

Third, any guidelines on resettlement policy and organisation should contain advice on the appropriate *language* of resettlement management. The language of policy optimism in the WBR should not obscure Aberle's point referred to at the beginning of this paper that resettlement is always a tragedy of varying degrees since it is the powerless who are being moved from their homes. The WBR does recognise this point when it refers to the dismantling of social ties and recognises that relocation is a process of disorganisation and, frequently, the restriction of opportunities at a time when better-placed social groups and categories are benefitting from infrastructure development and renovation. Special emphasis should be given to the way that displacement can corrode community relations and lead to distrust of all development interventions and to the selection of a style of discussion that recognises this conclusion. This adjustment of language is already underway (Cernea 1993: 30).

Fourth, the WBR urges that commentators do not lose themselves in case-by-case analyses but rise to the policy-level when considering resettlement options. My own recommendation is contrary to this advice. It is that analysis must start with the detail of options and processes in each case. Resettlement planning is essentially an ethnographic and management task in which legal and policy principles have an important role to play, but not as important at field level as they may seem in the context of donor-borrower policy dialogues.

My final recommendation is that further detailed analysis of the organisational models appropriate to resettlement should be undertaken by the World Bank. There is a considerable resource in institutional analysis in the Bank, and it would be most useful to see the WBR extended to consider how policy is best implemented. From my own experience I suggest that some detailed evidence on good practice and risks should be prepared and disseminated so that resettlement managers and administrators can better decide if they do want to raise the level of their commitment in the interests of a feasible set of resettlement objectives. At present I fear that the optimism in the WBR is a little too upstream in policy terms to counter the public sector manager's image of resettlement planning as a hornets' nest of problems.

13

Impoverishment Risks' Analysis

A METHODOLOGICAL TOOL FOR PARTICIPATORY RESETTLEMENT PLANNING

Sam Thangaraj

Introduction

Development-induced displacement and the resettlement and rehabilitation of displaced people (DPs) are two aspects of the process of development in a developing country like India. This is because of the very real needs for irrigation, electricity and infrastructure that are necessary for development.

The World Bank's resettlement policy, while taking into consideration the human-rights perspective, aims to resettle and rehabilitate the displaced and the project-affected persons (PAPs) with the provision of an appropriate and adequate 'resource base' such as land, and with a view to 'improve or at least restore' their incomes and livelihoods. For such a policy to be effective, I argue that it needs to be complemented by a methodological 'model' which could analyse, anticipate and articulate the risks of displacement and become a management and participatory tool for resettlement planning and the attainment of the Bank's policy objectives of restoring, and over a period improving, incomes and livelihoods, better housing with civic amenities and access to health care and education.

Cernea's 'impoverishment risks' analysis model (see Chapter Two) provides one tool for planners, other development practitioners and, of equal importance, relocated people themsleves, to analyse the impoverishment involved in development-induced displacement and to work towards sustainable redevelopment by consciously counteracting the anticipated and predictable risks.

This chapter aims to explain how the 'impoverishment risks' analysis model can be usefully used as a planning tool so that risks could be mitigated and/or avoided when planning for resettlement and rehabilitation. As stated earlier, the 'impoverishment risks' model has been devised to understand the complexity of the impoverishment process which, according to Cernea, is of particular importance because:

> the analysis of the vast evidence coming up from numerous displacement and resettlement processes reveals patterns of recurrent characteristics. While each one of these characteristics is distinct and irreducible to the others, they have a common denominator: all are dimensions of a multifaceted process of impoverishment. These characteristics may be linked into a coherent typology or descriptive model of impoverishment risks through displacement. Such a conceptualisation, or descriptive model, is a tool usable in strategy formulation and a device for practical planning, in that it points to the key sets of ill-effects that actual projects must purposely avoid.

The findings presented here are drawn from research and activities undertaken in a number of Bank-assisted projects in India, including the Upper Indravati Hydro-electric Project, Orissa Water Resources Consolidation Project (WRCP) and the Tamil Nadu Water Resources Consolidation Project where the model has been applied in both evaluation and project planning. I present the findings by looking at each of the levels of risk identified in the model and assess what action needs to be taken to best couteract the risk of impoverishment. The analysis reveals the inter-relatedness of the processes invloved and the usefulness of this model as a tool for participatory rural appraisal.

The Case Study

This case study is based on the Hariharjore sub-project of Orissa WRCP and Upper Indravati Hydroelectric Project.[1]

1. The importance of the use 'impoverishment risks' analysis was discussed with, among others, Anita Agnihotri, Additional Secretary, Department of Water Resources, and Mr. R.L. Jamuda, Additional Secretary, Department of Energy, of the Government of Orissa (GoO), Pradeep Jena, the Resettlement and Rehabilitation Officer (RRO) of the Resettlement and Rehabilitation Unit (RRU) and the staff of the Government's RRU. In Tamil Nadu WRCP, this was discussed with R.N. Krishnan, Project Management Group, Public Works Department, Government of Tamil Nadu. They all appreciated the need to carry out 'impoverishment risks' analysis so that such risks could be prevented while planning for the resettlement and rehabilitation of the displaced persons.

Landlessness

In total, 89.50 ha. of *patta* (title) lands were acquired from eighteen families ranging from 0.53 ha. to 29.90 ha. Of the eighteen families, twelve lost less than 2.00 ha. of land; one family lost 29.90 ha.; while two lost about 14 ha. of land each. The quality of these lands varied.

To prevent the risks of landlessness after displacement and relocation, compensation was paid to those displaced for the *patta* lands. The compensation included the 'market value' of the land, 30 per cent of that amount as solatium because of compulsory acquisition, and 12 per cent annual interest for the period of delay in the payment of compensation from the date of the publication of Section 4(i) notification to the date of payment.

However, it is known that cash compensation alone is often insufficient to prevent landlessness. Therefore, as part of rehabilitation, all displaced persons, including 'major' sons (over eighteen years of age), were provided 1.25 acres of irrigated land, the quality of which varied, as most of the lands were degraded and needed reclamation before they could become fully productive. It is obvious from this that landlessness is a very serious problem that contributes to the impoverishment of displaced communities over a period, as this would affect their resource base, livelihood and income.

Landlessness in Hariharjore can be compared with the Upper Indravati Hydro-electric Project, for which *patta*, revenue and forest lands had been acquired. According to the socio-economic study carried out the Centre for Education, Research and Training (CENDERET) of the Xavier Institute of Management (Bhubaneswar) based on the genealogy methodology, landlessness had been a major problem of the displaced community prior to their displacement. For instance, of the 4,119 displaced persons studied, only 559 (14 per cent) had land. Of these, 373 (67 per cent) had *patta* in their names, 154 (28 per cent) had joint *patta* while 32 (6 per cent) had individual and joint *patta* land. Many of the displaced persons also had access to forest land for *podu* (shifting) cultivation. The average land holdings were rather small: the average land holding of *patta* land was less than 2.5 acres and the average forest land holding less than 2 acres.

The Government of Orissa's (GoO) initial plan in 1989 was to resettle the displaced persons in such a way that they could be pro-

---

The use of 'impoverishment risks' analysis has also been recommended to other project managers and consultants who are responsible for planning, implementation and monitoring of resettlement and rehabilitation action plans. It is hoped that the use of 'impoverishment risks' analysis would become a regular feature of future planning.

vided with land-based rehabilitation in areas it had selected in the command area of Upper Indravati. This became difficult to implement, as those affected were very keen on resettling on their own initiative, moving closer to the forest and their relatives. The GoO finally agreed to finance the purchase of 1.25 acres of irrigated land or 2.5 acres of unirrigated land to each displaced person at the site of his choice. A total sum of 81.21 million rupees was spent by GoO to provide land to those displaced as a basic resource base. At present, 4,351 out of 5,344 people have either 1.25 acres of irrigated land or 2.5 acres of unirrigated land. The remaining have money in the bank to purchase land. Considering that most of these people were previously landless, this has given them the basic resource base on which efforts for the restoration of their livelihood could be built, by providing them further economic-rehabilitation assistance so that their income and living standards would further improve.

Loss of Access to Common Property

The risk of landlessness would have been greater if the displaced persons' loss of access to common property, governed by a land tenure system such as *podu* cultivation, was also taken into consideration when assessing land loss. Until the use of 'impoverishment risks' analysis, the assessment of the extent of the landlessness of the project-affected people had been limited only to calculating the loss of land due to land acquisition.

Almost all families in tribal areas use forest land for *podu* cultivation and also depend on forest for non-timber produce. The forest land or the village common land, though not owned by families, customarily belongs to the village clans or the lineage group. These common property resources are used or occupied on the basis of usufruct or similar occupation-based tenure and not based on ownership. Therefore, the extent of landlessness goes far beyond the *patta* holders and their *patta* land. However, families who depend on such common properties are not entitled to payment of compensation. Nevertheless, because of the need to prevent the risks that result as a consequence of loss of access to common property, those who depend on them have a way of coping with such risks on their own.

For example, the displaced families of Upper Indravati Hydro-electric Project have proven how important it is to prevent the risk of loss of access to common property. Though the GoO had planned to resettle them in the command area of the project so that they could enjoy the benefits of irrigation, the displaced families, as a community, decided to resettle in clusters closer to the forest so that they could reduce the risk of no longer enjoying access to the forest and could continue to have access to firewood, fodder and non-timber produce as well as timber. According to the CENDERET study, out of the 4,110 people surveyed, 3,711 (91 per cent) had access to fuel wood, 2,913 (71 per cent) to fodder, 2,596 (63 per cent) to timber and 3,553 (56 per cent) to non-timber produce. In order to further compensate for the loss of access to common property, the Resettlement and Rehabilitation Unit (RRU) of the project planned also to undertake social forestry programmes closer to some resettlement clusters where lands are available.

Joblessness

In the case of Gania, joblessness could be defined as the loss of employment opportunities created through the collecting of non-timber produce, share cropping and the working of individual's land, and employment arising from *podu* cultivation. Joblessness became a wide-spread problem affecting the income of the displaced people to the extent that the average annual income prior to the displacement was higher than it is today. According to the displaced, it has fallen to an amount between 7,000 rupees and 11,000 rupees, which is below the recognised 'poverty line'.

Joblessness also means that those who were owners of the means of production have now become wage earners. At present, eighteen resettled people are working as construction workers at the dam site. Thirty-seven people work as agricultural labourers in the villages close to the Littipalli Rehabilitation Colony where they have been resettled. In addition the collection of *kendu* leaves provides employment to all displaced persons for at least forty-five days a year.

There has been little change in the number of wage earners before and after displacement associated with the Upper Indravati project. There were 2,457 wage earners before displacement and 2,336 after. The low acreage of holding meant that the demand for extra labour has fallen. One hundred and seventy-eight of the resettled initially had jobs due to the project and this has now increased to one hundred and ninety. There are thirty-four who have regular employment outside the project. The RRU is now planning to provide productive assets and training to improve the productive skills of the displaced. These efforts may contribute to the creation of further employment opportunities.

Homelessness

The risk of homelessness is a very important one, as it causes displacement, loss of access to sources of livelihood and also affects social and community relations. To prevent the risk of relocated peo-

ple remaining without shelter and homes, the resettlement plan entitled each household to 0.20 acre of homestead land at 16,000 rupees
per acre in addition to 17,000 rupees towards the construction of a
house. As a result, sixty-one of the 108 displaced people of Gania
had resettled in Littipalli Rehabilitation Colony. The others had
gone off on their own to resettle.

The sixty-one displaced persons had been provided with homestead plots, along with 5,000 rupees out of 17,000 rupees. Most of the
displaced had spent the sum to meet their consumption needs, and
the quality of the mud houses built was poor. The rehabilitation
colony also had been provided with two hand pumps, a water tank,
classrooms and an approach road. In this case it would seem sensible to link the payment of the remaining 12,000 rupees with the construction of houses, to ensure the construction of quality dwellings as
in the Upper Indravati Project.

The number of displaced persons in Upper Indravati is 5,344, of
whom a vast majority are 'major' sons. Of the 4,119 studied, 3,433 are
'major' children and 658 are widows. It is clear from the findings of
the study that of the 4,119 displaced, 1,124 (27.3 per cent) live in their
own house, 1,571 (38.1 per cent) in their own house built on
encroached land, 954 (23.2 per cent) in their own house but on relatives' land, while 347 (8.4 per cent) live in the house of their relatives.
While some live in houses built on land that belongs to temples and
landlords, only 19 (0.5 per cent) live in a rented house. Though many
of them live without access to electricity, they do have civic amenities
and access to social infrastructure. It is important to point out that the
quality of construction of the houses that the community of the displaced has built is by far better than those found in the host villages.

This is an example of successful housing and resettlement where
a major risk, homelessness, has been reversed with the active participation of the displaced who chose their own resettlement sites, in
which the RRU of the project played a very active and supportive
role. The provision of 3,200 rupees for the purchase of homestead
land and 17,000 rupees for the construction of a house is also a casual
factor for reversing the risk so successfully.

Marginalisation

Marginalisation is here described as a severe erosion in the economic condition of households and often overlaps with landlessness,
joblessness and homelessness. In Sagjuri village of the Hariharjore
Medium Project area, there were ninety-three marginal farmers prior
to displacement. Their condition was worsened after displacement
and thirty-seven of them became landless. It was interesting to note,

however, that a minority of farmers – albeit a small minority – did make effective use of the compensation and other financial resources to purchase land to avoid marginalisation.

In Upper Indravati Project, even though a large number of the displaced were provided with land as a basic resource base, many of them remain marginalised, as the land is only sufficient to enable them to maintain their subsistence level. It is likely that this would change if they were helped further with other productive assets, sources of income and training to improve their skills, particularly women, in accordance with the 'cluster-based and family-oriented' Rehabilitation Action Plan which the RRU has prepared.

Food Insecurity

Food insecurity among displaced communities is the result of loss of land, livelihood, income and, in Littipalli, the loss of access to the forest from which they harvested tubers, fruits, plants, leaves, etc. The loss of cultivated land has affected food production and also the pattern of food consumption. The displaced women have little control over the money that has come in as compensation and rehabilitation assistance, and as the men who have the money tend to spend it on their own consumption needs, the women's ability to provide food has been reduced. This, in particular, affects their children.

Though the displaced have been provided with some land and the government has initiated a kitchen garden scheme, these measures need to be further supplemented so that their sources of livelihood and incomes are improved and their ability to purchase food increased. In Upper Indravati, for example, the risk of food insecurity of the displaced people has been addressed by the RRU of the project at two levels. Prior to displacement, the average landholding of *patta* land was less than 2.5 acres and the average forest landholding was less than 2 acres. In an attempt to accelerate the process of restoring the livelihoods of the displaced, the government planned to provide them with land in the command area of Upper Indravati.

However, the displaced people rejected the government's plan and decided to resettle on their own. The government subsequently decided to offer each displaced person either 1.25 acres of irrigated land or 2.5 acres of unirrigated land. As stated earlier, out of the 5,344 displaced persons, 4,351 have either 1.25 acres of irrigated land or 2.5 acres of unirrigated land. The remaining have money in the bank and are looking for land for purchase. Now that these displaced people have a basic land resource base, the RRU is planning to complement this with efforts for restoration of their livelihood. As a package of measures, they should increase the food security of the displaced families.

On another level, the RRU, with the active participation of AGRAGAMEE, a local NGO has organised Participatory Public Distribution Centres in many resettlement clusters, through which the displaced are provided essential commodities such as rice, sugar and kerosene. AGRAGAMEE has also enabled the resettled population in some villages to organise Grain Banks to meet their needs when the requirements for energy are high and the availability of food low. The children and pregnant mothers also enjoy the benefits of the nutrition programme of the Integrated Child Development Services. All these have contributed towards reducing the risk of food insecurity.

Morbidity

Displacement and involuntary resettlement in temporary shelters, lack of adequate food and unhygienic living and environmental conditions have adverse impacts on the health of the displaced. This is particularly true for women, children and the aged in Hariharjore project area in general, and Littipalli Rehabilitation Colony in particular. Malaria, diarrhoea, and skin diseases are some of the health problems faced by the displaced.

Health implications of involuntary resettlement were assessed in the Upper Indravati Project area. According to preliminary observations, morbidity and mortality were high due to diarrhoeal diseases, respiratory illnesses and malaria. Malnutrition was prevalent among the children in the age group of one to three years. The awareness of prevention of diseases was low among the displaced. An interesting aspect of the observations was that the fertility rate of tribal women was also low after displacement.

In order to minimise morbidity and to meet the health-care needs of the displaced people, the RRU is organising immunisation camps and also mobile health services in cooperation with the primary health centres in the area. Such measures have to be further strengthened with increased access to health care and health education if they are to improve the health of resettled populations.

Social Disarticulation

Social and kinship relations enable a group of people to remain a community, because they provide the bond that helps its members overcome periods of time beset with economic and social problems. Such relations also provide mutual help arrangements, labour exchange relationships, production-oriented informal organisations, etc. All these are very severely affected and often lost in the process of displacement, and such loss has implications for the ability of the community to manage its socio-economic and even cultural affairs due, in large part, to the weakening of traditional authority, leadership and social control.

In the Littipali Rehabilitation Colony, which is 7 kilometres from the main road, social disarticulation has occured because the resettled population was depived of the linkages with others and the loss of socio-economic status. The payment of compensation and rehabilitation assistance to 'major' sons appears also to have affected families and in particular the family support to vulnerable members of the family, notably the aged. The emotional bond which held the families together no longer exists, as the need for survival is greater than any other concern, and money is considered vital for survival.

The women of the *chasa* community, who have never worked in the fields because of their higher economic status, have now been reduced to the status of agricultural labourers due to the loss of their lands. Lack of quality housing, access to common resources, and the sense of inferiority and insecurity have markedly affected their relations with the host community resulting, in visible signs of social disarticulation.

It is interesting to see that social disarticulation, a very common risk of displacement, is not a problem today in Upper Indravati, though it did cause anxiety and trauma to the displaced persons at the time of displacement. In order to appreciate this, it is necessary to understand the process of resettlement itself.

There are about five hundred and sixty clusters of various sites spread over nineteen blocks of five newly created districts: Kalahandi, Koraput, Nowrangpur, Malkangiri and Rayagada. These sites have been chosen by the displaced because of access to forest resources and the presence of relatives and friends. The findings of the CENDERET study confirm that the displaced preferred to have social relations and an economic resource base in the area of their resettlement, rather than access to land and irrigation in the command area. Thus the resettlement that has taken place is the result of a participatory decision taken by the displaced and choices about the resettlement site were often a group decision. In this case, group decision-making and choice effectively reduced and almost eliminated social disarticulation.

Inasmuch as social articulation is a very important aspect of the displaced persons' ability to actively participate in the process of their rehabilitation, the RRU of the Upper Indravati Project, with the active participation of AGRAGAMEE, is planning to organise community groups in all the large resettlement clusters and host villages with a view to enabling them to regain their sense of community, leadership and mutual help arrangements, so that they are fully responsible for planning and implementation of the updated action plan. Since they have been successfully resettled with quality housing built with rehabilitation assistance and are almost integrated with the host community, the restoration of livelihood and community organisation will help the displaced to become socially articulate once more.

Conclusion

It is obvious from the case study that the 'eight key dimensions of impoverishment' are interlinked because of their causal relations and their resultant impacts on the displaced communities. It is important, therefore, to take these dimensions into consideration while planning for the resettlement and rehabilitation of the displaced. The advantage of the 'impoverishment risks' analysis model is that it also provides the much-needed conceptual framework for participatory planning.

This would mean that however appropriate and effective a policy framework may be, such as the Bank's policy, it is necessary to complement it with a conceptual framework so that the displaced are resettled with better housing, civic amenities, access to social infrastructure, including health-care services, and rehabilitated by restoring, or sometimes even improving, livelihoods and incomes so that the Bank's policy objectives are met. The 'impoverishment risks' analysis model is, therefore, a management tool for planning.

Rapid Assessment Procedures (RAP) has developed over the years four main processes and trends – fast repertoire enrichment, application in new sectors and sub-sectors through content adaptation and cross-fertilisation, geographic broadening in its elaboration and application and finally the shift from technique to substance. When practised correctly and creatively, these rapid techniques often develop the capacity to carry their practitioners further in a new substantive direction as participatory data generation techniques increase the opportunities for participatory planning. The 'impoverishment risks' analysis which we have started using in India is also an effective tool for RAP and for Participatory Rural Appraisal. The successful use of 'impoverishment risks' analysis as a tool for Participatory Rural Appraisal is also an indication that it could fit into any of the processes and trends related to Rapid Assessment Procedures and help with 'putting people first' and the displaced people first of all.

Bibliography

ABC News (1992) 'Hurricane Andrew: One Family's Struggle', ABC News videotape of Nightline, 1 September 1992.

Aberle, D. (1993) 'The Navajo-Hopi Land Dispute and Navajo Relocation' in Cernea, M. and Guggenheim, S. (eds) *Anthropological Approaches to Resettlement: Policy Practice and Theory*, Boulder, Colorado: Westview Press.

Acreman, M., Pirot, J-Y and Scudder, T. (forthcoming) 'The Role of Artificial Flooding in the Integrated Development of River Basins in Africa' in *Hydrological Management and Wetland Conservation in Africa*, Gland, Switzerland: IUCN/World Conservation Movement.

Adams, W. (1992) *Wasting the Rain: Rivers, People and Planning in Africa*, London: Earthscan Publications.

_____ (1993) 'Development's Deaf Ear: Downstream Users and Water Releases from the Bakalori Dam, Nigeria', *World Development*, Vol. 21 No. 9 pp.1405-1416.

Adu-Aryee, V. (1993) Resettlement in Ghana: From Akosombo to Kpong in Cernea, M. and Guggenheim, S. (eds) *Anthropological Approaches to Resettlement: Policy Practice and Theory*, Boulder, Colorado: Westview Press.

Alvares, C. and Billorey, R. (1987) 'Damning the Narmada: The Politics Behind the Destruction', *The Ecologist*, Vol. 17 Nos. 2/3 pp.62-75.

American Anthropological Association (1991) 'Draft of White Paper on Involuntary Resettlement', Prepared by the AAA Task Force on Involuntary Resettlement, 24 March 1991.

Appa, G. and Sridharan, R. (1992) 'A Report on the Canal Affected People and the Downstream Impact of the Sardar Sarovar Projects', Operational Research Working Paper Series, LSEOR.92.1.

Appell, G. (1985) 'The Bulusu of East Kalimantan: The Consequences of Resettlement', in Appell, G. (ed.) *Modernization and Emergence of a Landless Peasantry, Studies in Third World Societies,* Vol. 33 Williamsburg: College of William and Mary.

ASI (Anti-Slavery International/Anti-Slavery Society) (1983) 'The Philippines: Authoritarian Government, Multinationals and Ancestral Lands' Report 1 in *Indigenous Peoples and Development Series,* London.

ASI (Anti-Slavery International) (1984) 'The Chittagong Hill Tracts: Militarisation, Oppression and the Hill Tribes', in *Indigenous Peoples and Development Series 2,* London.

Aspelin, P. and Coelho dos Santos, S. (1981) 'Indian Areas Threatened by Hydroelectric Projects in Brazil', IWGIA Document 44, Copenhagen.

Ault, S. (1994) 'The Environmental Health Impacts of Resettlement: A Wealth of Systemic Problems, a Dearth of Comprehensive Responses', Lecture at the International Congress of Americanists, 7 July, Uppsala, Sweden.

Autumn, S. (1994) 'Anthropologists, Development and Situated Truth: The Uses of Debate', unpublished Ms.

Awachie, J. (1979) in Welcomme, R. (ed.) 'Fisheries Management in Large Rivers', FAO Technical Paper No. 194 Rome:United Nations Food and Agriculture Organisation.

Baboo, B. (1992) *Technology and Social Transformation: The Case of the Hirakud Multi-Purpose Dam Project in Orissa,* New Delhi, India: Concept Publishing Company.

Bandyopadhyay, J. (1992) 'From Environmental Conflicts to Sustainable Mountain Transformation: Ecological Action in the Garhwal Himalaya', in Dharam, G. and Vivian, J. (eds) *Grassroots Environmental Action,* London: Routledge.

Barabas, A. (1977) 'Chinantec Messianism: The Mediator of the Divine Western Expansion and Indigenous People', Sevilla Casas, E. (ed.) *World Anthropology Series,* The Hague: Mouton Publishers.

Bartolomé, L. (1992) 'Fighting Leviatan: The Articulation and Spread of Local Opposition to Hydrodevelopment in Brazil', 41st Annual Latin American Studies Conference: Involuntary Migration and Resettlement in Latin American, Center of Latin American Studies, University of Florida, Gainesville.

Bartolomé, M. (1992) 'Relocalizaciones de indígenas en América-Latina', 41st Annual Latin American Studies Conference: Involuntary Migration and Resettlement in Latin America, Center of Latin American Studies, University of Florida, Gainesville.

Bartolomé, M. and Barabas, A. (1973) 'Hydraulic Ethnocide: The Mazatec and Chinantec People of Oaxaca, Mexico', Copenhagen: IWGIA.

_____ (1990) 'La presa Cerro de Oro y el Ingeniero El Gran Dios. Relocalización y Etnocidio Chinanteco en México', Col. Presencias nums. 19 y 20, ConsejoNacional para la Cultura y las Artes, Instituto Nacional Indigenista, México.

_____ (1992) 'Antropología y relocalizaciones' *Alternidades*, Vol. 2 No. 4 pp.5-15.

Basso, K. (1984) 'Stalking with stories: Names, Places and Moral Narratives among the Western Apache' in Bruner, E. (ed.) *Text, Play and Story*, Washington, D.C.: American Ethnological Society.

Bauman, Z. (1989), *Modernity and the Holocaust*, Ithaca: Cornell University Press.

Bello, W., Kinley, D. and Elinson, E. (eds) n.d. 'Development Debacle: The World Bank in the Philippines', Institute for Food and Development Policy, Philippine Solidarity Network.

Berman, M. (1982) *All that is Solid Melts into Air*, New York: Simon and Schuster.

Bernstein, H., Crow, B. and Johnson, H. (eds) (1992*) Rural Livelihoods: Crisis and Response*, Oxford: OUP.

Besterman, C. and Roth, M. (1988) 'JESS Report on Land Tenure in the Middle Jubba Valley: Issues and Policy Recommendations', JESS Report No.34, Burlington, Vermont: Associates in Rural Development.

Blair, H. (1978) 'Rural Development, Class Structure and Bureaucracy in Bangladesh', *World Development*, Vol. 6 No.1 pp.65-82.

Bock, P. (1968) *Modern Cultural Anthropology*, New York: Alfred A. Knopf.

Bourassa, R. (1985) *Power from the North*, Ottawa: Prentice-Hall.

Brand, K-W. (1992) 'Aspectos cíclicos de los nuevos movimientossociales, Los Nuevos movimientos Sociales', in Dalton, R. and Kuechler, M. (eds) *Los Nuevos Movimientos Sociales: un reto al orden político*, Generalitat Valenciana: Ediciones Alfons el Manganim.

Brandon, K. and Wells, M. (1992) *People and Parks: Linking Protected Area Management with Local Communities*, Washington, D.C.: The World Bank.

Brokensha, D. and Scudder, T. (1968) 'Resettlement', in Rubin, N. and Warren, M. (eds) *Dams in Africa: An Interdisciplinary Study of Man-Made Lakes in Africa*, London: Frank Cass.

Brown, B. and Perkins, D. (1992) 'Disruptions in Place Attachment', in Low, S. and Altman, I. (eds) *Place Attachment,* New York: Plenum Press.

Burger, J. (1987) *Report from the Frontier: The State of the World's Indigenous Peoples,* London: Zed Books.

Butcher, D. (1971) 'An Operational Manual for Resettlement: A Systematic Approach to the Resettlement Problem Created by Man-Made Lakes, with Special Relevance for West Africa', FAO, Rome.

_____ (1990) 'Review of the Treatment of Environmental Aspects of Bank Energy Projects', The World Bank Industry and Energy Department, PRE Working Paper, March.

Cabañas, S. (1993) 'El Consejo de pueblos nahuas del Alto Balsas (CPNAB): Los primeros años 1989-1992', Cuadernos del Alto Balsas No.1, México: Ediciones GEO.

Carneiro da Cunha, M. (1987) *Os Direitos Do Indio,* São Paulo: Editora Brasiliense.

Cernea, M.M. (1988a) *Involuntary Resettlement in Development Projects: Policy Guidelines in World Bank-Financed Projects,* The World Bank Technical Paper No.80,. Washington, DC.

_____ (1988b) 'Involuntary Resettlement and Development', *Finance and Development,* Vol. 25 No. 3 pp.44-46.

_____ (1989) 'Metropolitan Development and Compulsory Population Relocation: Policy Issues and Project Experiences', *Regional Development Dialogue,* Vol. 10 No. 4.

_____ (1990a) 'Poverty Risks from Population Displacement in Water Resource Projects', Harvard University, HIID, DDP No.355, Cambridge, Mass.

_____ (1990b) 'Internal Refugee Flows and Development-Induced Population Displacement', *Journal of Refugee Studies,* Vol.3 No.4 pp.320-339.

_____ (1991a) *Putting People First: Sociological Variables in Rural Development,* 2nd edn, Oxford: OUP for The World Bank.

_____ (1991b) *Impoverishment Risks From Population Displacement in Water Resources Development: Policy and Operational Issues,* International Workshop on Regional Approaches to Reservoir Development and Management.

_____ (1991c) 'Involuntary Resettlement: Social Research, Policy, and Planning.' in Cernea, M. (ed.) *Putting People First: Sociological Variables in Rural Development,* 2nd edn, Oxford: OUP for The World Bank.

_____ (1992) Re-tooling in Applied Social Investigation for Development Planning: Some Methodological Issues: Some

Methodological Issues in Scrimshaw, N. and Gleason, G. (eds) *Rapid Assessment Procedures (RAP): Qualitative Methodologies for Planning and Evaluation of Health Related Programmes*, the International Nutrition Foundation for Developing Countries.

_____ (1993a) 'Disaster-Related Refugee Flows and Development-Caused Population Displacement' in Cernea, M. and Guggenheim, S. (eds) *Anthropological Approaches to Involuntary Resettlement: Policy, Practice and Theory*, Boulder, Colorado: Westview Press.

_____ (1993b) 'Anthropological and Sociological Research for Policy Development on Population Resettlement', in Cernea, M. and Guggenheim, S. (eds) *Anthropological Approaches to Resettlement: Policy, Practice and Theory* Boulder, Colorado: Westview Press.

_____ (1993c) 'African Resettlement in a Global Context' in Cook, C. (ed.) *Involuntary Resettlement in Africa*, The World Bank Technical Paper No. 227, Washington, DC.

_____ (1994a) 'Poverty Risks from Population Displacement in Water Resource Development' ICA-94. Uppsala, 6 July 1994.

_____ (1994b) 'Sociology, Anthropology, and Development: An Annotated Bibliography of World Bank Publications 1975-93', Washington, D.C.: The World Bank, Environmentally Sustainable Development Studies and Monographs Series Paper No.3.

_____ (1994c) 'Population resettlement and development', *Finance and Development*, Vol. 31 No. 1 pp.46-49.

_____ (1994d) 'Hydro-power Dams and Social Impacts: A Sociological Perspective' Paper Presented at the International Hydropower and Environment Conference, NORAD, Oslo, 12-14 September.

_____ (1995a) 'Public Policy Responses to Development-Induced Population Displacement' in Drèze, J., Samson, M. and Sing, S. (eds) *Displacement and Resettlement in the Narmada Valley.*

_____ (1995b) 'Understanding and Preventing Impoverishment from Displacement: Reflections on the State of Knowledge', Keynote address, First International Conference on Development-Induced Displacement and Impoverishment, Refugee Studies Programme, Oxford, January.

_____ (1996) 'Bridging the Research Divide: Studying Refugees and Development Oustees' in Allen, T. (ed.) *In Search of Cool Ground: Displacement and Homecoming in Northeast Africa*, London and New York: James Currey.

Cernea, M. and Guggenheim, S. (eds) (1993) *Anthropological Approaches to Resettlement: Policy Practice and Theory*, Boulder, Colorado: Westview Press.

Chambers, R. (ed.) (1970) *The Volta Resettlement Experience*, London: Pall Mall Press.

Chandler, W. (1984) *The Myth of TVA: Conservation and Development in the Tennessee Valley, 1933-1983*, Cambridge, Mass.: Ballinger.

Chawla, L. (1994) 'Childhood Place Attachments' in Low, S. and Altman, I. (eds) *Place Attachment*, New York: Plenum Press.

Chernela, J. (1988) 'Potential Impacts of a Proposed Amazon Hydropower Project', *Cultural Survival*, Vol. 12 No. 2 pp.20-24.

Chittagong Hill Tracts Commission (1991) '"Life is not Ours": Land and Human Rights in the Chittagong Hill Tracts, Bangladesh', the report of the Chittagong Hill Tracts Commission. IWGIA and Organising Committee, Chittagong Hill Tracts Campaign, London: Calvert's Press.

Colchester, M. (1987) 'The Tribal People of the Narmada Valley: Damned by the World Bank' in Sahabat Alam Malaysia (ed.) *Forest Resources Crisis in the Third World*, Pengang: Jutaprint.

Colchester, M. (1993) 'Changing World Bank Policies on Indigenous Peoples' *Third World Network Features*, 1093/93, Penang.

Clark, S., Colson, E., Lee, J. and Scudder. T (1994) 'Ten Thousand Tonga: A Longitudinal Anthropological Study from Southern Zambia, 1956-1991', unpublished.

Clay, J. (1988) 'Villagisation in Ethiopia' in Clay, J. Steingraber, S. and Niggli, P. (eds), *The Spoils of Famine. Ethiopian Famine policy and Peasant Agriculture*, Cambridge, Mass.: Cultural Survival.

Colson, E. (1971) *The Social Consequences of Resettlement: The Impact of the Kariba Resettlement Upon the Gwembe Tonga*, Manchester: Manchester University Press.

Crow, B. (1992) 'Rural Livelihoods: Action from Above' in Bernstein, H., Crow, B. and Johnson, H. (eds), *Rural Livelihoods: Crisis and Response*, Oxford: OUP.

Csikszentimihalyi, M. and Rochberg-Halton, E. (1981) *The Meaning of Things: Domestic Symbols and the Self*, New York: Cambridge.

Cummings, B. (1990) *Dam the Rivers, Damn the People: Development and Resistance in Amazonian Brazil*, London: Earthscan Publications.

Curle, A. (1971) *Making Peace*, London: Tavistock Publications.

Dalton, R. and Kuechler, M. (1992) *Los Nuevos Movimientos Sociales: un reto al orden político*, Generalitat Valenciana: Ediciones Alfons el Manganim.

Daniel, E. (1994) *The American Mosaic: The Impact of Space, Time and Culture on American Politics,* Boulder, Colorado: Westview Press.

Davidson, F., Zaijer, M., Peltenburg, M. and Rodell, M. (1993) *Relocation and Resettlement Manual: A Guide to Managing and Planning Relocation,* Institute for Housing and Urban Development Studies, the Netherlands.

de Pina Cabal, J. (1994) 'The Valuation of Time Among the Peasant Population of the Alto Minho, Northwestern Portugal' in Layton, R. (ed.) *Who Needs the Past? Indigenous Values and Archaeology,* London and New York: Routledge.

de Wet, C. (1993) 'A Spatial Analysis of Involuntary Community Relocation: A South African Cast Study' in Cernea, M. and Guggenheim, S. (eds) *Anthropological Approaches to Resettlement: Policy, Practice, and Theory* Boulder, Colorado: Westview Press.

Dhar, B. (1994) *'Impoverishment Risks' Analysis of Hariharjore Medium Irrigation Project Affected Persons,* a Field Report on Participatory Rural Appraisal.

Dieci, P. and Viezolli, C. (eds) (1992*) Resettlement and Rural Development in Ethiopia,* Milan: Franco Angeli.

Douglas, M. (1973) *Rules and Meaning,* Harmondsworth: Penguin.

Downing, T. and Kushner, G. (eds) (1988) 'Human Rights and Anthropology', Cultural Survival Report No. 24, Cambridge, Mass.: Cultural Survival Inc.

Downing, T. (1994) 'Social Geometrics: A Theory of Social Displacement in Resettlement' Paper Presented at the International Congress of the Americanists, Stockholm/Uppsala, Sweden.

_____ (1995) 'Mitigating Social Impoverishment when People are Involuntarily Displaced' Paper Presented at the First International Conference on Development-Induced Displacement and Impoverishment, Refugee Studies Programme, Oxford, January.

Drucker, C. (1985) 'Dam the Chico: Hydropower Development and Tribal Resistance', *The Ecologist,* Vol. 15 No. 4 pp.149-157.

_____ (1988) 'Dam the Chico: Hydropower Development and Tribal Resistance', in Bodley, J. (ed*.) Tribal Peoples and Development Issues: A Global Overview,* California:Mayfield Publishing Company.

Elazar, D. J. (1994) *The American Mosaic: The impact of space, time and culture on American politics* Boulder, Colorado: Westview.

Erhmann, H. (1975) 'Grupos de presión', *Enciclopedia Internacionalde las Ciencias Sociales,* Vol. 5, Madrid : Ed. Aguilar.

Escobar, A. (1991) 'Anthropology and the Development
Encounter: The Making and Marketing of Development
Anthropology,' *American Ethnologist*, Vol. 18 No. 4 pp. 658-682.

Escobar, A. and Alvarez S. (eds) (1992) *The Making of Social
Movements in Latin American: Identity, Strategy and Democracy*,
Boulder, Colorado: Westview Press.

Escudero, C. (1988) 'Involuntary Resettlement in Bank-Assisted
Projects: An Introduction to Legal Issues', Legal Department,
The World Bank, Washington.

Esteva, G. and Prakesh, M. (1992) 'Grassroots Resistance to
Sustainable Development: Lessons from the Banks for the
Narmada' *The Ecologist*, Vol. 22 No. 2 pp.45-51.

Fabian, S. (1992) *Space-Time of the Bororo of Brazil*, Gainesville,
Florida: University of Florida Press.

Falk, R. (1983) *The End of World Order*, London: Holmes and Meier.

Fantasia, R. (1988) *Cultures of Solidarity*, Berkeley: University of
California Press.

Feit, H. (1982) 'The Future of Hunters within Nation-States:
Anthropology and the James Bay Cree' in Leacock, E. and Lee,
R. (eds) *Politics and History in Band Societies*, Cambridge:
Cambridge University Press.

Fernandes, W., Das, J. and Rao, S. (1989) 'Displacement and
Rehabilitation: An Estimate of Extent and Prospects' in
Fernandes, W. and Ganguly-Thukral, E. (eds) *Development,
Displacement and Rehabilitation*, New Delhi: Indian Social
Institute.

Fernandes, W. and Ganguly-Thukral, E. (eds) (1989) *Development,
Displacement and Rehabilitation*, New Delhi: Indian Social
Institute.

Fernandes, W. and Ganguly-Thukral, E. (1989) 'A Draft National
Policy on Developmental Resettlement of Project Affected
People' in Fernandes, W. and Ganguly-Thukral, E. (eds)
Development, Displacement and Rehabilitation, New Delhi: Indian
Social Institute.

Fernandes, W. (1994) *Development-Induced Displacement in the Tribal
Areas of Eastern India*, New Delhi: Indian Social Institute.

Fisher, W. (1994) 'Megadevelopment, Environmentalism, and
Resistance: The Institutional Context of Kayapo Indigenous
Politics in Central Brazil', *Human Organisation*, Vol. 53 No. 3
pp.220-232.

Fixico, D. (1990) *Termination and Relocation: Federal Indian Policy*,
Albuquerque: University of New Mexico Press.

Frake, C. (1993) *Seafaring and the Medieval Construction of Time,*
Stanford: Stanford University Press.

Frederiksen, H. (1982) 'Water Resources Institutions: Some
Principles and Practices', The World Bank Technical Paper
No.191, Washington, DC.: The World Bank.

Friedlander, K. (1940) 'On the "Longing to Die"', *International
Journal of Psychoanalysis,* Vol. 16 No. 3 pp.416-468.

Ganguly-Thukral, E. and Singh, M. (1994) 'Dams and the displaced
in India' in Mathur, H.M. (ed.) *Development, Displacement and
Resettlement. Focus on Asian Experiences,* Delhi: Vikas Publishing
House.

Gans, H. (1968) *People and Plans: Essays on Urban Problems and
Solutions,* New York: Basic Books.

Garcia Canclini, N. (1993) *Transforming Modernity,* Austin:
University of Texas Press.

Ghai, D. and Vivian, J. (1992) *Grassroots Environmental Action,*
London: Routledge.

Ghosal, S.K. (1995) 'Issues in Resettlement and Rehabilitation
of Project-Affected Families - Experiences in India', Paper
Presented at First International Conference on Development-
Induced Displacement and Impoverishment, Refugee Studies
Programme, Oxford, January.

Gibson, D. (1993) 'The Politics of Involuntary Resettlement:
World Bank Supported Projects in Asia,' unpublished Ph.D.
dissertation, Department of Political Science, Duke University.

Giddens, A. (1984) *The Constitution of Society: Outline of the Theory of
Structuration,* Berkeley: University of California Press.

Glass, R., Urrutia, J., Sibony, S., Smith, H., Garcia , B., and Rizzo,
L. (1977) 'Earthquake Injures Related to Housing in a
Guatemalan Village' in *Science,* Vol.197 pp.638-643.

Glazer, N. and Moynihan, D. (ed.) (1975*) Ethnicity, Theory and
Experience,* Harvard: Harvard University Press.

Goldsmith, E. and Hildyard, N. (1984) *The Social and
Environmental Effects of Large Dams,* San Francisco: A Sierra
Club Book.

Gomez, T. (1993) 'Hacia un camino propio de los pueblos nahuas
del Alto Balsas', Cuadernos del Alto Balsas No.2, México:
Ediciones Gea.

Good, C. (1992) 'Making the Struggle One Big One: Nahuatl
Resistance to the San Juan Dam Mexico', Paper Presented at the
Yale seminar Programme on Agrarian Studies, Yale University:
New Haven.

Gray, A. (1994) 'From Bretton Woods to Indigenous Forests'
editorial in *Indigenous Affairs*, No. 2 April-June, 1994 pp. 2-4,
Copenhagen.
_____ (1995) 'The Indigenous Movement in Asia' in Barnes R.,
Gray, A. and Kingsbury, B. (eds) *Indigenous Peoples in Asia*, Asian
Studies Center, Ann Arbor, Michigan.
_____ (forthcoming) 'Development Policy - Development Protest:
The World Bank, Indigenous Peoples and NGOs' Ms.
Guggenheim, S. (1989) 'Development and the Dynamics of
Displacement' in Fernandes, A. (ed.) *Workshop on Rehabilitation
of Persons Displaced by Development Projects*, Bangalore: Myrada.
_____ (1990) 'Development and the Dynamics of Displacement'
in *Workshop on Rehabilitation of Persons Displaced by Development
Projects*, Institute for Social and Economic Change, Myrada,
Bangalore, India.
_____ (1993) 'Peasants, Planners, and Participation: Resettlement
in Mexico', in Cernea, M. and Guggenheim, S. (eds)
*Anthropological Approaches to Resettlement: Policy, Practice and
Theory*, Boulder, Colorado: Westview Press.
_____ (1994) *Involuntary Resettlement: An Annotated Reference
Bibliography For Development Research*, Environment Working
Paper No.64, The World Bank.
Gunaratna, M. (1988) *For a Sovereign State*, Ratmalana, Sri Lanka:
Sarvodaya Book Publishing Service.
Hadejia-Nguru Wetlands Conservation Project and the National
Institute for Policy and Strategic Studies (1993) 'Proceedings of
the workshop on the management of the water resources of the
Komadugu-Yobe basin, Kuru, 1-2 April', Kuru, Nigeria:
National Institute Press.
Hall, E. (1959) *The Silent Language*, Greenwich: Fawcett.
Hallward, P. (1992) 'The Urgent Need for a Campaign against
Forced Resettlement' in *The Ecologist*, Vol. 22 No. 2 March/April
pp.43-44.
Hann, C. (ed.) (1994) *When History Accelerates*, London: Athlone
Hansen, A. and Oliver-Smith, A. (eds) (1982) *Involuntary Migration
and Resettlement*, Boulder, Colorado: Westview Press.
Hildyard, N. (1989) 'Adios Amazonia? A Report from the Altamira
Gathering', *The Ecologist*, Vol. 19 No. 2 pp.53-62.
Horowitz, M., Salem-Murdock, M. et al. (1990) 'The Senegal River
Basin Monitoring Activity Synthesis Report', Binghampton, New
York: Institute for Development Anthropology.
Horowitz, M. (1991) 'Victims Upstream and Down', *Journal of
Refugee Studies*, Vol. 4 No. 2 pp.164-181.

Horowitz M., (1993) 'Resettlement at Manantali, Mali: Short-Term Success, Long-Term Problems' in Cernea, M. and Guggenheim, S. (eds) *Anthropological Approaches to Resettlement: Policy, Practice and Theory,* Boulder: Westview Press.

Hotchkiss, J. (1967) 'Children and Conduct in a Latino Community of Chiapas, Mexico', *American Anthropologist,* Vol. 69 No.2. Also in Romney, K. and DeVore, P. (eds) *You and Others,* Cambridge, Mass.: Winthrop Publishers.

Huang, Y. (1984) 'On the Reform of Resettlement Policies in China', *Chinese Journal of Water Conservation,* No.6.

Hydro-Quebec (1993) 'Grand Baleine Complex Feasibility Study', Quebec: Hydro-Quebec.

ICIHI (Independent Commission on International Humanitarian Issues), (1987) *Indigenous Peoples: A Global Quest for Justice,* London: ICIHI and Zed Books.

International Dams Newsletter (1985) 'Why This Newsletter?' Vol.1 No.1 p.1.

International Labour Organization Convention 107 (1958), on the Protection and Integration of Indigenous and Other Tribal Populations in Independent Countries.

Israel, A. (1987) *Institutional Development,* Baltimore, MD: Johns Hopkins University Press.

IUCN (The World Conservation Union) (ongoing) 'Newsletter: Wetlands Programme', Gland, Switzerland.

IWGIA (International Work Group for Indigenous Affairs), *Yearbook 1988: IWGIA 20 Years,* Copenhagen.

Jellinek, L. (1991) *The Wheel of Fortune: The History of a Poor Community in Jarkata,* ASAA. London: Allen and Unwin.

Johnson, B. (1994) *Who Pays the Price: The Sociocultural Context of Environmental Crisis,* Covelo,Ca.: Island Press.

Joshi, V. (1991) *Rehabilitation – A Promise to Keep. A Case of Sardar Sarovar Project,* Ahmedabad: Tax Publications.

Kardam, N. (1993) 'Development Approaches and the Role of Policy Advocacy: The case of the World Bank' *World Development,* Vol. 21 No.11 pp.1773-1789.

Kates, R. (1973) 'Human Impacts of the Mangua Earthquake' *Science,* Vol. 182 pp.981-990.

Khera, S. and Mariella, P. (1982) 'The Fort McDowell Yavapai: A Case of Long-Term Resistance to Relocation,' in Hansen, A. and Oliver-Smith, A. (eds) *Involuntary Migration andResettlement,* Boulder, Colorado: Westview Press.

Kleivan, H. (1978) 'Incompatible Patterns of Land Use: The Controversy over Hydroelectric Schemes in the Heartland

of the Sami People', in *IWGIA Newsletter* 20-21, December
pp.56-80.

Kottak, C. (1991) 'When People Don't Come First: Some
sociological lessons from completed projects', in Cernea, M. (ed)
Putting People First 2nd edn, Oxford: Oxford University Press.

Kushner, G. (1988) 'Powerless People: The Administered
Community', in Downing, T. and Kushner, G. (eds) *Human
Rights and Anthropology* (Cultural Survival Report 24),
Cambridge, Mass.: Cultural Survival Inc.

Lassailly-Jacob, V. (1986) 'Un Exemple Éphémère de
Planification du Développement: l'AVB en Côte d'Ivoire
Central (1969-1980)', *Cahiers d'Études Africaines*, Vol. 103 No.
26 pp.333-348.

_____ (1990) 'Grands Barrages Africains et Transferts de
Populations: La Question Foncière' in *Eau et Aménagement dans les
Régions Inter-Tropicales*, Talence: CEGET-CNRS.

_____ (1994) 'Government-Sponsored Agricultural Schemes for
Involuntary Migrants in Africa: Some Key Obstacles to Their
Economic Viability' in Adelman, H. and Sorenson, J. (eds)
African Refugees: Development Aid and Repatriation, Boulder,
Colorado: Westview Press.

Lane, C. and Jules, P. (1990) 'Displaced Pastoralists and
Transferred Wheat Technology in Tanzania,' IIED, Sustainable
Agriculture Programme, Gate Keeper Services, No.SA20.

Lawrence, R. (1986) 'Showdown at Big Mountain,' in *These Times*,
Vol.10 No.14.

Layton, R. (ed.) (1994) *Who Needs the Past? Indigenous Values and
Archaeology*, London and New York: Routledge.

Leonel, M., Mindlin, B. and Junquera, C. (1992) 'The Joint
Responsibility of the International Community in the
Indigenous and Environmental Issues of the Brazilian Amazon',
IWGIA Newsletter 3/92 July-September, pp.6-20, Copenhagen.

Levine, S. and Lurie, N. (eds) (1968) *The American Indian Today*,
Baltimore: Penguin Books.

Lightfoot, P. (1979) 'Spatial Distribution and Cohesion of Resettled
Communities' in Gosling, L. (ed.) *Population Resettlement in the
Mekong River Basin*, Studies in Geography No.10, Chapel Hill,
North Carolina: University of North Carolina.

Low, S. (1992) 'Symbolic Ties that Bind: Place Attachment in the
Plaza' in Low, S. and Altman, I. (eds) *Place Attachment*, New
York: Plenum Press.

Low, S. and Altman, I. (eds) (1992) *Place Attachment*, New York:
Plenum Press.

Magee, P. (1989) 'Peasant Political Identity and the Tucurui Dam: A Case Study of the Island Dwellers of Para, Brazil', *The Latinamericanist*, Vol. 24 No.1 pp.6-10.

Males, A. (1994) 'Past and Present of Andean Indian Society: the Otavalos', in Layton, R. (ed.) *Who Needs the Past? Indigenous values and archaeology*, London and New York: Routledge.

Malkki, L. (1992) 'National Geographic: The Rooting of Peoples and the Territorialisation of National Identity Among Scholars and Refugees,' *Cultural Anthropology*, Vol. 7 No.1 pp.24-44.

Marcus, C. (1994) 'Environmental memories' in Low, S. and Altman, I. (eds) *Place Attachment*, New York: Plenum Press.

Marris, P. (1975) *Loss and Change*, New York: Anchor Books.

Marshall, G. (1983) 'Some Remarks on the Study of Working Class Consciousness', *Politics and Society*, Vol.12 No.3.

Mathur, H. M. (ed.) (1994) *Development, Displacement and Resettlement. Focus on Asian Experiences*, Delhi: Vikas Publishing House.

_____ (1995) 'Struggling to Regain Lost Livelihood – the Case of People Displaced by Pong Dam in India', Paper Presented at First International Conference on Development-Induced Displacement and Impoverishment, Refugee Studies Programme, Oxford, January.

Mburugu E. (1994) 'Dislocation of Settled Communities in the Development Process: The Case of Kiambere Hydroelectric Project', in Cook, C. (ed.) 'Involuntary Resettlement in Africa' The World Bank Technical Paper No.227.

McAdam, D., McCarthy, J. and Zald, M. (1988) 'Social Movements', in Smelser, N. (ed) *Handbook of Sociology*, Newbury Park, Ca.: Sage Publications.

McDowell, C. (1995) 'Development-Induced Displacement', *The Courier*, No.150, March-April pp.56-57.

_____ (1996) 'Review - Resettlement and Development: The Bankwide Review of Projects Involving Involuntary Resettlement, 1986-1993', *Journal of Refugee Studies*, Vol.9 No.1 pp.104-106.

Merton, R. K. (1957) *Social Theory and Social Structure*, New York: Free Press.

Mey, W. (1984) 'They Are Now Burning Village after Village: Genocide in the Chittagong Hill Tracts, Bangladesh', *IWGIA Document* No. 51, Copenhagen.

Moore, M. (1992) 'Competition and Pluralism in Public Bureaucracies', IDS Bulletin No. 23 No. 4 pp.65-77.

Moran, E. (1981) *Developing the Amazon*, Bloomington: Indiana University Press.

Morse, B. and Berger, T. (1992a) *Sardar Sarovar: Report of the Independent Review*, Ottawa: Resource Futures International, Inc.

Morse, B, Berger, T. Gamble, D. and Brody, H. (1992b), 'The Report of the Independent Review', (commissioned by the The World Bank and published by Resource Futures International INC).

Myers, N. (1995) *Environmental Exodus: An Emergent Crisis in the Global Arena*, Washington, DC.: Climate Institute.

Nachowitz, T. (1988) 'Repression in the Narmada Valley,' *Cultural Survival Quarterly*, Vol. 12 No. 3 pp.22-24.

National Irrigation Authority, Files and Documents on Pantabangan Dam and Resettlement, 1969-1994, The Philippines.

Negrete, G. (1993) 'El Consejo de Pueblos Nahuas del Alto Balsas (CNPAB): Los primeros años 1989-1992', Cuadernosdel Alto Balsas No.1, México,D.F.: Ediciones Gea.

NGO, (1994) 'NGO Letters on Bankwide Resettlement Review', Ms., Bank Information Center.

Odidi Okidi, C. (1992) *Policy and Legal Framework in Development-Driven Involuntary Resettlement in African Countries*, draft, Kenya: Moi University, School of Environmental Studies.

Okavango Observer 'Dream of a Dam', 30 June 1995 p.1.

Oliver-Smith, A. (1982) 'Here There Is Life: The Social and Cultural Dynamics of Resistance to Resettlement in Post-Disaster Peru', in Hansen, A. and Oliver-Smith, A. (eds) *Involuntary Migration and Resettlement*, Boulder, Colorado: Westview Press.

_____ (1986) *The Martyred City: Death and Rebirth in the Andes*, Albuquerque: The University of New Mexico Press.

_____ (1991a) 'Involuntary Resettlement, Resistance and Political Empowerment', *Journal of Refugee Studies*, Vol. 4 No. 2 pp.132-149.

_____ (1991b) 'Successes and Failures in Post-Disaster Resettlement', *Disasters* Vol.15 No.1 pp.12-23.

_____ (1995) 'Resistance to Resettlement: The Formation and Evolution of Movements', *Research in Social Movements, Conflict and Change*, Vol.17 pp.197-219.

Organization for Economic Co-Operation and Development. (OECD) Guidelines for Aid Agencies on Involuntary Displacement and Resettlement in Development Projects. Development Assistance Committee, Paris, 1991, CODE/GAD (91) 201.

Oxfam, (1994) 'Response to Resettlement and Development Review of the World Bank', Ms.

Paine, R. (1982) 'Dam a River Damn a People? Saami (Lapp) Livelihood and the Alta/Kautokeino Hydro-electric Project and the Norwegian Parliament', *IWGIA Document 45*, Copenhagen.

Pandey, B. (1995) *Development Induced Displacement: An Agenda for the Social Summit,* Institute for Socio-Economic Development: Bhubaneswar, Orissa.

Pankhurst, A. (1992) *Resettlement and Famine in Ethiopia - The Villagers' Experience*, Manchester, New York and Manchester: Manchester University Press.

Partridge, W., Brown, A. and Nugent, J. (1982) 'The Papaloapan Dam and Resettlement Project: Human Ecology and Health Impacts', in Hansen, A. and Oliver-Smith, A. (eds) *Involuntary Migration and Resettlement*, Boulder, Colorado: Westview Press.

Partridge, W. (1989) 'Population Displacement Due to Development Projects', *Journal of Refugee Studies*, Vol. 2 No. 3 pp.373-384.

_____ (1993) 'Successful Involuntary Resettlement: Lessons from Costa Rica Arenal Hydroelectric Project' in Cernea, M. and Guggenheim, S. (eds) *Anthropological Approaches to Resettlement: Policy Practice and Theory,* Boulder, Colorado: Westview Press.

Paul, J. (1988) 'International Development Agencies, Human Rights and Human Development Projects', *Denver Journal of International Law and Policy,* Vol.17 No. 1 p.67.

Pearce, D. (1993) 'The Economics of Involuntary Resettlement', consultant report to the Task Force for the Bankwide Resettlement review, Ms.

Peeler, D. and Winter, M. (1993) *Tiempo Sagrado, Espacio Sagrado: Astronomia, calendario y arquitectura en Monte Alban y Teotihuacan,* Oaxaca, Mexico: Instituto Oaxaqueño de las Culturas.

Pellow, D. (1994) 'Spaces that Teach', in Altman, I. and Low, S. *Place Attachment,* New York: Plenum Press.

Posey, D. (1989) 'The Kayapó: On Trial for Speaking Out', *Index on Censorship*, Vol. 18 Nos. 6/7 pp.16 - 20.

_____ (1989) 'From Warclubs to Words', *Journal of The North American Centre on Latin America,* Vol. 23 No. 1 pp.13-19.

Quebec Government (1991) *The James Bay and Northern Quebec Agreement and Complementary Agreement,* Quebec: Publications of Quebec.

Qureshi, M. (1989). 'Resettlement, Development, and the World Bank', *The Bank's World,* May, pp.12-13, Washington, DC.: The World Bank

Radovich, J. and Balazote, A. (1992) 'La etnicidad mapuche en un contexto de relocalización', *América Indígena*, Vol. 2 No.1, Instituto Indigenista Interamericano, México.

Ramaiah, S. (1994) *Health Implications of Involuntary Resettlement and Rehabilitation, Upper Indravati Hydroelectric Project*, Preliminary Observations.

Ramirez, A., Celestino, E., and Cabañas, I. (1992) 'Los pueblos nahuas del Alto Balsas y su entorno ecológico', Ce-Acatl 31/32, Tecuilhuitl, México, D.F.

Ravindran, L. (1994) *Impoverishment Risks' Analysis of Displaced Persons in Upper Indravati Hydroelectric Project*, Field Notes.

_____ (1994) *Socio-economic study of displaced persons under Upper Indravati Project, Orissa*, CENDERET, Xavier Institute of Management, Bhubaneswar, Orissa.

Redclift, M. (1987) *Sustainable Development: Exploring the Contradictions*, London: Methuen.

_____ (1992) 'Sustainable Development and Popular Participation: A Framework for Analysis', in Ghai, D. and Vivian, J. (eds) *Grassroots Environmental Action*, London: Routledge.

Redford, K. (1991) 'The Ecologically Noble Savage', *Cultural Survival Quarterly*, Vol.15 No.1 pp.46-48.

Resettlement and Rehabilitation Officer (1994) *Brochure on Resettlement and Rehabilitation Activities of Upper Indravati Project*, September.

Rew, A. (1994) 'Social Standards and Social Theory' in Hann, C. (ed) *When History Accelerates*, London: Athlone.

Riberio, G. (1994) *Transnational Capitalism and Hydropolitics in Argenta: The Yacyretá High Dam*, Gainesville: University Press of Florida.

Riley, R. (1994) 'Attachment to the Ordinary Landscape' in Low, S. and Altman, I. (eds), *Place Attachment*, New York: Plenum Press.

Robinson, S. (1992) 'Participation and Accountability: Understanding the Political Culture of Involuntary Resettlement in Mexico', Paper Presented at the 41st Annual Conference of the Center for Latin American Studies, Involuntary Migration and Resettlement in Latin America, University of Florida, Gainesville, April 2-4.

_____ (1994) 'Involuntary Resettlement: Just So Stories', Paper Presented at the Symposium on Operational Resettlement Theories, 48th ICA Conference, Uppsala, Sweden, July.

Roder, W. (1994) *Human Adjustment to Kainji Reservoir in Nigeria: An Assessment of the Economics and Environmental Consequences of a*

Major Man-Made Lake in Africa, Lanham: University Press of America.

Rodman, M. (1992) 'Empowering Place: Multilocality and Multivocality', *American Anthropologist*, Vol. 94 No. 3 pp.640-656.

Roy-Burman, B. (1961) *Social Processes in the Industrialisation of Rourkhela*, New Delhi: Census of India.

Rutz, H. (ed.) (1992) *The Politics of Time*, Washington, D.C.: American Anthropological Association, American Ethnological Society Monographs, No. 4.

Sachs, W. (ed.) (1993) *The Development Dictionary: a Guide to Knowledge as Power*, London: Zed Books.

Salem-Murdock, M. (1989) *Arabs and Nubians in New Halfa*, Salt Lake City: University of Utah Press.

Salisbury, R. (1986) *A Homeland for the Cree: Regional Development in James Bay, 1971-1981*, Quebec: McGill-Queens University Press.

Scherer-Warren, I. and Reis, M. J. (1986) 'As barragens do Urugua: A dinnamica de un movimento social', *Boletim de Ciencias Sociales*, No. 41, UFSC, Brasil.

Scott, R.P. (1992a) 'Etnia y Nacao en dois movimentos de resistencia a barragens: México y Brazil', ponencia presentada en la Reunión del Grupo de Trabajo sobre Identidades en América Latina, CLACSO, Brasilia, Brasil.

_____ (1992b) 'Dams, Forced Resettlement and the Transformation of the Peasant Economy in the São Francisco River Valley, Brazil', Paper Presented at the XVII International Congress of LASA, Los Angeles.

_____ (1995) 'Rethinking Resettlement Phases: Questions for Administrators and for Social Movements' Paper Presented at First International Conference on Development-Induced Displacement and Impoverishment, Refugee Studies Programme, Oxford, January.

Scudder, T. (1962) *The Ecology of the Gwembe Tonga*, Manchester: Manchester University Press.

_____ (1973) 'The Human Ecology of Big Projects: River Basin Development and Resettlement', in *Annual Review of Anthropology*, Vol. 2 pp. 45-55.

_____ (1980) 'River-Basin Development and Local Initiative in African Savanna Environments' in Harris, D. (ed.) *Savanna Environments*, London: Academic Press.

_____ (1983) 'The Relocation Component in Connection with the Sardar Sarovar (Narmada) Project', prepared for the World Bank, quoted in Morse, B., Berger, T., Gamble, D. and Brody, H. 'The Report of the Independent Review', (commissioned by the

The World Bank and published by Resource Futures
International Inc).

_____ (1991a) 'A Sociological Framework for the Analysis of New
Land Settlements' in Cernea, M. (ed.) *Putting People First:
Sociological Variables in Rural Development,* New York: Oxford
University Press.

_____ (1991b) 'The Need and Justification for Maintaining
Transboundary Flood Regimes: The Africa Case', *Special Issue of
Natural Resources Journal on the International Law of the Hydraulic
Cycle,* Vol. 31 No. 1 pp.75-107.

_____ (1993) 'Development-induced Relocation and Refugees
Studies: 37 Years of Change and Continuity among Zambia's
Ovenbe Tonga' *Journal of Refugee Studies,* Vol. 6 No. 2 pp.123-152.

_____(1994) 'Recent experiences with river basin development in
the tropics and subtropics', *Natural Resources Forum,* Vol. 18 No.2
pp.101-113.

Scudder, T. and Colson, E. (1982). 'From Welfare to Development:
A Conceptual Framework for Analysis of Dislocated People' in
Hansen, A. and Oliver-Smith, A. (eds), *Involuntary Migration and
Resettlement: The Problems and Responses of Dislocated People,*
Boulder, Colorado: Westview Press.

Scudder, T. with Manley, R.E., Coley, R.W., Davis, R.K., Green, J.,
Howard, G.W., Lawry, S.W., Martz, D., Rogers, P.P., Taylor,
A.R.D., Turner, S.D., White, G.F. and Wright, E.P. (1993) *IUCN
Review of the Southern Okavango Integrated Water Development
Project,* Gland, Switzerland: Samara Publishing Company.

Seabrook, J. (1993*) Victims of Development: Resisitance and
Alternatives,* London: Verso.

Serra, M. (1993) 'Resettlement Planning in the Brazilian Power
Sector: Recent Changes in Approach', in Cernea, M. and
Guggenheim, S. (eds) *Anthropological Approaches to Resettlement,*
Boulder, Colorado: Westview Press.

Shihata, I. (1991a) 'The World Bank and Human Rights', pp.97-
134; also 'The World Bank and the Environment - A Legal
Perspective', pp.135-180, in *The World Bank in a Changing World,*
the Netherlands: Martinus Nijhoff Publishers.

_____ (1991b) *The World Bank in a Changing World: Selected Essays,*
Compiled by Tschofen, F. and Parra, A. Dordrecht: Martinus
Nijhoff Publishers.

_____ (1993) 'Legal Aspects of Involuntary Population
Resettlement' in Cernea, M. and Guggenheim, S. (eds)
*Anthropological Approaches to Resettlement: Policy, Practice, and
Theory,* Boulder, Colorado: Westview Press.

Sigaud, L. (1986) 'Feitos Sociais de Grandes Projectos Hidroeletricos: As Barragems de Sobradinho e Machadinho', P.P. *Antropología Social, Comunicao* No. 9, Museu Nacional, UFRJ, R.J., Brasil.

Solem, E., (1982) 'Supreme Court Rejects Appeal over Alta Case', *IWGIA Newsletter*, No. 30 pp.103-106.

Sutro, L. and Downing, T. (1988) 'A Step Toward a Grammar of Space in Zapotec Villages' in Wilk, R. and Ashmore, W. (eds) *House and Household in the MesoAmerican Past*, Albuquerque: University of New Mexico Press.

Tamondong, S. Field Work Notes on Pantabangan Research, Nueva Ecija, 1992-1994.

Treece, D. (1987) *Bound in Misery and Iron: the Impact of the Grande Carajas Programme on the Indians of Brazil*, London: Survival International.

Turnbull, C. (1987) *The Mountain People*, London: Touchstone Books.

Turner, A. (ed.) (1990) *Time*, The Hague: Ten Brink Meppel.

Turner, T. (1991) 'Major Shift in Brazilian Yanomami Policy', *Anthropology Newsletter*, Vol. 32 No. 6 p.1 and p.46.

Umali, D. Ahl, (1993) *Tracing Marcos Gold, The True Story of Yamashita Treasure*, THAPI: Manila.

United Nations General Assembly (1986) *Declaration on the Right to Development, Resolution 41/128.*

Waldram, J. (1980) 'Relocation and Political Change in a Manitoba Native Community,' *Canadian Journal of Anthropology*, Vol.1 No.2 pp.173-178.

Wali, A. (1989) *Kilowatts and Crisis: Hydroelectric Power and Social Dislocation in Eastern Panama*, Boulder, Colorado: Westview Press.

Wangxiang, C. (1993) 'Resettlement Associated with Hydro Projects in China', *International Water Power and Dam Construction*, Vol. 45 No.2 pp.19-20.

Waterbury, J. (1979) *Hydropolitics of the Nile Valley*, Syracuse, NY: Syracuse University Press.

Weber, M. (1947) *The Theory of Social and Economic Organization*, translated by Henderson, A. and Parsons, T., Glencoe, Illinois: The Free Press.

West, P. and Brechin, S. (eds) (1991) *Resident Peoples and National Parks*, Tucson: University of Arizona Press.

Wilmer, F. (1993) *The Indigenous Voice in World Politics*, Newbury Park: Sage Publications.

Wittfogel, K. (1963) *Oriental Despotism*, New Haven: Yale University Press.

The World Bank. (1980) Operational Manual Statement 2.33. *Social Issues Associated with Involuntary Resettlement in Bank-Financed Projects*, Washington, DC.

_____ (1982) 'Tribal Peoples and Economic Development', Washington: The World Bank (sometimes placed under Goodland, R.).

_____ (1990) Operational Directive 4.30: *Involuntary Resettlement*, Washington, D.C., June.

_____ (1994a) *Resettlement and Development: The Bankwide Review of Projects Involving Involuntary Resettlement 1986-1993*, The Environment Department, Washington, D.C.

_____ (1994b) 'Sectoral Environmental Assessment is Needed for Power Sectors - and the Big Dams Debate', Ms. (paper circulated for discussion by Robert Goodland).

_____ (1994c) 'Status Report: Remedial Action Planning for Involuntary Resettlement', Washington, D.C.

World Rivers Review (1988) 'Activists Put IRN on the Map', *World Rivers Review,* Vol. 3 No. 3 p.1.

Zaman, M. (1982) 'Crisis in Chittagong Hill Tracts: Ethnicity and Integration', *Economic and Political Weekly*, Vol. 17 No. 3 pp.75-80.

Zerubavel, E. (1985*) The Seven Day Circle: the History and Meaning of the Week,* London: The Free Press.

Notes On Contributors

Dr Gautam Appa is a Senior Lecturer in Operational Research at the London School of Economics and Political Science, specialising in mathematical programming. His research interests include the effects of development policies on people and the environment, and the political economy of India.

Dr Alicia M. Barabas is a Senior Research Professor at the National Institute of Anthropology and History, Mexico. She has worked for twenty years with Indian people displaced by the Cerro de Orro dam in Mexico and has published widely on inter-ethnic relations and development in Mexico and Latin America.

Dr Miguel A. Bartolomé is a Senior Research Professor at the National Institute of Anthropology and History, Mexico. His research focuses on inter-ethnic relations and development issues in Mexico and Latin America with a concentration on the displacement arising out of the construction of the Cerro de Orro dam.

Dr Michael Cernea is the World Bank's Senior Adviser on Social Policy and Sociology in Washington. His work and main research focuses on the application of sociology and anthropology to development policies and programmes, migration, population settlement, the social organisation of natural resource management and public policy. He received the Solon T. Kimball Award in 1988 and the Bronislav Malinowski Award in 1995 for his work applying social science knowledge to development policies and programmes and to the formulation of public policies.

Dr Theodore E. Downing is Research Professor of Social Development at the University of Arizona, former President of the Society for Applied Anthropology and frequent consultant to major international organisations. His social development specialisations are in indigenous affairs, resettlement, human rights and participatory programme evaluation. He is currently working with the Pehuenche Indians in southern Chile.

Dr Andrew Gray is a researcher for the World Rainforest Movement and the International Workgroup on Indigenous Affairs, and he teaches Human Sciences at the University of Oxford. He has recently published a series of three books on the Arakmbut of the Peruvian Amazon examining history, culture and indigenous rights.

Dr Véronique Lassailly-Jacob is a French geographer and research fellow at the National Centre for Scientific Research in Paris. Her research field includes forced migration and rural development in Africa. She specialises in the study of land resettlement schemes implemented for involuntary migrants.

Dr Christopher McDowell is an anthropologist and researcher at the Refugee Studies Programme, University of Oxford. He has recently published a monograph on the movement of Tamils from Sri Lanka to Europe in pursuit of asylum.

Dr Anthony Oliver-Smith is Professor of Anthropology and Co-Director of the Displacement and Resettlement Studies Programme at the University of Florida. His research focuses on environmental refugees, disaster-caused displacement, development-induced displacement and resistance to displacement, primarily in Latin America.

Girish Patel is a human rights Advocate at the Gujarat High Court, India. He pioneered the field of public interest litigation on behalf of the poor and underprivileged in Gujarat. He is president of the Human Rights Association in Gujarat and is involved in a large number of peoples' movements involving tribals, minorities, scheduled castes people and women.

Dr Darrell A. Posey is currently Director of the Working Group on Traditional Resource Rights and a Fellow of Linacre College, Oxford. He is also Titled Researcher for the Brazilian Council for Science and Technology, and Professor at the Federal Universities of Para and Maranhao. Dr Posey was founding President of the International Society for Ethnobiology (ISE) and is Executive Director of the ISE's Global Coalition for Bio-Cultural Diversity, under whose auspices he established the Working Group on Traditional Resource

Rights. He is author of more than 150 scientific and technical publications on ethnoecology, indigenous knowledge, human rights and sustainable development.

Dr Alan Rew is an anthropologist, Professor of Development Policy and Planning and Director of the Centre for Development Studies, University of Wales at Swansea. He has researched the anthropology of development in the Pacific, the Philippines and, more recently, in India and China. His studies of resettlement management include an evaluation of the Victoria Dam Project in Sri Lanka.

Dr Thayer Scudder is Professor of Anthropology at the California Institute of Technology, Pasadena. His research is related to new land settlement, river-basin development, and long-term community studies. His publications deal particularly with the Kariba Dam Project in central Africa and with dam relocation world-wide. He has worked as a consultant for leading international organisations in a number of countries.

Susan Tamondong-Helin is a resettlement expert and currently a full-time social science consultant at the World Bank in Washington, D.C. Her doctoral research examined the consequences of displacement arising out of the construction of Pantabangan Dam in the Philippines.

Sam Thangaraj is a social scientist and a specialist in resettlement and rehabilitation at the World Bank in India. He was previously Oxfam's Assistant Field Director for northern India and Nepal.

Index

REFUGEE AND FORCED MIGRATION STUDIES

General Editors: **Barbara Harrell-Bond**, *Refugee Studies Programme, International Development Centre, University of Oxford,* and **Roger Zetter**, *School of Planning, Oxford Brookes University*

This new series, published in association with the Refugee Studies Programme, University of Oxford, reflects the multidisciplinary nature of the field and includes within its scope international law, anthropology, medicine, geography, geopolitics, social psychology and economics.

Volume 1
A TAMIL ASYLUM DIASPORA
Sri Lankan Migration, Settlement and Politics in Switzerland

Christopher McDowell, *Research Officer, Refugee Studies Programme, International Development Centre, University of Oxford*

During twelve years of ethno-nationalist secessionist violence in the north and east of Sri Lanka, insurrection in the south, and island-wide state repression, many Tamils were forced to seek political asylum overseas. At least 200,000 Tamils, primarily from the Jaffna Peninsula, have escaped to Europe of whom ca. 25,000 (the largest group relative to the population), have settled in Switzerland, the focus of this study. The author examines the conditions in Sri Lanka that led to the flight, the phases and technicalities of the emigration and resettlement in Switzerland. Based on anthropological fieldwork and on completely new archival material, the author not only looks at the development of the Tamil community in all its diversity but also at the impact of federal and cantonal policy and practice, at the economic situation and broader changes in Switzerland which led to demands for reforms to the country's asylum and immigration rules. In this respect Switzerland set an example that other governments were soon to follow.

"...based on good use of existing literature, documentary research, and ethnographic interviewing... has major implications for those concerned with repatriations and the way in which asylum-seekers are channeled to different countries."
Elizabeth Colson

ca. 288 pages · 4 maps, 16 tables., 5 figs, bibliog., index
ISBN 1-57181-917-7 · hardback ca. $49.95/£35.00
Anthropology/Development Studies/Refugee Studies

165 Taber Avenue • Providence, Rhode Island 02906
Phone: 401-861-9330 • Fax: 401-521-0046 • E-mail: BerghahnBk@aol.com

TURKISH CULTURE IN GERMAN SOCIETY TODAY

Edited by **David Horrocks** and **Eva Kolinsky,** *Department of Modern Languages, Keele University*

Provides valuable information on the social and cultural life of the Turkish minority in Germany.

For many decades Germany has had a sizeable Turkish minority that lives in an uneasy co-existence with the surrounding German community and as such has attracted considerable interest abroad where this tends to be seen as a measure of German tolerance. However, little is known about the actual situation of the Turks. This volume provides valuable information, presented in a most original manner, which combines literary and cultural studies with social and political analysis. It focuses on the Turkish-born writer Emine Sevgi Özdamar, who writes in German and whose work, particularly her highly acclaimed novel *Das Leben ist eine Karawanserei*, is examined critically and situated in the context of German "migrant literature." An interview with the author and a sample of her work are followed by a sociological survey of the general situation of minorities in Germany today; their views and experiences, official government policy towards, and popular perceptions of them. The volume furthermore includes a study of a particular Turkish community, that of Frankfurt am Main, which is supported by a collection of documents and statistical data. General surveys and detailed analyses thus combine to provide a multi-faceted picture in which the life and cultural activity of the Turks in Germany is set against the background of other minorities in the country.

Contents: E. Kolinsky/D. Horrocks, Between Acceptance and Exclusion: Culture, Society and Minorities in Contemporary Germany – M. McGowan/S. Fischer, The Literature of Ethnic Minorities in Contemporary Germany – D. Horrocks, Turkish Germans, German Turks? Language, Culture and Identity in Emine Sevgi Özdamar's Work – E. S. Özdamar, Living and Writing in Germany – D. Horrocks/F. Krause, Emine Sevgi Özdamar: her Voice and her Life – E. Kolinsky, Non-German Minorities in Germany Today – E. Kürsat-Ahlers, The Turkish Minority in German Society – H.-P. Waldhoff/D. Tan, Everyday Life and Turkish Everyday Culture – Y. Karakasoglu, Turkish Youth between German and Islamic Traditions.

ca. 160 pages ca. 20 tables and diagrams, 1 photograph, bibliog., index
ISBN 1-57181-899-5 · hardback · ca. **$29.95/£22.00**
ISBN 1-57181-047-1 · paperback · ca. **$12.50/£9.95**
Culture and Society in Germany, Volume 1
German Studies/Literature/Sociology

165 Taber Avenue • Providence, Rhode Island 02906
Phone: 401-861-9330 • Fax: 401-521-0046 • E-mail: BerghahnBk@aol.com

www.ingramcontent.com/pod-product-compliance
Lightning Source LLC
Chambersburg PA
CBHW060031030426
42334CB00019B/2278